Guess Who's Coming to Dinner

Entertaining at the Georgia Governor's Mansion

Menus, Recipes, & Anecdotes

MARY BETH BUSBEE
with
JAN BUSBEE CURTIS

Peachtree Publishers, Ltd.

Published by
PEACHTREE PUBLISHERS, LTD.
494 Armour Circle, N.E.
Atlanta, Georgia 30324

Copyright © 1986 Mary Beth Busbee and Jan Busbee Curtis

All rights reserved. No part of this book may be reproduced in any form or by any means without the prior written permission of the Publisher, excepting brief quotes used in connection with reviews, written specifically for inclusion in a magazine or newspaper.

Manufactured in the United States of America

1st printing

Library of Congress Catalog Number 86-61543

ISBN 0-934601-06-2

CONTENTS

PREFACE 1
INTRODUCTION 3
MEMORIES, MENUS, AND RECIPES 7
Burt Reynolds 9
Legislative Dinners 15
Ansel Adams 19
His Royal Highness, Prince Charles 25
Freshman Legislators 31
New First Ladies 35
Congressional Aides Nostalgia Party 39
His Majesty, King Hussein I 43
Entertaining for Industry and Trade 49
Georgia House Speaker Tom Murphy 53
Minister President Filbinger of Germany 57
Our First Family Wedding 65
President-elect Jimmy Carter 73
Visiting Ambassadors from Foreign Countries .. 77
Rev. Billy Graham 87
Secretary of Transportation William Coleman ... 91
Busbee Family Thanksgiving 95
Signora Maria Pia Fanfani 101
Dr. Henry Kissinger 105
Western Buffet for the Office of Planning and
    Budget 109
Vice Premier Deng Xiaoping 113
Joan Mondale: "Joan of Art" 115
Sharky's Machine Premiere Reception 119
Prime Minister Nouira of Tunisia 129
Van Cliburn 133
Governor's Staff Family Christmas Party 135
Her Majesty, Queen Beatrix of the
    Netherlands 141

FAMILY FAVORITES 145
Appetizers 147
Salads 151
Soups and Stews 155
Seafood 159
Meats 165
Poultry 173
Vegetables 177
Side Dishes 181
Sweets 185
Potpourri 193

INDEX 197

GUESS WHO'S COMING TO DINNER

PREFACE

From 1975 until 1983, it was my family's privilege to live in the beautiful Georgia governor's mansion. Those were exciting years for our family and also for the entire Southeast. During that time, the Sunbelt emerged as the economic darling of the United States and the nation sent a Georgian to the White House. The great new interest in all things Southern prompted a number of dignitaries to visit the Georgia governor's mansion during the time we lived there.

With each passing day, I realize more and more what a unique opportunity our family had during the eight years we lived in the mansion. I have been asked so many times, "What was it like to live there? What was it like to entertain all of those dignitaries and famous people? Did you serve turnip greens to Prince Charles or grits to Henry Kissinger? What kind of guy is Burt Reynolds?"

This book will answer some of these questions — and share some of the memories, menus, and recipes from our time in the Georgia governor's mansion.

M.B.B.

INTRODUCTION

Living in the Georgia governor's mansion can be, at times, like living in a fishbowl. But no fish have been so privileged. It is the highest honor for a family to represent its fellow citizens in the state's official residence, especially when that residence is one of the most beautiful governor's mansions in the United States.

An incoming first family needs to bring very little on move-in day. When the Busbee family arrived at the mansion in January 1975, we brought clothes, George's scruffy old reclining chair, most of our books, and our thirteen-year-old dog.

The governor's mansion is an extension of the governor's office, a place where he can meet in a home-like atmosphere with business leaders, legislators, and constituents. We also used the mansion as a place to receive and lodge distinguished visitors to Georgia. The entertaining that we did in eight years (on average, more than one function a week) was designed to provide nourishment and hospitality to this broad range of guests.

The nourishment and hospitality required breakfasts, luncheons, dinners (casual and formal), and receptions. The mansion is well suited to accommodate all these functions, large and small. The most formal dining room, called the state dining room, is on the main floor and seats eighteen people. Meals for the family and for groups of eight or less were served in the family dining room, also on the main floor. French doors open both dining rooms to the porches and provide easy access to the mansion gardens. On many occasions, the weather permitted us to have seated dinners in the east and west gardens.

Large crowds were entertained in the ball-

HELEN AND JIM LEE

room, located in the mansion's lower level. Up to two hundred people can be seated there for a meal. In addition, the ballroom was frequently used for receptions. The state drawing room is a large, beautifully decorated room on the main floor, which we used for smaller receptions and as a receiving room before dinners.

As I settled into my new role of first lady, the responsibility for planning and directing the entertaining for such a diverse collection of events was, at first, rather intimidating. I drew great comfort through the years by relying on a simple philosophy of entertaining — my primary objective was to make our guests feel comfortable and welcome. I came to learn that if I accomplished that objective, then occasional foibles of entertaining would be taken in stride. For example, we survived salt used instead of sugar in a dessert, candy mints mistaken for molded butter and placed by the staff on the bread plates, and a cook who quit in the middle of preparing a dinner for forty.

In addition to comfort and a welcoming atmosphere, our guests needed to be fed. We enjoyed offering the kinds of menus which, where possible, represented the variety and quality of foods produced in Georgia, coupled with the highest caliber of preparation and presentation. This all begins with good recipes.

Along with a large personal collection of cookbooks, I brought a hefty file of family recipes with me to the mansion and started the kitchen off with proven favorites. Many other recipes used in entertaining at the mansion were collected during our eight years there.

We offered our guests the best of Southern cooking, both down home and uptown. For that reason, you will not find many menus in this cookbook for fancy six and seven-course dinners. Our guests were always interested in and delighted by the traditional foods of the South.

Almost weekly, we received Georgia products from friends around the state. Autumn brought apples from north Georgia, and pecans and peanuts from south Georgia. With winter and the Christmas season came Claxton fruitcakes and Bob's Candies. In the spring and summer, melons, peaches, blueberries, Vidalia onions, and fresh produce arrived. Friends also shared homemade jams, jellies, preserves, and pickles.

I am sure we converted a few non-Southerners to the virtues of grits. One visitor from far away was so taken with them he asked, "What tree do grits come from?" I suppressed a grin and replied, "A corn tree."

Since, in formal entertaining, an equal partner with the food is protocol and etiquette, the first book I purchased after moving into the man-

GARY WOMACK

sion was a complete guide to protocol. Protocol is an essential element in entertaining visiting heads of state. It is the common denominator within which they feel most comfortable. I must also admit that in 1975 I harbored a conviction that many foreign visitors did not think Southerners knew a fish knife from a cocktail fork. Therefore, it was even more important to me that the food we served was properly and beautifully presented.

Obviously, entertaining at the governor's mansion cannot be a one-person show. One of the first (and best) steps I took as first lady was to employ a full-time mansion manager, Mary Dwozan. With a staff of ten, Mary handled day-to-day housekeeping details and acted as my right hand in planning and implementing the many events over eight years.

Although this book relates anecdotes of entertaining the people I am most asked about, thousands of Georgians were entertained as well at the governor's mansion. From the piedmont plains to the Atlantic coast to the mountains of north Georgia, the people of Georgia enjoyed and took pride in visiting the official residence of the state. And on the personal side, the mansion was our home for eight years, where we celebrated weddings, rehearsal dinners, graduation parties, the first visit of new grandchildren, and so much more.

To all of you who have not asked me personally whether we fed turnip greens to Prince Charles and other similar questions, this book is for you. And if all you are seeking is menus and recipes that have stood the test of time, you are also in the right pew. With my best wishes, I hope you enjoy this collection of memories, menus, and recipes from the Georgia governor's mansion.

Mary Beth Busbee

MEMORIES, MENUS, AND RECIPES

BURT REYNOLDS

Movie-making came to Georgia in the early 1970s and was a rapidly growing industry in the state when George Busbee came into office in January 1975. The Department of Industry and Trade does an excellent job of "selling" Georgia to movie makers. As a part of this effort, we entertained a number of producers and "movie stars" at the governor's mansion.

One of Georgia's best friends in the industry is Burt Reynolds. By 1975, he had already made several movies in the state and had many friends here. In the summer of that year, Burt came to Georgia to scout locations for the filming of *Gator*. We were asked by the Department of Industry and Trade to host a small dinner party for him, his producer, and a few friends.

By the afternoon of the dinner, July 18, we still had not received a final guest list. So a call from someone identifying himself as "Miss Benton's agent" did not seem unusual, and we simply

COURTESY OF WARNER BROS.

answered his questions about the time and dress for dinner. We assumed "Miss Benton" was an invited guest whose name had not yet been given to my secretary.

At the appointed time, Burt and his producer arrived. Other guests, as they arrived, were brought into the drawing room where we talked for a while before dinner. Burt said that we were missing one member of his party, and I asked the cook to put dinner on hold. About that time, in walked Barbi Benton, the entertainer and former *Playboy* bunny. I could tell by the look on Burt's face that she was *not* the missing guest. She was in Atlanta for an engagement at Six Flags and was crashing our party.

We continued to wait for our last invited guest, but still there was no sign of him. After I had made several nervous trips to the kitchen, Burt suggested that we go on into the family dining room. Dinner was served, and I finally began to relax and enjoy the evening.

Well into the main course, we suddenly heard laughter and great commotion in the foyer outside the dining room. The double doors flew open, and in strode Burt's good friend and movie sidekick Jerry Reed, holding a big sack of Krystal hamburgers. Throwing his leg over the back of a chair, he said, "Don't worry about me, folks. I brought my own supper!"

It did, indeed, turn out to be an informal evening. I learned that, at times, there is nothing one can do but roll with the punches. In one evening, a *Playboy* bunny crashed my party, and an invited guest came an hour late and brought his own dinner.

After our guests left, George asked, "Who was that Benton woman? She kept saying we would have to stay at the mansion next time we came to Los Angeles." Poor George. He had an invitation to Hugh Hefner's *Playboy* mansion and didn't even know it.

Although the evening was full of the unpredictable, we had a wonderful time. Burt Reynolds is a delightful person and a true gentleman. ■

DINNER IN HONOR OF BURT REYNOLDS

MENU

Seafood Fancy

Shanghai Salad

Charcoal Sirloin Cubes

Sautéed Mushrooms   Crunchy Baked Potatoes

Cheese Biscuits

Coupe Champagne

SEAFOOD FANCY

¾ cup finely chopped celery
¾ cup finely chopped onion
¾ cup finely chopped green pepper
½ teaspoon salt
⅛ teaspoon ground pepper
1 teaspoon worcestershire sauce
1 cup bread crumbs
1 cup mayonnaise
1 (6½-ounce) can crab meat, drained
1 (6½-ounce) can shrimp, drained
seasoned bread crumbs

Preheat oven to 350 degrees.

Mix celery, onion, green pepper, salt, ground pepper, worcestershire sauce, bread crumbs, and mayonnaise in a large bowl. Add crab meat; mix well. Add shrimp to crab meat mixture and mix thoroughly.

Spoon mixture into 2-quart casserole. Sprinkle with seasoned bread crumbs. Bake, uncovered, for 40-45 minutes. (Note: Instead of baking this in a casserole, we frequently portioned it into individual shells before baking.)

Yield: 6 servings

SHANGHAI SALAD

1 large head crisp lettuce, shredded
2 (16-ounce) cans bean sprouts, drained well
2 green peppers, coarsely chopped
2 (5-ounce) cans water chestnuts, thinly sliced
Shanghai Dressing
½ cup toasted almonds, chopped

Place first 4 ingredients in very large bowl. Right before serving, pour dressing over all and toss well. Sprinkle almonds over top.

Yield: 12-15 servings

SHANGHAI DRESSING:

⅔ cup mayonnaise
1 teaspoon prepared mustard
½ teaspoon Tabasco sauce
2 teaspoons chili powder
1 clove garlic, crushed
2 teaspoons grated onion
5 tablespoons tarragon vinegar
1½ teaspoons dried marjoram
½ teaspoon dried thyme
¼ teaspoon coarsely ground pepper
1 teaspoon salt
2 teaspoons soy sauce

Blend all ingredients in bowl. Transfer to jar with tight-fitting lid. Cover and shake vigorously. Refrigerate overnight.

Yield: 1 cup

CHARCOAL SIRLOIN CUBES

1 (12-ounce) bottle barbecue sauce
2 cups vegetable oil
1 (5-ounce) bottle soy sauce
2 cloves garlic, crushed
4 cups water
dash ground ginger
5 pounds sirloin steak

Combine first 6 ingredients; mix well. Cut steak into 2-inch cubes. Pour barbecue sauce mixture over meat. Cover and refrigerate for several hours. Grill steak over medium-hot coals to desired doneness, turning to brown on all sides.

Yield: 10-12 servings

SAUTÉED MUSHROOMS

2 tablespoons butter
1 tablespoon olive oil
½ pound mushrooms, washed, dried, and sliced
½ teaspoon lemon juice
¼ teaspoon seasoned salt
dash pepper

Heat butter and oil in large skillet over high heat. Butter will foam. When foam begins to subside, butter is hot enough. Add mushrooms; toss them and shake pan, or keep them moving with spatula until lightly browned (3-4 minutes). Remove from heat.

Sprinkle mushrooms with lemon juice, seasoned salt, and pepper. Toss to distribute seasonings.

Yield: 2-3 servings (Note: To increase number of servings, make recipe twice, instead of doubling it.)

CRUNCHY BAKED POTATOES

3 baking potatoes, baked
⅓ cup instant nonfat dry milk
⅓ cup water
¼ cup finely chopped onion
1 egg, well beaten
1 teaspoon salt
dash cayenne pepper
1 cup crumbled corn flakes
½ cup grated parmesan cheese
3 tablespoons melted butter

Preheat oven to 375 degrees.

Cut baked potatoes in half. Scoop out pulp, reserving shells. Mash potatoes; reserve.

In large bowl of electric mixer, whip milk and water until thick and smooth. Mix in mashed potatoes, onion, egg, salt, and cayenne pepper. Beat until light and fluffy. Stuff potato shells with mashed potato mixture. Place shells in baking dish.

Mix corn flakes, parmesan cheese, and butter; sprinkle over stuffed potatoes. Bake, uncovered, for 20-25 minutes.

Yield: 6 servings

CHEESE BISCUITS

1 cup margarine, at room temperature
1 cup sour cream
2 cups self-rising flour
1 cup grated sharp cheddar cheese

Preheat oven to 400 degrees.

Cream margarine in large bowl of electric mixer; add sour cream and mix well. Gradually add flour; mix. Add grated cheese and mix well.

Drop dough by teaspoonfuls into greased miniature muffin tins. Bake for 20 minutes. Immediately remove biscuits from tins.

Yield: 4 dozen small biscuits

COUPE CHAMPAGNE

2 ripe Georgia peaches
lemon juice
small bunch seedless green grapes
1 pint strawberry ice cream
16 ounces pink champagne, chilled

Peel, pit, and slice peaches. Sprinkle with small amount of lemon juice to prevent darkening. Divide peaches among 4 stemmed sherbert glasses or individual glass dessert dishes.

Add a few stemmed grapes and a large scoop of ice cream to each glass. Fill to brim with champagne and serve at once.

Yield: 4 servings

LEGISLATIVE DINNERS

It has become a tradition for Georgia's governor and first lady to entertain members of the legislature and their spouses once during each legislative session. Since this is such a large group, legislative dinners are usually held on three consecutive evenings.

As a legislative wife for eighteen years, I always looked forward to the big "do" at the governor's mansion. Frequently it was the only occasion that brought me to Atlanta during the legislative session — four children kept me close to home during those years.

So with great enthusiasm and excitement, I planned our first dinner for the state legislators in January 1975. Time was short between George's inauguration and the first series of legislative dinners, so we decided to have them catered. I wanted the dinner to be the most elegant ever.

Initially there had been a little grumbling from some of the legislators about the "black tie" on the invitation. But once our guests arrived, they began to enjoy themselves. The musical entertainment that evening was a big hit, and the food was beautifully presented and served. Faces really lit up when the dessert appeared — flaming baked Alaska.

Feeling quite confident now with the menu selection for the evening, I watched contentedly as our guests began to eat their baked Alaska. Suddenly I noticed something strange. On some faces a look of pure pleasure — on others a look of confusion and a certain pucker of the lips. I tasted my dessert and realized, to my complete horror, that some of the baked Alaska had been made with salt instead of sugar.

George was seated at another table and realized what had happened about the same time that I went into shock. Always one to enjoy the humor in any situation, George went up to the microphone and said, "You are not being poisoned. I want you to at least have a chance to pass my legislative programs. If this had been intentional, I would have seen to it that *only* our beloved Speaker of the House, Tom Murphy, got a dessert made with salt."

George and our guests had a good laugh over the baked Alaska that night, but it took a while for me to be able to look back on that night and laugh. On learning of the mix-up, the poor chef from the catering company burst into tears. I am quite sure that he is still not able to muster a smile about that evening.

After the baked Alaska incident, there were many more less eventful legislative dinners. Following is a menu for one of the buffets prepared by our mansion staff in later years. ■

LEGISLATIVE BUFFET

MENU

Seafood Casserole

Orange-Glazed Cornish Hen Halves

Broccoli-Stuffed Tomatoes   Rice Mingle

Squash Casserole

Curried Fruit   Garden Aspic

Hard Rolls

Grasshopper Pie

SEAFOOD CASSEROLE

1 (16-ounce) package frozen flounder or cod filets, thawed
1 pound shrimp, peeled and deveined
2 (8-ounce) cans minced clams
3 (8-ounce) packages small shell macaroni
5 cups coarsely chopped celery
1½ cups butter or margarine
1½ cups all-purpose flour
4 cups whole milk
6-7 green onions, cut into 1-inch pieces
3 chicken bouillon cubes
5 teaspoons salt
¼ teaspoon pepper

Cut flounder filets into serving-sized pieces; drain filets and shrimp on paper towels. In strainer over 4-cup measure, drain clams; add enough water to clam liquid to measure 4 cups.

In large saucepan, cook macaroni according to package directions; drain well. Set aside.

In 8-quart Dutch oven over medium-high heat, cook celery in butter until tender, about 10 minutes, stirring occasionally. With large spoon, stir flour into celery mixture until well blended. Gradually stir in reserved clam liquid, milk, green onions, bouillon cubes, salt, and pepper. Cook, stirring constantly, until mixture is thickened, about 15 minutes. In meantime, preheat oven to 350 degrees.

Gently stir in cooked macaroni, filets, shrimp, and clams. Spoon mixture into 2 lightly greased 3-quart casseroles. Cover and bake for 25 minutes, or until shrimp are tender when tested with a fork.

Yield: 12 servings

ORANGE-GLAZED CORNISH HEN HALVES

4 Cornish hens, split in half
salt and pepper to taste
4 medium onions, cut in half
6 tablespoons butter or margarine
2 tablespoons Kitchen Bouquet
4 ounces orange marmalade

Preheat oven to 350 degrees.

Rinse hen halves; salt and pepper. Place hen halves, skin side down, in shallow 13 x 15-inch roasting pan. Place an onion half in cavity of each hen half.

In small saucepan, combine butter, Kitchen Bouquet, and orange marmalade. Cook over medium heat until butter is melted and mixture is blended. Spoon half of marmalade mixture over hen halves.

Bake in open roasting pan for 30 minutes. Remove from oven and turn hen halves over. Brush remaining marmalade mixture over hens and bake an additional 30 minutes, basting often.

Yield: 8 servings

BROCCOLI-STUFFED TOMATOES

6 medium, unpeeled ripe tomatoes
salt
1 (10-ounce) package frozen chopped broccoli
2 tablespoons minced onion
¼ cup butter
½ cup all-purpose flour
½ teaspoon dried basil
¼ teaspoon ground nutmeg
½ cup chicken broth
½ cup dry sherry
salt and pepper to taste

With sharp knife, cut thin slice from top of each tomato. Scoop out center pulp; discard. Sprinkle insides of tomatoes with salt; turn tomatoes upside down to drain for an hour.

Preheat oven to 350 degrees.

Cook broccoli in boiling salted water for 5 minutes; drain well. Sauté onion in butter until soft. Remove from heat. Stir in flour, basil, and nutmeg. Cook over medium-low heat, stirring, for 3 minutes. Do not brown. Gradually add chicken broth and sherry. Cook 3 minutes, stirring constantly. Add broccoli, salt, and pepper. Cook until mixture is heated through.

Stuff each tomato with broccoli mixture. Bake, uncovered, for about 20 minutes, or until tomatoes are tender when pricked with a fork. Do not overcook. (Note: Instead of using ½ cup chicken broth and ½ cup sherry, 1 cup chicken broth can be used if desired.)

Yield: 6 servings

RICE MINGLE

1 cup wild rice
1 teaspoon salt
1 medium onion, chopped
½ cup butter or margarine
2 (10½-ounce) cans beef consommé
1 soup can water
1½ cups regular long-grain white rice
½ teaspoon salt
1 tablespoon butter or margarine

Place wild rice in colander and rinse with cold water. Bring 2 cups salted water to boil; add wild rice. Cover and reduce heat; cook until tender (about 1 hour), stirring occasionally.

In large saucepan over medium-high heat, sauté onion in butter. Stir in consommé and soup can of water. Bring to boil; add long-grain rice and ½ teaspoon salt. Bring back to boil; cover and reduce heat. Cook for 20-25 minutes.

Drain wild rice; add 1 tablespoon butter. Mix wild rice with long-grain rice and serve.

Yield: 8-10 servings

SQUASH CASSEROLE

(recipe on page 28)

GRASSHOPPER PIE

(recipe on page 86)

CURRIED FRUIT

1 (16-ounce) can peach or apricot halves
1 (16-ounce) can pear halves
1 (20-ounce) can pineapple slices or chunks
6 maraschino cherries, halved
¼ cup butter or margarine
¾ cup dark brown sugar
4 teaspoons curry powder

Preheat oven to 325 degrees.

Drain fruit thoroughly. Meanwhile, in small saucepan over low heat, melt butter; stir in brown sugar and curry powder.

Place fruit in shallow 1½-quart casserole. Spoon sugar mixture over fruit. Bake, uncovered, for 1 hour. Serve warm.

Yield: 12 servings

GARDEN ASPIC

4 envelopes unflavored gelatin
1 (46-ounce) can cocktail vegetable juice
2 cups sliced celery
¾ cup chopped ripe olives
½ cup diced green peppers
½ teaspoon seasoned salt
½ teaspoon garlic salt
lettuce leaves
1 (8-ounce) bottle French salad dressing

Day before serving: In Dutch oven, sprinkle gelatin over 1 cup water. Cook over medium heat, stirring constantly, until gelatin is completely dissolved. Stir in cocktail vegetable juice and next 5 ingredients. Pour mixture into 9 x 13 x 2-inch dish; refrigerate overnight.

Cut aspic into 12 portions; arrange on lettuce leaves. Spoon 1½ tablespoons French dressing over each serving.

Yield: 12 servings

ANSEL ADAMS

A photography buff for twenty-five years, George has long been an admirer of Ansel Adams. His majestic black-and-white landscape photographs of the American West made Mr. Adams the most famous and respected photographer in the United States.

In the fall of 1977, the newspaper tipped me off that Ansel Adams would be in Atlanta in early October for a lecture at the High Museum of Art. Knowing that George would be thrilled, I invited Mr. Adams to be our house guest during his stay in Atlanta. He accepted the invitation and arrived at the mansion on October 2 for two very interesting days.

Mr. Adams was seventy-five years old at the time of his visit, but he possessed the energy and enthusiasm of a much younger person. What a charming and delightful man. He told us with excitement of his plans for several new books, and he spoke just as enthusiastically about his interest in and work for environmental causes.

For two days, Mr. Adams had a captive audience in my husband, who delighted in the opportunity to spend time at the feet of the master. If Mr. Adams had known how many questions he'd have to answer just for room and board, he would never have accepted. The two discussed at length the zone system for black-and-white photography, which Mr. Adams created and made famous. They even spent some time in George's darkroom, developing and printing film they had taken together.

In this short time, they became fast friends. Until his death in 1984, Ansel Adams corresponded regularly with George. They talked by telephone or wrote notes to each other at least

GEORGE BUSBEE

once a month. Mr. Adams's typewritten notes frequently came on postcards bearing his famous photographs. He used the typewriter for correspondence because arthritis in his hands made it difficult for him to write.

Ansel Adams's hands and brilliant mind were busy until his last day. His art has moved millions to appreciate the natural world around us. ■

DINNER FOR ANSEL ADAMS

MENU

Cream of Broccoli Soup

Shrimp Salad

Beef Bourguignonne over Noodles

Vegetable Medley

Herb Bread

Fruit Parfait

CREAM OF BROCCOLI SOUP

1 (14½-ounce) can chicken broth
½ cup chopped onion
2 cups cut fresh broccoli
2 tablespoons butter
3 tablespoons all-purpose flour
¼ teaspoon celery salt
¼ teaspoon white pepper
⅛ teaspoon garlic salt
1½ cups half-and-half

Combine first 3 ingredients in saucepan. Bring mixture to boiling. Reduce heat. Cover and simmer for 10 minutes, or until broccoli is tender. Cool slightly. Place vegetable mixture in blender or food processor. Cover and blend for 30-60 seconds or until smooth. Set aside.

In same saucepan, melt butter. Blend in flour, celery salt, pepper, and garlic salt. Add half-and-half. Cook and stir until mixture is thickened and bubbly. (Do not boil.) Stir in blended vegetable mixture. Cook and stir until soup is heated through. Season to taste.

Yield: 4-6 servings

SHRIMP SALAD

1 pound fresh shrimp, boiled, peeled, deveined, and chopped
2 large stalks celery, chopped
1 small white onion, minced
2 hard-boiled eggs, chopped
½ cup mayonnaise
2 tablespoons lemon juice
salt and pepper to taste
4 ripe tomatoes, quartered most of the way through
lettuce leaves
1 hard-boiled egg, sliced

Combine first 6 ingredients; salt and pepper to taste. Mix lightly. Place tomatoes on salad plates lined with lettuce leaves. Fill each tomato with shrimp salad; garnish with egg slices. Chill thoroughly before serving.

Yield: 4 servings

BEEF BOURGUIGNONNE OVER NOODLES

4-5 pounds beef tenderloin, sliced
all-purpose flour
3 tablespoons olive oil
3 tablespoons butter
5 shallots, minced
1 large onion, coarsely chopped
¾ pound fresh mushrooms, sliced
8 slices bacon, cut into ½-inch pieces
¼ cup cognac, warmed
1½ cups burgundy wine
1½ cups beef stock
1 (16-ounce) package wide egg noodles

Roll beef lightly in flour; shake off excess. In Dutch oven over medium-high heat, sauté beef slices in olive oil and butter with shallots and onion. Add mushrooms and bacon; sauté until mushrooms are soft.

Add warmed cognac and light. Stir in wine and beef stock. Cover and simmer until beef is tender. In meantime, cook egg noodles according to package directions. Serve beef on bed of noodles.

Yield: 8-10 servings

VEGETABLE MEDLEY

1 (10-ounce) package frozen green peas
2 medium carrots, sliced
1½ cups sliced celery
2 summer squash, sliced
salt and pepper to taste
butter or margarine

Cook peas according to package directions. In covered saucepan, cook carrots, celery, and squash in small amount of boiling salted water until tender. Do not overcook. Celery should be slightly crisp. Drain and combine vegetables. Season with salt and pepper. Serve with melted butter.

Yield: 6-8 servings

HERB BREAD

loaf of French bread
½ cup butter or margarine, at room temperature
1 teaspoon dried parsley
¼ teaspoon dried oregano, crumbled
1 clove garlic, minced
¼ teaspoon dried dill
grated parmesan cheese

Preheat oven to 400 degrees.

Cut bread diagonally into 1-inch slices. Mix butter and herbs; spread mixture on both sides of each slice of bread. Place bread on baking sheet; sprinkle liberally with parmesan cheese. Bake for 8-10 minutes.

Yield: 10-12 servings

FRUIT PARFAIT

1 (16-ounce) package frozen sliced strawberries (sweetened)
2 cups whipping cream
3 tablespoons XXXX confectioners' sugar
½ cup cream sherry or rum
3 cups navel orange sections, with membranes removed

Thaw strawberries. Whip cream, gradually adding confectioners' sugar. Fold in cream sherry. Layer in parfait glasses: orange sections, whipped cream, strawberries, and whipped cream. Repeat, ending with whipped cream.

Yield: 8 servings

BREAKFAST FOR ANSEL ADAMS

MENU

Orange Sections and Sliced Bananas

Cheese Omelettes

Crisp Bacon

Toasted Homemade Bread with Blackberry Jelly

GEORGE BUSBEE

CHEESE OMELETTE

3 eggs
1½ tablespoons cream (or 1 teaspoon water)
dash salt
dash pepper
1 teaspoon butter
cooking oil (preferably peanut oil)
⅓ cup grated sharp cheddar cheese

Beat eggs, cream, salt, and pepper together until mixture begins to froth. Add butter in tiny pieces while continuing to beat. When blended, let mixture stand 10 minutes.

Lightly brush omelette pan (or heavy iron skillet) with cooking oil. Place over high heat just until oil starts to smoke. Remove pan from heat and allow smoking to stop. Return pan to heat and pour in egg mixture. Reduce heat slightly.

With narrow spatula, lift edges of egg mixture away from pan as soon as a bottom skin begins to form; at same time, tilt pan to allow any liquid in center to trickle between cooked part of omelette and hot pan. Drop edge of omelette at once. Sprinkle cheese over half of omelette. As soon as top of egg mixture begins to solidify, use spatula to fold plain side of omelette over cheese side. Turn onto warm plate and brush lightly with butter.

Yield: 1 large serving

HOMEMADE BREAD

5½ to 6½ cups all-purpose flour, divided
3 tablespoons sugar
2 teaspoons salt
1 package active dry yeast
1½ cups water
½ cup whole milk
3 tablespoons margarine

In large bowl of electric mixer, thoroughly mix 2 cups flour, sugar, salt, and undissolved yeast. Combine water, milk, and margarine in saucepan; heat over low heat until warm. (Margarine does not have to melt.) Gradually add liquid mixture to dry ingredients; beat for 2 minutes with electric mixer at medium speed, scraping bowl occasionally. Add ¾ cup flour, or enough to make a thick batter. Beat at high speed for 2 minutes, scraping bowl occasionally.

With spoon, stir in enough of remaining flour to make soft dough. Turn out onto lightly floured board. Knead until smooth and elastic, about 8-10 minutes. Place in greased bowl; turn dough over to grease top. Cover; let rise in warm place, free from draft, until doubled (about 1 hour).

Punch down dough; turn onto lightly floured board. Cover and let rest for 15 minutes. Divide dough in half; shape each half into a loaf. Place in greased 8½ x 4½ x 2½-inch loaf pans. Cover; let rise in warm place until doubled (about 1 hour).

In meantime, preheat oven to 400 degrees.

Bake bread for 25-30 minutes, or until done. Remove from pans and cool on wire racks.

Yield: 2 loaves

GARY WOMACK

HIS ROYAL HIGHNESS, PRINCE CHARLES

"Who was the most exciting person you ever entertained at the governor's mansion?" To this question asked so many times, I have always given a diplomatic answer — "All of our guests were interesting in different ways."

Now, I confess. In first place by a healthy margin, His Royal Highness, Prince Charles, the Prince of Wales, was *the* most exciting of all. In October 1977, Prince Charles was our house guest for two days and nights. His visit was the first ever made to the Southeast by British royalty.

As always, the worldwide press was insanely interested in every facet of Prince Charles's trip to Georgia. His visit came "B.D." (before Diana), so media speculation was ever-present about romantic links in America. Our royal guest was paired by the international press with dozens of eligible young ladies long before he arrived in this country.

One of these was our daughter, Jan. (Our older daughter, Beth, was already married.) In advance of Prince Charles's trip to Georgia, a few members of the British press, known for its persistence, waited in the lobby of The Coca-Cola Company, where Jan worked, trying to get an interview or photograph. Knowing the reputation of some of the British press, Jan provided few comments and those were royally misquoted. For example, she was quoted in several publications as saying, "I don't see why a Southern girl shouldn't marry the Prince and become

GARY WOMACK

Queen of England." She never made such a statement.

Preparations for the royal visit required hours of work and attention to detail. Our staff worked closely with Atlanta's British Consul General, Francis Kennedy, who was in frequent communication with Buckingham Palace. All schedules, guest lists, and royal appearances were approved by Buckingham Palace prior to the prince's arrival.

His Royal Highness, Prince Charles, the Prince of Wales, arrived in Atlanta on a Friday afternoon. He was welcomed to Georgia by members of the General Assembly, who had convened in a special session in his honor. After a brief ceremony at the Capitol, Prince Charles arrived at the governor's mansion in time to change clothes for a formal dinner. As he was introduced to our family, the prince turned to Jan and asked with a smile, "Are you the one I'm supposed to be romancing?" A bit embarrassed, Jan replied, "I'm afraid so."

The visit of Prince Charles is a kaleidoscope of memories for me. As the cliché goes, it was an experience I will never forget — the kind that gives clichés their meaning.

One of my most vivid recollections is a conversation with Prince Charles right before George and I escorted him into the ballroom for dinner. After gallantly complimenting me on my appearance, the prince said, in a brief, unguarded moment, "You know, there are times when I really wish I were a bit taller."

With equal sincerity, I responded, "I understand. At 5'10", there are times when I wish I were a bit shorter."

Years later, after learning that Prince Charles would be married, I thought about this conversation. His bride-to-be was described by the British press as a "willowy 5'10" tall."

The next morning, a Saturday, Prince Charles flew to Charleston, South Carolina, for a quick tour of that city with Governor and Mrs. James Edwards. From there, he went to Athens for a University of Georgia football game. George enjoyed explaining American football to him. Although the prince might not have understood everything happening on the football field, he understood the rousing welcome he received from the Georgia football fans.

Later that afternoon, Prince Charles returned to Atlanta to "receive" the city's British community at the Swan House. That night, the city of Atlanta hosted an evening of special entertainment at the Fox Theatre in honor of the prince. Before the performance, we had a small, informal, family dinner at the mansion.

Buckingham Palace had indicated, through Consul General Kennedy, that our royal guest would like to sample some "real Southern food."

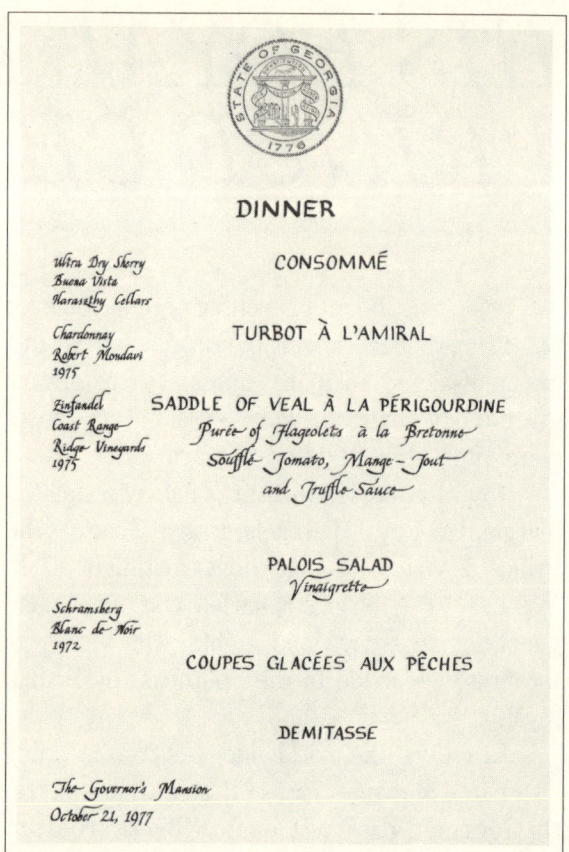

Since Prince Charles had asked to have breakfast of cold cereal and tea in his room each morning, we were unable to introduce him to grits. However, we were able to plan a dinner meal for him which included some traditional Southern favorites.

We kept the number in our dinner party to a minimum, since our guest was surrounded by crowds during the rest of his trip. Only our immediate family; George's executive secretary, Norman Underwood, and his wife, Linda; and two of Prince Charles's aides were invited to the family dinner.

Our guest of honor was not intimidated by the array of "strange" foods on the buffet. He served himself generously — until he came to the fried okra. He warily put two pieces of okra on his plate. As he walked back to his place at the dining table, he popped a piece into his mouth, whirled around, and served himself some more. The dinner conversation was filled with explanations about the food we had chosen to serve him.

The dessert was also a new experience for Prince Charles. When his pecan pie was served, he stared at it for a moment and reached for the coffee cream. As he poured cream over his pie, he asked, "Is this permitted?"

"Yes, of course," I said, pouring cream over *my* pie.

We told him that American pies are frequently served with a scoop of vanilla ice cream on top, so his instincts were in line with Southern palates.

The next morning, Prince Charles attended services at the Cathedral of St. Phillip before leaving for Texas, the next stop on the royal itinerary. As we exchanged good-byes at the airport, he said, "Mrs. Busbee, this has been a most enjoyable visit. It is the first time that I have ever stayed with a family during a foreign visit."

JESSIE SAMPLEY

In comparing "firsts," I think our family got the better end of the deal. It was the first time we ever had a future King of England as a house guest. ■

FAMILY DINNER FOR PRINCE CHARLES

M E N U

Fried Chicken

Fresh Pole Beans   *Squash Casserole*

Creamed Corn   *Fried Okra*

Misty Salad

Corn Sticks

Southern Pecan Pie

M E N U

FRIED CHICKEN

1 (3 to 4-pound) chicken, cut into serving pieces
seasoned salt to taste
lemon & pepper seasoning (optional)
6-7 cups vegetable oil
2 tablespoons butter
1 egg, beaten
½ cup whole milk
2 cups all-purpose flour
2 teaspoons salt
½ teaspoon pepper

Lightly sprinkle each side of chicken pieces with seasoned salt and lemon & pepper seasoning. Cover and refrigerate for 8-10 hours.

In large deep skillet or Dutch oven, heat vegetable oil and butter over medium-high heat. (Oil should be deep enough to completely cover chicken.)

Meanwhile, mix egg and milk in small bowl. Mix flour, salt, and pepper in large bowl. Dip each piece of chicken in egg-milk mixture, turning to coat; place in flour mixture and turn several times to coat well.

When vegetable oil reaches 350 degrees, carefully drop chicken pieces in 1 at a time. Do not crowd chicken in skillet. Cook 7 minutes and turn. Cook an additional 7-8 minutes, or until brown and crisp. Remove chicken to pan lined with paper towels. Repeat procedure with remaining chicken. (Note: Allow oil to return to 350 degrees before cooking remainder of chicken.)

Yield: 6-8 servings

FRESH POLE BEANS

(recipe on page 98)

SQUASH CASSEROLE

1 pound yellow squash
1 large onion, grated
1 cup grated cheddar cheese
¼ cup heavy cream
2 tablespoons butter, melted
1 egg, beaten
dash ground nutmeg
salt and pepper to taste
½ cup cracker crumbs
paprika

Preheat oven to 350 degrees.

Cut squash into ½-inch slices. In medium saucepan, cook squash and onion in small amount of boiling salted water for 12-15 minutes, or until tender. Drain well in colander.

In medium bowl, combine squash, onion, cheese, cream, butter, egg, nutmeg, salt, and pepper; mix well. Pour into lightly greased 1½-quart casserole. Top with cracker crumbs; sprinkle lightly with paprika. Bake, uncovered, until center is set and crumbs are lightly browned, about 30 minutes.

Yield: 4-6 servings

CREAMED CORN

12 ears tender fresh white corn
3 tablespoons bacon drippings
½ teaspoon salt
pepper to taste
½ teaspoon sugar
whole milk, if needed
2 tablespoons butter

With sharp knife, cut tips of kernels off each ear of corn. Over a bowl, scrape each ear to remove the "milk" and remaining pulp.

Heat bacon drippings in large heavy skillet over medium-high heat. Add corn. Cook, stirring constantly, for several minutes. Add salt, pepper, and sugar. If corn is dry, add small amount of whole milk.

Reduce heat to low. Simmer for 15-20 minutes. Watch carefully and stir often to avoid scorching corn. Stir in butter 5 minutes before serving.

Yield: 6-8 servings

FRIED OKRA

4 cups cut fresh okra
1 egg, beaten
1 cup plain cornmeal
1 cup vegetable oil
salt to taste

In bowl, stir okra and egg together, coating okra well. Place cornmeal in paper bag. Pour okra into bag; shake bag to thoroughly coat okra with cornmeal.

Heat vegetable oil in large heavy skillet over medium-high heat. When oil is hot, spoon half of okra into skillet. Cook, turning once, until okra is golden brown. Remove with slotted spoon to paper towels to drain. Salt while very hot. Repeat with remaining okra.

Yield: 6 servings

MISTY SALAD

1 (20-ounce) can crushed pineapple, in heavy syrup
1 (3-ounce) package lime-flavored gelatin
1 (3-ounce) package lemon-flavored gelatin
¼ teaspoon salt
1 cup small curd cottage cheese
1 cup mayonnaise
½ cup chopped pecans
¼ cup lemon juice
lettuce leaves

Drain pineapple, reserving syrup. Add water to syrup to make 2 cups. In large saucepan, heat syrup and water just to boiling; remove from heat. Add lime gelatin, lemon gelatin, and salt. Stir until gelatin is dissolved. Cool until slightly thickened.

Fold in crushed pineapple, cottage cheese, mayonnaise, pecans, and lemon juice. Pour into lightly oiled 6-cup mold. Cover with plastic wrap. Refrigerate overnight or until firm. To serve, unmold onto lettuce leaves.

Yield: 12 servings

CORN STICKS

1 cup plain cornmeal
1 tablespoon baking powder
½ teaspoon salt
½ teaspoon sugar
pinch baking soda
1 cup buttermilk
1 egg
¼ cup vegetable oil

Preheat oven to 450 degrees.

Pour ½ teaspoon vegetable oil into each slot of 2 cast-iron corn stick pans. Heat pans in oven for 30 minutes. Meanwhile, combine cornmeal, baking powder, salt, and sugar in medium bowl; stir to mix.

Remove corn stick pans from oven. Pour out excess oil; return pans to oven. Add baking soda to buttermilk. Pour buttermilk into dry ingredients. Quickly and vigorously beat in egg. Add vegetable oil and beat into mixture with spoon. Working quickly, remove heated pans from oven to wire rack. With serving spoon, fill each slot with cornbread batter.

Bake for 15-20 minutes, or until lightly browned. Remove from oven. With a fork, loosen corn sticks from pans. Serve hot.

Yield: 14 corn sticks

SOUTHERN PECAN PIE

3 eggs
1 cup light corn syrup
½ cup dark brown sugar
¼ teaspoon salt
1 teaspoon vanilla extract
2 teaspoons lemon juice
1 cup broken pecan halves or small pecan halves
1 (9-inch) Pie Crust (recipe on page 194)

Preheat oven to 425 degrees.

In small bowl of electric mixer, beat eggs. Add corn syrup, sugar, salt, vanilla extract, and lemon juice. Beat thoroughly. Stir in pecans and pour into unbaked Pie Crust.

Bake for 10 minutes. Reduce oven temperature to 325 degrees. Bake for 35-40 minutes, or until filling is set and crust is golden.

Yield: 6-8 servings

FRESHMAN LEGISLATORS

Every two years while George was in office, we invited all the newly elected state legislators to dinner at the mansion. They were a great group to entertain. These new senators and representatives had all recently arrived in Atlanta for their first legislative session and were most appreciative of the welcome they received at the mansion.

We always wanted these occasions to be memorable for the fledgling legislators. I know one young man who will never forget his first dinner at the governor's mansion — although not for the reasons you might expect. His reputation as an egregious practical joker had preceded the gentleman from the 139th district and his colleagues were ready for him.

As dessert was being served, there was a whispered conversation between George and one of our guests. (I later learned that a plan was being proposed which required George's cooperation.) He excused himself from the table as if to take an important telephone call. In reality, he made a call to the state troopers at the front gate.

After dinner, as the new legislators began to leave, George and I walked onto the front porch to say good-night to our guests. A few cars passed through the gate when suddenly the trooper-controlled "arm" came down to block the driveway. The young legislator from the 139th district got out of his car and was promptly frisked by a state trooper. A silver spoon, planted by George's co-conspirator, was removed from his coat pocket. A long minute passed as the red-faced legislator gestured wildly. The pantomime slowed as it gradually dawned on him — he had finally met his match. ■

FRESHMAN LEGISLATIVE DINNER

MENU

Baked Ham

Green Beans Amandine Candied Yams

Waldorf Salad

Small Corn Muffins

Ice Cream with Crème de Cassis

Shortbread Cookies

BAKED HAM

Preheat oven to 325 degrees.

Place a 10 to 14-pound smoked baked ham fat side up on rack in open roasting pan. Bake for 20 minutes per pound. About 30 minutes before ham is done, trim skin and excess fat from top. Spread with Glaze and return to oven. When ham is done, slice into serving pieces. Garnish each serving with pineapple slice and cherry, if desired.

GLAZE FOR BAKED HAM:

1 cup dark brown sugar
1 tablespoon all-purpose flour
1 teaspoon dry mustard
1 tablespoon cider vinegar
3 tablespoons frozen concentrated orange juice

Combine all ingredients. Stir until smooth and spread over ham.

Yield: 16-20 servings

GREEN BEANS AMANDINE

2 pounds fresh green beans
½ teaspoon salt
½ cup slivered almonds
3 tablespoons butter or margarine
2 teaspoons lemon juice
½ teaspoon salt

Cut each bean in half lengthwise. In large saucepan, bring 3 cups salted water to boil. Add beans; return to boil. Cover; reduce heat. Simmer 20 minutes; drain.

In small skillet, sauté almonds in butter until golden. Reduce heat; stir in lemon juice and ½ teaspoon salt. Toss with beans.

Yield: 6-8 servings

CANDIED YAMS

6 medium yams
½ cup dark brown sugar
¼ cup butter
½ cup miniature marshmallows

Wash yams and cut off tough ends. Cook, covered, in boiling salted water for 30-40 minutes.

In meantime, preheat oven to 375 degrees. Drain yams; cool slightly and peel. Cut into ½-inch slices.

Layer yams in lightly greased 2-quart casserole with brown sugar and bits of butter, ending with sugar and butter. Bake, uncovered, for 30 minutes. Sprinkle with marshmallows and bake an additional 5 minutes.

Yield: 6 servings

WALDORF SALAD

1 envelope unflavored gelatin
⅓ cup sugar
½ teaspoon salt
1½ cups water, divided
¼ cup vinegar or lemon juice
2 cups diced tart apples
½ cup chopped celery
¼ cup chopped pecans

Mix gelatin, sugar, and salt in small saucepan. Add ½ cup of water. Place over low heat, stirring constantly until gelatin is dissolved. Remove from heat and stir in remaining cup of water and vinegar. Chill mixture until it is consistency of unbeaten egg white. Fold in apples, celery, and pecans.

Turn into 4-cup mold or 8 individual molds. Cover and refrigerate until firm. Unmold by dipping mold into warm water. Loosen edge with tip of knife. Place serving dish on mold and turn upside down. Shake, holding serving dish tightly to mold. Garnish with fruit, if desired.

Yield: 8 servings

SMALL CORN MUFFINS

1 cup all-purpose flour
1 cup plain cornmeal
4 teaspoons baking powder
¾ teaspoon salt
2 eggs
1 cup whole milk
¼ cup vegetable oil

Preheat oven to 425 degrees.

Stir together flour, cornmeal, baking powder, and salt. Add eggs, milk, and oil. Beat just until smooth. (Do not overbeat.) Spoon into greased miniature muffin tins. Bake for 15 minutes.

Yield: 2½ dozen

ICE CREAM WITH CRÈME DE CASSIS

1 quart of vanilla ice cream
crème de cassis

Place large scoop of vanilla ice cream in each of 8 stemmed glasses. Pour 2 teaspoons of crème de cassis over each scoop of ice cream. Serve immediately.

Yield: 8 servings

SHORTBREAD COOKIES

2¼ cups sifted all-purpose flour
¼ teaspoon baking powder
1 cup butter, at room temperature
½ cup plus 1 tablespoon sugar

Resift flour twice with baking powder. In large bowl of electric mixer, cream butter until shiny. Gradually add sugar, creaming well. Stir in flour in 2 or 3 portions, mixing until smooth after each addition.

Preheat oven to 325 degrees.

Shape dough into ball and knead several times with hands to blend well. On lightly floured board, roll to ¼-inch thickness, keeping shape as nearly rectangular as possible.

Cut dough into 2-inch squares. Place on ungreased baking sheet ½ inch apart. Prick each cookie diagonally with tines of large serving fork. Bake for 18-20 minutes, or until cookies are a delicate golden color. Immediately remove from baking sheet to wire racks to cool.

Yield: 3 dozen

NEW FIRST LADIES

Governors from all fifty states are banded together through the National Governors Association. They meet annually in a different state, with a meeting also held in Washington, D.C., each year.

Governors' spouses have no formal organization, but they do share many common interests. A special kind of closeness forms among them over the years. However, the differences in our states and the differences in people dictate that the role of first lady can vary greatly.

Just as women's interests in general have changed dramatically over the last fifteen to twenty years, so have the interests of governors' wives. (And due to these changes, we are seeing more and more governor's *husbands*!) The "tea-pouring" role is virtually extinct now. In my eight years as first lady, I found most of the other women in this position to be articulate, vocal, and active people — not only in their supportive roles, but in their individual interests, as well.

Every four years, the National Governors Association sponsors a seminar for newly elected governors. These seminars are working sessions for the governors and their spouses, and they are usually held in a resort area. The new governors are, for the most part, coming out of a long, hard, and exhausting campaign.

In November 1978, during George's term as Chairman of the National Governors Association, the new governors seminar was held at Georgia's Pine Isle. It was my privilege to entertain a dozen new governors' wives and their aides at a luncheon at the mansion.

My guests were, of course, interested in seeing the Georgia governor's mansion. After a tour of the house, we had an informal time of discussion. Each one of them was apprehensive about her new job but eager to begin . . . just as I had been four years earlier. They had many questions about mansion staffing, entertaining, and the effects of their new roles on their families. This time of sharing was followed by lunch in the mansion ballroom. ∎

NEW FIRST LADIES LUNCHEON

MENU

Avocado Mousse

Creamed Shrimp in Puff Pastry Shells

Crisp Green Beans

Apple Nut Cake

AVOCADO MOUSSE

1 envelope unflavored gelatin
¼ cup cold water
¾ cup chicken bouillon, boiling
1 teaspoon worcestershire sauce
½ teaspoon lemon juice
¼ teaspoon onion salt
½ teaspoon sugar
¼ teaspoon salt
cayenne pepper to taste
½ cup whipping cream
1 large, very ripe avocado
½ cup mayonnaise
lettuce leaves
2 pimiento-stuffed green olives, sliced

Dissolve gelatin in cold water. Add bouillon, worcestershire sauce, lemon juice, onion salt, sugar, salt, and cayenne pepper. Chill until slightly thickened.

Whip cream. Purée avocado. Fold whipped cream, avocado, and mayonnaise into gelatin mixture. Pour into lightly oiled individual salad molds. Cover with plastic wrap; refrigerate for at least 3 hours. Unmold onto lettuce leaves. Garnish with olive slices.

Yield: 6 servings

CREAMED SHRIMP IN PUFF PASTRY SHELLS

1 (10-ounce) box Pepperidge Farm frozen Patty Shells (6 shells)
2 tablespoons unsalted butter
1 pound fresh shrimp, peeled and deveined
3 green onions, chopped
2 teaspoons all-purpose flour
½ teaspoon fresh chopped dill (or ¼ teaspoon dried dill)
¾ cup half-and-half, heated
2 egg yolks
1 teaspoon lemon juice
salt and pepper
chopped parsley for garnish

Bake patty shells according to package directions. Cool on wire rack.

Melt butter in skillet. Cut each shrimp in half; add to butter. Cook, stirring, over medium-high heat for 3-4 minutes. Remove with slotted spoon and set aside. Add green onions to skillet and cook for 30 seconds. Stir in flour and dill; cook for 1 minute. Add half-and-half; stir until thickened. Remove from heat.

Beat egg yolks lightly in a bowl. Gradually stir warm sauce into beaten egg yolks. Return mixture to skillet and cook over low heat, stirring constantly, until thickened. (Do not boil.)

Add shrimp and lemon juice. Season with salt and pepper. Cook until shrimp are heated through. Fill patty shells with creamed shrimp; garnish with chopped parsley.

Yield: 3-6 servings

CRISP GREEN BEANS

2 pounds small, tender green beans
1 teaspoon salt
2 cups water
6 tablespoons butter
salt
coarse ground pepper

Leave beans whole, removing only ends; wash. Bring salted water to boil. Drop in beans; cover and reduce heat. Cook for 10-15 minutes, until beans are just tender. Drain beans and set aside.

Melt butter in skillet. Sauté beans for 1-2 minutes. Add salt and coarse ground pepper to taste.

Yield: 8 servings

APPLE NUT CAKE

1¼ cups vegetable oil
2 cups sugar
3 eggs
3 cups all-purpose flour
1 teaspoon baking soda
1 teaspoon salt
2 teaspoons vanilla extract
3½ cups peeled, cored, and finely chopped cooking apples
1 cup chopped pecans
Glaze for Apple Nut Cake

Preheat oven to 350 degrees.

Mix oil and sugar. Add eggs; beat well. Sift flour, baking soda, and salt together. Add to sugar mixture, mixing well. Stir in vanilla extract, apples, and pecans. Pour into greased and floured 9 x 13 x 2-inch baking dish. Bake for 40-45 minutes, or until center of cake tests done. Pour Glaze over cake while cake is still warm. Cool. Cut cake into squares.

Yield: 15 servings

GLAZE FOR APPLE NUT CAKE:

1 cup sugar
½ teaspoon baking soda
½ cup buttermilk
1 tablespoon light corn syrup
¼ cup butter or margarine
1 teaspoon vanilla extract

Combine sugar, baking soda, buttermilk, syrup, and butter in large saucepan. Cook until soft ball stage (234 degrees on candy thermometer), stirring occasionally. Remove from heat. Add vanilla extract. Beat until almost cool. Pour over cake.

BILL BIRDSONG

CONGRESSIONAL AIDES NOSTALGIA PARTY

For George and me, a mansion event that rated high on the fun meter was the annual congressional aides party. Each year Washington-based aides to Georgia's U.S. senators and representatives were our guests at an informal gathering at the mansion. These people handle constituent services for Georgia citizens in Washington and are responsible for many of the governor's legislative concerns "on the hill."

The purpose of this annual function was simple: We wanted to create a relaxed atmosphere in which various state department officials could put a face with a name for the congressional aides with whom they usually dealt by long-distance telephone. The congressional aides received a better understanding of how Georgia's state government works, and we felt that this resulted in a more effective team working on behalf of the state.

Capable of creating the most formal of dinners, our mansion staff was also adept at putting on delicious, yet informal buffets. In 1979, the congressional aides were treated to a nostalgia party which had all of the elements of the rock-and-rolling fifties, right down to the jukebox. Everyone involved liked the idea of planning something different — everyone, that is, except the "dignified" governor. He balked when we suggested that he dress like "The Fonz." George didn't object to the character — he just didn't know who "The Fonz" was. Never one to be on top of the latest television hits, he was given a "briefing" on this phenomenon by our youngest son and was finally coaxed into wearing the appropriate attire.

Who had the best time of all? You guessed it — "The Fonz"! ■

BILL BIRDSONG

NOSTALGIA PARTY

MENU

Lasagna

Pizza

Tossed Green Salad   Relish Tray

Brennan's Garlic Bread

Pineapple and Lime Sherbert

Sugar Cookies

LASAGNA

2 pounds lean ground beef
1 pound sweet Italian sausage
1 clove garlic, minced
2 (16-ounce) cans Italian-style tomatoes
4 (6-ounce) cans tomato paste
¼ cup chopped fresh parsley
2 tablespoons chopped fresh basil or 1 teaspoon dried basil
4½ teaspoons salt
1½ teaspoons sugar
1 teaspoon coarsely ground pepper
½ teaspoon dried oregano leaves, crumbled
14 ounces lasagna noodles (about 18 noodles)
1 tablespoon olive oil
3 eggs
2 (15-ounce) containers ricotta cheese
4 (8-ounce) packages mozzarella cheese

In 7-quart Dutch oven, cook ground beef, sausage, and garlic, stirring frequently, until browned. Drain.

Add tomatoes and their liquid and the next 7 ingredients. Heat to boiling over high heat. Reduce heat to low; simmer about 25 minutes, stirring frequently, until sauce is slightly thickened.

Preheat oven to 350 degrees.

Meanwhile, cook lasagna noodles with olive oil according to package directions; drain. In medium bowl, beat eggs with fork. Stir in ricotta cheese.

Grease 2 (12 x 9 x 2½-inch) baking pans. Thinly slice mozzarella cheese. Into each pan, spoon about 1 cup tomato sauce. Arrange 3 noodles in layer over sauce. Spread ¼ of ricotta cheese mixture over noodles in each pan. Top with layer of sliced mozzarella. Repeat layers once. Top with remaining noodles and tomato sauce. Cut remaining mozzarella into strips and arrange in attractive pattern on top.

Bake for about 1 hour, or until hot and bubbly. Let stand 10-15 minutes before serving.

(Note: This freezes nicely. To bake frozen lasagna, thaw wrapped lasagna overnight in refrigerator. Cover pan with aluminum foil and bake at 350 degrees for 1½ hours, or until hot and bubbly. Uncover during last 10 minutes of baking to slightly brown top.)

Yield: 16 servings

Pizza for the nostalgia party came from Franco's — we did not attempt to compete with their delicious Italian pie. Franco not only delivered two dozen pizzas to the mansion, but he stayed to serve them.

BRENNAN'S GARLIC BREAD

1 loaf French bread
4 cloves garlic
½ cup butter, melted
¼ cup grated parmesan cheese
1 tablespoon minced fresh parsley
½ teaspoon paprika

Preheat oven to 350 degrees.

Thoroughly rub outside crust of bread with 2 slightly crushed cloves of garlic. Split loaf in half lengthwise; place each half, crust down, on ungreased baking sheet.

Crush remaining cloves of garlic in garlic press; combine with melted butter. Brush over cut surfaces. Mix remaining ingredients; sprinkle over buttered bread surfaces.

Cut bread diagonally into 2-inch slices. Bake for 12-15 minutes, until very hot.

Yield: 12 servings

SUGAR COOKIES

1 cup butter or margarine, at room temperature
2 cups sugar
3 eggs
2 teaspoons vanilla extract
4 cups sifted all-purpose flour
2 teaspoons baking powder
colored or plain sugar

In large bowl of electric mixer, cream butter and sugar. Add eggs; beat until fluffy. Add vanilla extract, flour, and baking powder; mix well. Cover and refrigerate until dough is very firm.

Preheat oven to 325 degrees.

Roll about ¼ of dough out at a time on floured board. Roll to ⅛-inch thickness; do not overwork or dough will stick to board. Cut out cookies with 2-inch cookie cutter. Sprinkle with colored or plain sugar.

Place cookies on ungreased baking sheets. Bake for 10 minutes, or until lightly browned.

Yield: 6½ dozen

HIS MAJESTY, KING HUSSEIN I

His Majesty Hussein I, King of the Hashemite Kingdom of Jordan, after meeting with President Carter in Washington and Secretary General Kurt Waldheim at the United Nations, arrived in Atlanta on April 29, 1977. A meeting with members of the Southern Center for International Studies was the primary item on his agenda. We were privileged to have King Hussein as our house guest on the evening of his arrival in Georgia.

King Hussein appeared at the mansion gates in kingly fashion — a long black limousine sporting flags on each fender. Soon after being escorted through the front door, His Majesty asked for a tour of the governor's mansion. We ended the tour at the presidential suite, where he would be spending the night.

At all times, King Hussein was accompanied by the Commander in Chief of the Jordan Armed Forces, who acted as his personal bodyguard. Of all our many guests, there was no one as security conscious as King Hussein. Not surprising, when you consider that at the age of sixteen he saw his grandfather, King Abdullah I, assassinated. And since that time he had seen many attempts on his own life.

GARY WOMACK

King Hussein's bodyguard selected fruit for him from the family fruit bowl in the kitchen, instead of from the fruit bowl in the presidential suite. The fresh fruit we had placed in our guest's room remained untouched throughout his visit, apparently as a precaution against poisoning.

Preparations for His Majesty's visit began weeks in advance of the occasion. A lengthy file of background information sent to us from the Office of the Chief of Protocol at the Department of State in Washington included pronunciations of proper names, correct forms of address, and even placecard information.

GARY WOMACK

We were given strict guidelines on the types of foods which should be served to our guest. Dietary restrictions and personal food preferences were considered in planning our menus. For example, we were told that "out of deference to Muslim religious prohibitions, pork and pork products should not be served to King Hussein and his party. He does not eat snails or shellfish. . . . Alcoholic beverages may, however, be served."

According to the State Department, certain toasting procedures were to be adhered to at all functions honoring King Hussein. "The first toast should be made by the host to His Majesty, the King of the Hashemite Kingdom of Jordan." We were told that King Hussein would respond with a toast to the President of the United States, and that "subsequent toasts, if any, may be made in declining order of precedence." Before our guest's arrival, George rehearsed his toast, so that "Hashemite" would come out with the emphasis on the right syllable.

On April 29, following weeks of planning, a black-tie dinner was given at the governor's mansion in honor of King Hussein. The sixteen guests included Dean Rusk, former Secretary of State; Milton Folds, Georgia's Commissioner of Industry and Trade; and Peter White, President of the Southern Center for International Studies.

The detailed file of briefing papers and our weeks of planning paid off. The evening went smoothly — right down to the toasts. George initiated the toasting procedures, and the guest of honor reciprocated as we had been told he would.

The conversation that evening ranged from very serious discussions about world affairs to the lighter subjects of hobbies and travel experiences. During the evening, we learned that King Hussein shared a number of mutual interests with my husband. (Both are avid pilots and photographers.) His Majesty was particularly amused to learn that the flounder served at dinner was gigged by George in the coastal waters of Georgia. ■

DINNER IN HONOR OF KING HUSSEIN

MENU

Onion Soup

Flounder Veronique

Spinach Mushroom Salad

Filet Mignon Sauté

Parsleyed New Potatoes   Fresh Green Beans

Southern Angel Biscuits

Savannah Trifle

ONION SOUP

5 cups thinly sliced onions
3 tablespoons butter
1 tablespoon vegetable oil
1 teaspoon salt
¼ teaspoon sugar
3 tablespoons all-purpose flour
2 quarts beef bouillon, boiling
½ cup dry white wine or vermouth
salt and pepper to taste

Cook onions slowly with butter and oil in covered saucepan for 15 minutes. Uncover. Raise heat to moderate, and stir in salt and sugar.

Cook for 30-40 minutes, stirring frequently, until onions have turned deep golden brown. Sprinkle in flour and stir for 3 minutes.

Remove from heat and blend in boiling bouillon. Add wine and season to taste. Simmer, partially covered, for 30-40 minutes, skimming occasionally.

Set aside, uncovered, until ready to serve. Reheat to simmer before serving.

Yield: 6-8 servings

FLOUNDER VERONIQUE

¼ cup cognac
1 cup seedless white grapes
6 filets of flounder
1 tablespoon minced onion
1 teaspoon lemon juice
½ cup dry white wine
2 tablespoons butter
2 tablespoons all-purpose flour
1 cup light cream
¼ teaspoon salt
dash white pepper
½ cup small shrimp, cooked and peeled

Preheat oven to 350 degrees.

Pour cognac over grapes. Roll filets and place in baking dish. Sprinkle with onion and lemon juice. Pour wine over all. Cover and bake for 15 minutes.

Meanwhile, melt butter in saucepan over medium heat; stir in flour until smooth. Slowly add cream; stir constantly until thickened. Add salt, pepper, and shrimp. Cook, stirring constantly, until shrimp are heated through.

Pour shrimp sauce over filets and sprinkle with grapes.

Yield: 6 servings

SPINACH MUSHROOM SALAD

3 quarts fresh spinach, washed and dried
12 fresh mushrooms, washed and sliced
½ cup Vinaigrette
2 hard-boiled eggs, finely chopped
1 (2-ounce) jar diced pimiento, drained
seasoned croutons

Tear spinach into bite-sized pieces. Toss with sliced mushrooms and Vinaigrette. Place on 6 chilled salad plates. Sprinkle each salad with chopped eggs. Garnish with diced pimiento and croutons.

Yield: 6 servings

VINAIGRETTE:

½ teaspoon salt
⅛ teaspoon freshly ground pepper
¼ cup vinegar or lemon juice
¼-½ teaspoon prepared mustard
¾ cup olive oil

Place first 4 ingredients in jar with tight-fitting lid. Cover and shake until blended. Add olive oil gradually, shaking between additions. If made in advance, cover Vinaigrette and refrigerate. Shake well before using.

Yield: 1 cup

FILET MIGNON SAUTÉ

3-4 tablespoons butter
8 (1-inch) filets of beef
½ cup dry red wine
¼ cup beef bouillon

Melt butter in large skillet over medium heat. Sauté filets in butter for 3-4 minutes a side; remove to warm serving platter. Deglaze skillet with mixture of wine and bouillon. Pour deglazing liquid over filets before serving.

Yield: 8 servings

PARSLEYED NEW POTATOES

12 small new potatoes
1 teaspoon salt
4-6 tablespoons butter
4 tablespoons chopped fresh parsley

Wash potatoes and peel a ½-inch strip of skin from around the center of each potato. Drop potatoes into boiling, salted water. Cover and reduce heat. Cook for 20-25 minutes, or until tender.

While potatoes are cooking, melt butter in skillet. When potatoes are done, drain and add them to butter. Sprinkle parsley over potatoes and toss well to coat. Serve immediately.

Yield: 4 servings

FRESH GREEN BEANS

1½ pounds fresh green beans
1 quart water
¼ pound salt pork
2 teaspoons salt

String beans and break into 1½-inch pieces. Wash. Heat water to boiling and add meat. Cover and cook 15 minutes. Add beans and salt. Cook over medium-low heat until beans are fork tender, about 30 minutes.

Yield: 4-6 servings

SOUTHERN ANGEL BISCUITS

(recipe on page 99)

SAVANNAH TRIFLE

1½ quarts whole milk
1½ cups sugar
2 tablespoons cornstarch
6 eggs
¾ cup dry sherry, divided
1 pint whipping cream
1 loaf pound cake
raspberry preserves
¼ cup slivered almonds

Pour milk into large saucepan or double boiler. In large bowl of electric mixer, beat together sugar, cornstarch, and eggs until smooth; add to milk. Heat until mixture is thickened, stirring constantly. Set aside to cool.

Add half of sherry to cooled custard. Whip cream and set aside. Cut cake into ¾-inch-thick slices. Arrange single layer of cake slices in bottom of glass trifle bowl. (A deep, 3-quart glass bowl can be used instead of a trifle bowl.)

Sprinkle cake layer with part of remaining sherry. Spread with thin layer of preserves and layer of custard. Sprinkle with part of almonds. Spread layer of whipped cream over all. Repeat layers until all ingredients are used, ending with whipped cream. Cover and refrigerate overnight before serving.

Yield: 12 servings

On the morning following the black-tie dinner, King Hussein was treated to an old-fashioned Southern breakfast. One item on the menu was a slight variation from the standard fare. Beef bacon, instead of pork, was served out of respect for His Majesty's religious affiliation. (Beef bacon can be purchased at any large grocery store, and is cooked in the same manner as pork bacon.)

BREAKFAST FOR KING HUSSEIN

MENU

Strawberries and Cream

Scrambled Eggs

Fried Grits

Beef Bacon

Buttermilk Biscuits   Fig Preserves

STRAWBERRIES AND CREAM

1 quart fresh strawberries, washed and hulled
¼ cup sugar
1½ cups heavy cream

Combine strawberries and sugar; mix gently. Cover and chill for several hours.

Spoon strawberries into individual fruit bowls. Pour ¼ cup chilled cream over each serving.

Yield: 6 servings

SCRAMBLED EGGS

8 large eggs
½ cup whole milk
½ teaspoon salt
dash pepper
3 tablespoons butter or margarine

Beat together eggs, milk, salt, and pepper, mixing thoroughly. Heat butter in frying pan over medium heat, until just hot enough to sizzle a drop of water. Pour in egg mixture.

As mixture begins to set, turn a spatula over and draw it across the bottom of the pan, forming large soft curds. Do this until eggs are thickened and cooked through, but still moist. (Note: Do not stir constantly.)

Yield: 4 servings

FRIED GRITS

4 cups water
½ teaspoon salt
1 cup uncooked, quick-cooking grits
2 eggs
¼ cup butter or margarine

Bring water and salt to a boil; stir in grits. Cook grits until done, according to package directions. Remove from heat, and pour into a greased 8½ x 4½ x 3-inch loaf pan. Cool. Cover and refrigerate.

Remove grits by inverting pan. Cut loaf into ½-inch slices. Beat eggs. Melt butter in large skillet. Dip each slice in egg. Fry over medium heat 5-7 minutes or until lightly browned, turning once.

Yield: 8 servings

BUTTERMILK BISCUITS

4 cups self-rising flour
1 tablespoon baking powder
1 tablespoon sugar
⅔ cup vegetable shortening
2 cups buttermilk
melted butter or margarine

Preheat oven to 450 degrees.

Combine flour, baking powder, and sugar; mix well. Cut in shortening with pastry blender until mixture resembles coarse meal. Add buttermilk, stirring until dry ingredients are mixed in.

Turn dough onto lightly floured board. Knead lightly 6-8 times, or until enough flour is worked in to roll out dough. Roll dough to ½-inch thickness. Cut with 2½-inch biscuit cutter.

Place biscuits on greased baking sheet. Brush tops with melted butter. Bake for 10-12 minutes, until golden brown. Brush with additional butter.

Yield: approximately 2 dozen

ENTERTAINING FOR INDUSTRY AND TRADE

Milton Folds, Georgia's Commissioner of Industry and Trade, was encouraged by George to utilize the mansion to meet with industrialists and business leaders who were interested in building plants or investing in Georgia. We entertained and provided lodging for business people from all parts of the United States and the world. A week seldom passed in which we did not have such a group at the mansion for a dinner or reception.

We found that the most effective way to entertain these guests was to have a seated dinner for eighteen in the state dining room. Keeping the group small enabled George and Milt Folds to talk easily with all of our guests.

Following is a menu for one of the dinner parties held in honor of visiting industrialists. This particular meal was planned and prepared by Lee Hopper, our first "chef/food manager." A native Atlantan, Lee graduated from Georgia Southern College and studied at the Cordon Bleu in London. ∎

DINNER FOR VISITING INDUSTRIALISTS

MENU

Duck Terrine

Romaine and Spinach Salad with Caesar Sour Cream Dressing

Veal with Mustard Sauce

Duchess Potatoes on Artichoke Bottoms   Crisp Green Beans

Herb Biscuits

Macedoine of Fruit   Butter Cookies

DUCK TERRINE

6 (3½ to 4-pound) ducks, skinned and boned, with whole breasts set aside and skin from 2 ducks reserved
2 pounds ground lean pork
1 pound ground lean veal
½-¾ pound ground pork fat
2 pounds bacon, simmered 10 minutes to remove smoke flavor
4 eggs
1 cup chopped onion, sautéed
2 cloves garlic, mashed into a paste with 1½ tablespoons salt
1 tablespoon salt
1½ teaspoons dried thyme
½ teaspoon allspice
½ teaspoon black pepper
4 bay leaves

Preheat oven to 350 degrees.

Grind all meat and fat together with exception of 6 whole duck breasts and bacon. Line 13 x 4 x 4-inch loaf pan with bacon, allowing for overlay which will be folded over top of duck mixture. In large bowl, combine ground meat mixture with eggs, onion, garlic, salt, thyme, allspice, and pepper. Place ½ of mixture in pan; arrange reserved breast meat down center. Place remaining mixture on top. Fold bacon over top. Drop onto counter to settle. Place bay leaves down center; cover with duck skin. Wrap tightly in aluminum foil.

Place loaf pan in a larger, deep-sided pan. Weight loaf pan on top. Fill larger pan with enough water to come up to rim of loaf pan. Bake for 1½ to 2 hours, or until juices run clear. Cool. Refrigerate overnight, weighted on top. To serve, cut into slices.

Yield: 20 first-course servings

ROMAINE AND SPINACH SALAD WITH CAESAR SOUR CREAM DRESSING

1 pound fresh romaine lettuce, washed, dried, and torn into bite-sized pieces
1 pound raw spinach, washed, dried, and torn into bite-sized pieces
alfalfa sprouts for garnish
cracked black pepper
Caesar Sour Cream Dressing

Toss romaine and spinach in large salad bowl. Place on chilled salad plates. Garnish with alfalfa sprouts and sprinkle lightly with pepper. Serve with Caesar Sour Cream Dressing.

Yield: 12 servings

CAESAR SOUR CREAM DRESSING:

2 cups mayonnaise
1¼ cups sour cream
½ cup minced fresh parsley
⅓ cup minced capers
¼ cup minced green onion
1 clove garlic, minced
1 tablespoon dried tarragon soaked in 2 tablespoons tarragon vinegar for 15 minutes
2 tablespoons fresh lemon juice
1 anchovy filet, minced

Combine all ingredients in large bowl of electric mixer; blend well. Cover and refrigerate until ready to use.

Yield: 1 quart

VEAL WITH MUSTARD SAUCE

8 veal scaloppine (about 1 pound)
⅓ cup all-purpose flour
salt and pepper to taste
4 tablespoons butter
2 tablespoons finely minced shallots
¼ cup dry white wine
½ cup heavy cream
1 tablespoon Dijon mustard

Place scaloppine on flat surface; pound with flat mallet until thin. Blend flour with salt and pepper; dredge scaloppine on all sides.

Heat butter in large, heavy skillet until it is quite hot, but not brown. Add scaloppine. Cook over medium-high heat until golden on one side, about 2 minutes. Turn and cook until golden on second side. Remove scaloppine to warm platter; cover with aluminum foil and keep warm.

Add shallots to skillet and cook over medium-high heat until tender, stirring constantly. Add wine and cook, stirring, until wine is almost totally evaporated. Add cream and allow to boil, stirring constantly. Cook 30 seconds and remove from heat. Stir in mustard. Spoon sauce over veal and serve.

Yield: 4 servings

DUCHESS POTATOES ON ARTICHOKE BOTTOMS

4-5 large Idaho baking potatoes
1 teaspoon garlic salt
1 teaspoon monosodium glutamate (Ac'cent)
1 drop Tabasco sauce
2 tablespoons butter
3-4 egg yolks
¼ cup grated parmesan cheese
8-10 artichoke bottoms

Peel and quarter potatoes. In large saucepan, cook potatoes, covered, in boiling salted water for 20-30 minutes, until tender; drain. In meantime, preheat oven to 350 degrees.

In large bowl of electric mixer, whip potatoes. Add all ingredients except artichoke bottoms. Beat until light and fluffy.

Place potato mixture in pastry bag with a star tube tip. Pipe potato mixture onto each artichoke bottom, swirling it into conelike shape. Arrange in buttered 9 x 13 x 2-inch baking dish. Bake, uncovered, for 20-30 minutes.

Yield: 8-10 servings

CRISP GREEN BEANS

(recipe on page 37)

HERB BISCUITS

1½ cups all-purpose flour
1 teaspoon salt
½ teaspoon baking soda
2 teaspoons baking powder
¼ cup vegetable shortening, chilled
2 tablespoons minced fresh parsley
2 tablespoons minced fresh chives (or 1 tablespoon freeze-dried)
1 egg
¾ cup buttermilk (may need a few more drops)

Preheat oven to 450 degrees.

Combine flour, salt, baking soda, and baking powder in mixing bowl. Rapidly cut in shortening with pastry blender until pieces are size of kosher salt grains.

Stir herbs into flour mixture. Beat egg and buttermilk together in small bowl. Pour into flour mixture, mixing rapidly with rubber spatula, turning and pressing ingredients together to form dough. Turn dough out onto lightly floured board. Knead dough quickly with floured hands to give it enough body to roll it out (the less kneading, the better).

Roll dough out to ½-inch thickness. Cut into rounds with 2-inch biscuit cutter. Place 1 inch apart on ungreased baking sheets. Bake for 10-15 minutes, or until biscuits are lightly browned.

Yield: 1½ dozen

MACEDOINE OF FRUIT

1 cup seedless grapes, halved lengthwise
1 (11-ounce) can mandarin orange sections, drained
1½ cups fresh, hulled strawberries
½ cup fresh blueberries
½ cup sliced kiwi fruit
¼ cup Cointreau liqueur
1 ripe banana

Combine all fruits except banana in bowl. Pour Cointreau over fruit. Stir gently to mix. Cover and refrigerate for several hours.

Just before serving, slice banana and add to fruit mixture; stir gently to mix. Serve in individual stemmed glasses.

Yield: 8 servings

BUTTER COOKIES

1 cup butter or margarine, at room temperature
¾ cup sugar
1 egg
½ teaspoon vanilla extract
2½ cups all-purpose flour
1 teaspoon baking powder
¼ teaspoon salt
2 drops yellow food coloring

Preheat oven to 350 degrees.

In large bowl of electric mixer, cream butter. Gradually add sugar, beating until light and fluffy. Add egg and vanilla extract; beat well. Combine flour, baking powder, and salt; gradually add to creamed mixture. Mix well. Add food coloring and mix well.

Using a cookie press, press dough into desired shapes onto ungreased baking sheets. Bake for 10-12 minutes. Remove cookies to wire racks to cool.

Yield: 6 dozen (2-inch) cookies

GEORGIA HOUSE SPEAKER TOM MURPHY

No member of the Georgia State Legislature is wined and dined during the legislative session more than the Speaker of the House of Representatives, the Honorable Tom Murphy. Frequently attending two or three functions an evening, the Speaker is the center of one "mob scene" after another.

Early in my husband's first administration, he suggested that we invite the Speaker to a quiet, relaxed meal with us at the mansion. Since George had some state business to discuss with Tom, we limited the dinner to the three of us.

I really wanted to serve a meal that Tom would enjoy — not something that he would get on the legislative dinner circuit. Having spent the last twenty-five years of my life in south Georgia, I felt there was no meal as special as a quail dinner. Our menu for the evening was planned around this delicacy.

When Tom's quail was placed before him, I don't know who was more surprised — the Speaker or George. Everyone in the state knows that Tom Murphy does not eat quail — everyone, that is, except Mary Beth.

After turning down my offer to have another meat prepared, the Speaker enjoyed the rest of his meal and politely shoved the poor quail around on his plate. Fortunately, the success of George's legislative programs was not determined by that dinner.

In the ensuing years, Tom and I have laughed many times over the quail dinner. Each year after that December night ten years ago, we invited the Speaker over for roast beef. You can bet that I know how he likes his beef cooked. (Well-done, if you're curious.)

If you have never eaten quail, I hope you will give the following recipe a try. The meat is mild and delicate. I think you will find it delicious. The Speaker would too, if he'd just try it. ■

DINNER FOR SPEAKER TOM MURPHY

MENU

Oyster Stew

Fresh Mushroom and Romaine Salad

Baked Quail

Wild Rice   Steamed Broccoli with Wine Sauce

Yam Balls

Buttermilk Biscuits

Puff Shells filled with Vanilla Ice Cream and Fudge Sauce

OYSTER STEW

4 tablespoons butter
1 medium onion, chopped
2 (12-ounce) containers fresh oysters in their liquor
1 teaspoon dried parsley flakes
½ teaspoon worcestershire sauce
¼ teaspoon Tabasco sauce
salt and pepper to taste
2 cups whole milk

Melt butter in large saucepan. Sauté onion in butter. Add oysters and their liquor, parsley, worcestershire sauce, Tabasco sauce, salt, and pepper. Cook over medium heat, stirring occasionally, until oysters curl.

Meanwhile, heat milk in small saucepan to just under boiling. Pour into oyster mixture. Stir and serve at once.

Yield: 4-6 servings

FRESH MUSHROOM AND ROMAINE SALAD

½ pound fresh mushrooms
lemon juice
2-3 heads romaine lettuce
Herb Dressing

Wash, dry, and slice mushrooms; sprinkle with lemon juice.

Wash and drain romaine lettuce. Tear into bite-sized pieces and arrange on salad plates. Place sliced mushrooms on romaine. Serve with Herb Dressing.

Yield: 6 servings

HERB DRESSING:

1 cup white vinegar
2 tablespoons sugar
1 teaspoon salt
1 teaspoon paprika
1 tablespoon Salad Herbs
1 tablespoon worcestershire sauce
½ cup vegetable oil
3 cloves garlic, crushed

Mix first 6 ingredients in saucepan. Cook

over medium-low heat for 8 minutes, stirring occasionally. Cool.

Add vegetable oil and garlic. Pour into jar with tight-fitting lid. Shake well before using.

Yield: 1 cup

BAKED QUAIL

salt and pepper
6 quail
6 tablespoons butter
3 tablespoons all-purpose flour
2 cups chicken broth
½ cup dry sherry

Preheat oven to 350 degrees.

Salt and pepper quail. Brown in butter in heavy skillet or Dutch oven. When golden, remove quail to deep baking dish.

Add flour to butter in skillet and stir well. Slowly add chicken broth and sherry; blend well. Bring to boil and pour over quail. Cover tightly and bake for 1 to 1½ hours, until tender.

Yield: 3-4 servings

WILD RICE

(prepare according to package directions)

STEAMED BROCCOLI WITH WINE SAUCE

1 large head broccoli
Wine Sauce

Remove large leaves and tough parts of broccoli stalks. Wash broccoli thoroughly and separate into stalks. Arrange broccoli in steamer rack with stalks to center. Place over boiling water.

Cover and steam for 10 minutes, or until crisp-tender. Serve with Wine Sauce.

Yield: 6 servings

WINE SAUCE:

1 cup mayonnaise
¼ cup dry white wine
1 teaspoon lemon juice
¼-½ teaspoon curry powder

Combine all ingredients in small saucepan. Cook over low heat until sauce is heated through, stirring frequently. Do not boil.

Yield: 1¼ cups

YAM BALLS

¼ cup butter, melted
¼ cup whole milk
2 tablespoons sugar
½ teaspoon salt
¼ teaspoon pepper
4 cups mashed, cooked yams
18-20 miniature marshmallows
3 cups coarsely crushed corn flakes

Preheat oven to 375 degrees.

Beat butter, milk, sugar, salt, and pepper into yams. Form 2-inch balls with marshmallow centers; roll in corn flakes.

Place in greased 13 x 9 x 2-inch baking pan. Bake for 25-35 minutes. (Note: These can be prepared ahead, frozen, and baked without defrosting. If frozen, bake yam balls for 45 minutes.)

Yield: 6 servings

BUTTERMILK BISCUITS

(recipe on page 48)

PUFF SHELLS FILLED WITH VANILLA ICE CREAM AND FUDGE SAUCE

½ cup water
¼ cup butter or margarine
½ cup all-purpose flour
⅛ teaspoon salt
2 eggs
1 quart vanilla ice cream
Fudge Sauce

Preheat oven to 400 degrees.

In medium saucepan, combine water and butter. Bring to boil. Add flour and salt all at once; stir vigorously. Cook and stir until mixture leaves sides of pan and forms a ball. Remove from heat; cool slightly, about 5 minutes.

Add eggs, 1 at a time. Beat well after each addition for 1 minute, or until smooth. Drop dough by heaping tablespoonfuls 3 inches apart onto greased baking sheet. Bake for 30-35 minutes, or until golden and puffed.

Remove puffs to cake rack. Cut off top ⅓ of each puff with serrated knife. Remove any soft dough inside. Cool puffs and fill each with a scoop of vanilla ice cream. Replace top. Serve warm Fudge Sauce over each.

Yield: 6 servings

FUDGE SAUCE:

2 (1-ounce) squares unsweetened chocolate
¼ cup plus 2 tablespoons water
½ cup sugar
dash salt
6 tablespoons butter or margarine
½ teaspoon vanilla extract

Combine chocolate and water in small saucepan. Cook over low heat until chocolate melts. Stir in sugar and salt. Simmer for 5 minutes. Stir in butter and vanilla extract.

Yield: 1¼ cups

MINISTER PRESIDENT FILBINGER OF GERMANY

Bringing new industry and trade into Georgia was an important part of George's job as governor. We made annual treks to Europe with officials from the Georgia Department of Industry and Trade. Government officials, businessmen, and industrialists in many European countries were all fair game for George's sales pitch.

Without exception, we received gracious hospitality wherever we went, and European interest in Georgia was keen. As we left each place, George invited our new friends to come to Georgia. I often accused him of going all over the world saying, "Y'all come!" And come they did.

In early 1976, we met Minister President Hans Filbinger and his wife in Stuttgart, Germany. Minister President Filbinger held an office equivalent to a governor in the United States. His state, or province, was Baden-Wurttemberg.

The Filbingers accepted our invitation to visit Georgia and arrived in October 1976, soon

BILL BIRDSONG

after the weather had turned cold. Each room in the mansion has its own thermostat for temperature control, so George showed the Filbingers how to operate the one in their room, the presidential suite.

At breakfast the next morning, the Filbingers said they had slept fine, but later asked if they could have a few more blankets for the remaining nights. We gathered extra blankets from other bedrooms in the mansion and put them on our guests' bed.

The following morning, the conversation again turned to how they had slept, and again they wanted more blankets. There was only one more blanket in the house — the one on our bed. I took it to the Filbingers' room and turned up the heat in our room.

Our guests said they slept fine that last night. After they left, we checked the thermostat in the presidential suite for a possible malfunction and discovered why they needed so many blankets. Our hale and hearty German friends had turned off the heat in their room and slept with all the windows open. It must have been toasty under all those blankets, but the getting in and out had to be a little brisk. ■

Mansion Manager Mary Dwozan inspects the table setting

BILL BIRDSONG

DINNER FOR MINISTER PRESIDENT AND MRS. FILBINGER

MENU

Oysters Thomas

Golden Pheasant Salad

Filet of Beef Stephanie

Crusty Baked Potatoes   Spinach-Stuffed Tomatoes

Herb Bread

Prune Cake

OYSTERS THOMAS

16-24 unshucked oysters
4-5 slices bread, toasted
2 green onions
1 sprig fresh parsley
¼ pound King crab meat
2 tablespoons butter, melted
2-3 tablespoons grated parmesan cheese

Preheat oven to 375 degrees.

Shuck oysters and leave on halfshell. Finely chop toasted bread, onions, and parsley tops; mix together. Add crab meat, butter, and parmesan cheese; mix well.

Place oysters on jellyroll pan and bake until slightly curled. Remove from oven. Form crab meat mixture into 16-24 thin patties; cover each oyster with a crab meat patty. Return oysters to oven until slightly brown and hot through. Serve on folded napkins on plates.

Yield: 4-6 servings

GOLDEN PHEASANT SALAD

1 clove garlic
½ teaspoon salt
¼ teaspoon black pepper
6 tablespoons vegetable oil
4 ounces blue cheese
dash cayenne pepper
dash worcestershire sauce
3 tablespoons red wine vinegar
1 head lettuce, broken into bits
1 medium onion, sliced into ¼-inch rings
6 stemmed fresh mushrooms, sliced
¼ cup finely chopped walnuts

Crush garlic in wooden salad bowl, rubbing into wood grain. Remove bulk. Add salt, black pepper, and oil; mix well. Add cheese and crush with fork, mixing well with oil (leaving a few small lumps of cheese whole). Add cayenne pepper, worcestershire sauce, and vinegar; mix well.

Add lettuce, onion rings, and mushrooms. Toss gently, mixing well. Sprinkle with walnuts and serve on chilled salad plates.

Yield: 6-8 servings

FILET OF BEEF STEPHANIE

6 (7 to 8-ounce) filets of beef
salt and pepper
Veal Farce
2 (17¼-ounce) packages Pepperidge Farm Puff Pastry
Béarnaise Sauce
2 fresh mushrooms, sliced

Season filets with salt and pepper; grill lightly on both sides. Let cool. In meantime, preheat oven to 450 degrees.

Spread a ¼-inch layer of Veal Farce around outside of each filet (not top and bottom). Wrap a strip of puff pastry around each filet. Pastry should come up a little higher than top of filet. Bake for about 15 minutes. Pastry should be nicely browned and meat medium rare to medium. While filets are baking, make Béarnaise Sauce.

Just before serving, spoon small amount of Béarnaise Sauce over each filet, keeping sauce inside of pastry. Garnish with mushroom slice.

Yield: 6 servings

VEAL FARCE:

1 cup finely ground cooked veal
salt and white pepper to taste
2 tablespoons chopped shallots
4 tablespoons heavy cream
2-3 tablespoons chopped fresh mushrooms
½ ounce cognac

Mix all ingredients together.

BÉARNAISE SAUCE:

3 tablespoons white wine vinegar
1 teaspoon finely chopped shallot or green onion
4 whole black peppercorns, crushed
dash dried tarragon, crushed
dash dried chervil, crushed
1 tablespoon cold water
4 egg yolks
½ cup butter, at room temperature, divided
1 teaspoon snipped fresh tarragon or ¼ teaspoon dried tarragon, crushed

Mix vinegar, shallot, peppercorns, tarragon, and chervil in saucepan. Bring to boil. Reduce heat and simmer until reduced to half. Strain, discarding solids; add cold water to herb liquid.

Beat egg yolks in top of double boiler (not over heat). Slowly add herb liquid. Add 2 tablespoons of the butter to egg yolks; place over simmering water. Cook and stir until butter melts and sauce begins to thicken. Continue adding remaining butter, 2 tablespoons at a time, while stirring constantly. Cook and stir until sauce is consistency of thick cream. Remove from heat. Stir in tarragon.

Yield: ¾ cup

CRUSTY BAKED POTATOES

4 tablespoons butter
4 medium baking potatoes
1 cup fine dry bread crumbs
1 teaspoon salt
1 teaspoon paprika

Preheat oven to 350 degrees.

Melt butter in saucepan. Wash and peel potatoes; pat dry. Mix bread crumbs, salt, and paprika together. Roll potatoes in butter; coat evenly with bread crumb mixture.

Place potatoes in buttered 2-quart casserole. Cover and bake for 45-50 minutes. Remove cover; turn potatoes. Bake another 15-20 minutes, until potatoes are tender. Serve with butter and sour cream, if desired.

Yield: 4 servings

HERB BREAD

(recipe on page 21)

SPINACH-STUFFED TOMATOES

8 medium, unpeeled ripe tomatoes
salt
8 slices bacon
2 (10-ounce) packages frozen chopped spinach
¾ cup soft bread crumbs
salt and pepper to taste
dash ground nutmeg
dash garlic powder
melted butter
sour cream

With sharp knife, cut thin slice from top of each tomato. Scoop out center pulp; discard. Sprinkle insides of tomatoes with salt; turn tomatoes upside down to drain for an hour.

Preheat oven to 350 degrees.

Cook bacon until crisp; crumble and set aside. Cook frozen spinach according to package directions, until thawed. Drain thoroughly.

Combine spinach with crumbled bacon, bread crumbs, salt, pepper, nutmeg, and garlic powder. Stuff tomatoes with this mixture; place in buttered baking dish. Drizzle small amount of melted butter over tomatoes.

Bake, uncovered, for about 20 minutes, or until tomatoes are tender when pricked with a fork. Do not overcook. Before serving, top each tomato with dollop of sour cream.

Yield: 8 servings

PRUNE CAKE

2½ cups sifted all-purpose flour
1 teaspoon baking soda
1 teaspoon ground cinnamon
1 teaspoon ground allspice
1 teaspoon ground nutmeg
1 teaspoon salt
1 cup vegetable oil
3 eggs, beaten
1½ cups sugar
1 cup buttermilk
1 cup chopped cooked prunes
1 cup chopped pecans
1 teaspoon vanilla extract
Glaze for Prune Cake

Preheat oven to 300 degrees.

Mix together flour, baking soda, cinnamon, allspice, nutmeg, and salt. In large bowl of electric mixer, combine oil, eggs, and sugar; mix well. Alternately add flour mixture and buttermilk until all is used; mix. Add prunes, pecans, and vanilla extract. Mix well with spoon. Pour into 9 x 13 x 2-inch baking dish. Bake for 1 hour. Pour Glaze over cake. Cool and cut into squares.

Yield: 15 servings

GLAZE FOR PRUNE CAKE:

1 cup sugar
½ cup buttermilk
½ teaspoon baking soda
1 teaspoon light corn syrup
½ cup margarine
1 teaspoon vanilla extract

Mix all ingredients in saucepan. Boil for 2 minutes, stirring occasionally. Cool slightly before pouring over warm cake.

BREAKFAST FOR MINISTER PRESIDENT AND MRS. FILBINGER

MENU

Fresh Pineapple Chunks

Baked Eggs   Crisp Bacon

Workhorse Waffles

Georgia Honey and Cane Syrup

BAKED EGGS

6 teaspoons butter
6 eggs
6 teaspoons grated cheddar cheese
6 teaspoons minced fresh parsley
salt
pepper
worcestershire sauce
paprika
Tabasco sauce

Preheat oven to 350 degrees.

Place 1 teaspoon butter into each of 6 oven-proof custard cups. Break 1 egg into each cup. Sprinkle each egg with 1 teaspoon cheese and 1 teaspoon parsley. Add salt, pepper, worcestershire sauce, paprika, and Tabasco sauce to taste.

Place custard cups on baking sheet and bake for 15 minutes, or until eggs are cooked to desired doneness.

Yield: 3-6 servings

WORKHORSE WAFFLES

1¾ cups all-purpose flour
1 tablespoon baking powder
½ teaspoon salt
2 egg yolks
1¾ cups whole milk
½ cup vegetable oil
2 egg whites

In large mixing bowl, stir together flour, baking powder, and salt. In small mixing bowl, beat egg yolks with a fork. Beat in milk and vegetable oil. Add to flour mixture all at once. Stir mixture until blended, but still slightly lumpy.

In small bowl of electric mixer, beat egg whites until stiff peaks form. Gently fold beaten egg whites into flour-milk mixture. Do not overmix.

Pour batter onto grids of preheated, lightly greased waffle iron. Close lid quickly; do not open during baking. When waffles are done, lift off of grid with a fork.

To keep waffles hot for serving, place in warm oven in single layer on wire rack placed on baking sheet.

Yield: 3-4 (8-inch) waffles

LARRY PATRICK

OUR FIRST FAMILY WEDDING

Few times are as exciting as getting ready for a family wedding, but our first one was more than we bargained for.

As soon as we moved into the mansion, our new staff was thrust into planning a wedding reception for one thousand people. Our first child, Beth, was to be married in a June wedding on the mansion grounds. On March 24, while Beth was visiting her future in-laws in Valdosta, Georgia, a vicious tornado roared through northwest Atlanta, the worst to hit the city in decades.

The governor's mansion was directly in harm's way. George and I and our younger son, Jeff, were home when the tornado came through in the early morning hours of that day. Our other son, Buz, was living in Albany. Jan, our younger daughter, was driving back to Atlanta after a beach trip.

Damage to the mansion was extensive. Within seconds, scores of beautiful hundred-year-old oak trees were reduced to splinters. Others were totally uprooted. The huge columns on the front side of the mansion were ripped off and deposited throughout the surrounding area. The roof was heavily damaged. Debris littered the sculptured grounds.

Jan heard the news on her car radio minutes before a state trooper pulled her over to tell her we were OK. As soon as telephone communications were restored, we called the rest of our family to let them know we were unhurt.

Beth was relieved to hear our voices, but then came the tearful question, "What about my wedding?" The ceremony was to take place in the west garden of the mansion just two months later. I reassured Beth that the wedding would go on as planned, but as we spoke, I looked around the room for someone to reassure me.

BILL BIRDSONG

LARRY PATRICK

The "clean-up" that took place over the next few weeks was truly a miracle, wrought by Steve Polk and his staff at the Georgia Building Authority. Thanks to many wonderful, hard-working people — all giving above and beyond the call of duty — our daughter was not disappointed. Indeed, on June 7, in the beautiful gardens of the Georgia governor's mansion, Beth became the bride of Robert Hugh Wiggins.

As a result of this union, George and I are the proud grandparents of twins, Brian Christopher and Patrick Busbee Wiggins, and triplets, Stuart Allen, Ashley Elizabeth, and Brooke Lauren Wiggins. I think the good Lord knew what He had planned for Beth and Bob, and He provided the tornado as a preview. ■

BILL BIRDSONG

WEDDING RECEPTION

MENU

Spiced Pineapple Chunks

Toasted Pecans   Cheese Wafers

Chicken Salad in Toast Cups

Assorted Sandwiches

Fresh Fruit

Cheese Dreams

Angel Food Rum Strips   Orange Balls

Frosted Cake Squares

Wedding Mints

Betty Sanders's Peach Punch

Golden Summer Punch

SPICED PINEAPPLE CHUNKS

3 (20-ounce) cans pineapple chunks, in heavy syrup
2½ cups sugar
1½ cups cider vinegar
16 whole cloves
2 short cinnamon sticks
dash salt

Day or two before serving: Into large saucepan, drain syrup from pineapple; reserve pineapple. Add remaining ingredients to syrup. Cook over medium heat for 10 minutes. Add pineapple chunks; heat to boiling. Remove from heat; cool slightly and refrigerate.

Before serving, drain pineapple. Serve with cocktail picks.

Yield: 16 appetizer servings

TOASTED PECANS

3 cups pecan halves
¼ cup butter or margarine
1 teaspoon Angostura bitters
1 teaspoon seasoned salt

Preheat oven to 300 degrees.

Place pecans in 13 x 9-inch pan. Bake for 20 minutes, stirring once or twice.

Meanwhile, melt butter in small saucepan. Add bitters and seasoned salt; stir to blend. Pour butter mixture over pecans; stir to evenly coat pecans. Toast 15 minutes, or until done, stirring occasionally. (Pecans should darken and be cooked through.)

Sprinkle with additional seasoned salt, if desired. Spread pecans on paper towels to dry and cool.

Yield: 3 cups

CHEESE WAFERS

(recipe on page 88)

CHICKEN SALAD IN TOAST CUPS

(recipe on page 137)

ASSORTED SANDWICHES

Most party sandwiches should be made with day-old bread, which is easier to slice than very fresh bread. Following are recipes for three types of sandwiches frequently used at the mansion for large receptions. These can be made ahead, wrapped tightly, and refrigerated. When preparing sandwiches in advance, spread a small amount of softened butter on the bread before spreading the filling. This will prevent moist fillings from soaking into the bread and making it soggy.

RIBBON PIMIENTO CHEESE SANDWICHES

1 (4-ounce) jar pimientos, undrained
3 cups (12 ounces) grated sharp cheddar cheese, at room temperature
3 tablespoons mayonnaise
½ teaspoon prepared mustard
12 thin slices white bread
6 thin slices dark bread

Drain pimientos, reserving liquid. Finely chop pimientos. In large bowl of electric mixer, blend cheese, pimientos and their liquid, mayonnaise, and mustard until smooth. (Note: This makes 2 cups of pimiento cheese spread.)

Spread thin layer of pimiento cheese on slice of white bread; cover with a slice of dark bread. Spread with pimiento cheese; cover with a slice of white bread. Start again and repeat this process until all ingredients are used. Wrap each "sandwich" tightly and refrigerate for several hours or overnight.

Remove sandwiches from refrigerator and unwrap. With sharp bread knife trim crusts from bread. Slice each sandwich into 6 (½-inch wide) strips.

Yield: 3 dozen

CREAM CHEESE OPEN-FACED SANDWICHES

1 (8-ounce) package cream cheese, at room temperature
½ teaspoon grated onion
2 teaspoons mayonnaise
1 (4½-ounce) jar pimiento-stuffed olives, drained and divided
butter, at room temperature
20 thin slices of bread

Beat cream cheese in small bowl of electric mixer. Add onion and mayonnaise; mix well. Finely chop 12 olives; stir into cream cheese mixture.

Lightly butter bread slices and spread with thin layer of cream cheese mixture. With 1½-inch sandwich cutter, cut 4 rounds from each bread slice. Slice remaining olives. Garnish each sandwich with olive slice.

Yield: 6½ dozen

HAM PINWHEELS

1 cup chopped cooked ham
½ teaspoon grated onion
1 teaspoon prepared mustard
2 tablespoons mayonnaise
¼ cup whole milk
loaf of unsliced bread
butter, at room temperature

Combine ham, onion, mustard, mayonnaise, and milk in bowl. Mix well. Trim crusts from bread. Slice bread lengthwise into 8 long slices. Lightly roll each slice with rolling pin and spread lightly with butter. Spread each piece of bread with thin layer of ham mixture. Carefully roll each slice in jellyroll fashion. Place seam side down in small pan. Cover tightly and refrigerate for several hours.

Remove sandwich rolls from refrigerator. With sharp bread knife, cut each roll into 6 pinwheel sandwiches.

Yield: 4 dozen

CHEESE DREAMS

¾ cup butter, at room temperature
1 pound grated sharp cheddar cheese, at room temperature
dash cayenne pepper
dash salt
3 cups all-purpose flour
3 (8-ounce) boxes pitted dates
approximately 2 cups pecan halves

In large bowl of electric mixer, cream together butter and cheese. Add cayenne pepper, salt, and flour. Mix well; chill.

Preheat oven to 350 degrees.

Stuff each date with a pecan half. Pinch off small pieces of dough and wrap around stuffed dates, completely encasing the dates with a thin layer of dough. Press dough firmly onto dates.

Place on ungreased baking sheet and bake for 20 minutes, or until light golden.

Yield: approximately 9 dozen

ANGEL FOOD RUM STRIPS

1 cup butter, melted
½ cup rum
12-16 ounces XXXX confectioners' sugar
14-ounce angel food cake (loaf is preferable)
14 ounces shredded, sweetened coconut, toasted

Mix butter and rum. Gradually add confectioners' sugar, stirring, until mixture is slightly thickened.

Cut angel food cake into ¾ x 3-inch strips. Dip cake strips, 1 at a time, into icing. Roll in toasted coconut. Place on sheets of wax paper to dry and firm up. Store in covered container.

Yield: 3-4 dozen

ORANGE BALLS

1 (12-ounce) package vanilla wafers
2 cups XXXX confectioners' sugar, divided
1 (6-ounce) can frozen orange juice concentrate, thawed
¾ cup chopped pecans

Crush vanilla wafers. Add 1 cup confectioners' sugar; mix well. Add orange juice concentrate; mix well. Add pecans; mix well. Shape mixture into balls the size of walnuts. Roll balls in remaining cup of confectioners' sugar and lay out on wax paper. Allow to firm up for 1-2 hours. Store in covered container.

Yield: 3 dozen

FROSTED CAKE SQUARES

2 cups all-purpose flour
1 tablespoon baking powder
1 teaspoon salt
¾ cup vegetable shortening
1½ cups sugar
1½ teaspoons vanilla extract
1 cup whole milk
5 egg whites
Butter Frosting

Preheat oven to 375 degrees.

Grease and lightly flour a 9 x 13 x 2-inch baking pan. Combine flour, baking powder, and salt. In large bowl of electric mixer, beat shortening on medium speed for about 30 seconds. Add sugar and vanilla extract; beat until fluffy. Alternately add dry ingredients and milk to beaten mixture, beating on low speed after each addition.

Wash beaters. In small mixer bowl, beat egg whites until stiff peaks form. Gently fold into flour mixture. Turn into prepared pan.

Bake for 30 minutes. Cool for 10 minutes on wire rack; remove from pan. Cool. Frost top of cake with Butter Frosting. Cut into 2-inch squares.

Yield: 24 servings

BUTTER FROSTING:

6 tablespoons butter, at room temperature
4½ to 4¾ cups sifted XXXX confectioners' sugar, divided
¼ cup whole milk
1½ teaspoons vanilla extract
additional whole milk, as needed

In small bowl of electric mixer, beat butter until light and fluffy. Gradually add half of confectioners' sugar, beating well. Beat in milk and vanilla extract. Gradually beat in remaining sugar, then additional milk if necessary, to make frosting of spreading consistency.

WEDDING MINTS

1 (3-ounce) package cream cheese, at room temperature
½ teaspoon peppermint extract
3 cups sifted XXXX confectioners' sugar
1-2 drops food coloring

In small bowl of electric mixer, cream softened cream cheese and peppermint extract. Gradually add confectioners' sugar, heaping tablespoonfuls at a time, beating after each addition until smooth. Knead in last additions of sugar with hands. Knead in food coloring until evenly distributed.

If using rubber molds to form mints, press ½ to ¾ teaspoon cream cheese-sugar mixture into each mold. To roll out and cut, place mixture between 2 sheets of wax paper; roll out to ⅛-inch thickness. Cut diagonally with metal spatula into diamond-shaped pieces, or cut with small round cutter.

Allow mints to dry overnight at room temperature. Store in airtight container. Mints keep for 2 weeks at room temperature and 1 month in freezer.

Yield: 6-8 dozen molded mints (10 dozen small diamonds or rounds)

BETTY SANDERS'S PEACH PUNCH

24 (12-ounce) cans peach concentrate, or 9 quarts fresh peach purée
1¾ gallons water
2¼ quarts ginger ale
1½ pints orange juice
¾ cup pineapple juice
¾ cup lemon juice
1 quart champagne
1½ quarts fresh peach halves and slices

Mix all ingredients except champagne and fresh peaches; chill. Pour punch into chilled punch bowls. Add champagne; float peach halves and slices in punch.

Yield: 130 servings (5 gallons)

GOLDEN SUMMER PUNCH

3 (12-ounce) cans frozen orange juice concentrate
3 (12-ounce) cans frozen lemonade concentrate
6¾ quarts water
6 (12-ounce) cans apricot nectar
3 (46-ounce) cans pineapple juice

Mix orange juice and lemonade concentrates with water. Combine with apricot nectar and pineapple juice; chill. Serve in chilled punch bowls.

Yield: 100 servings (4 gallons)

PRESIDENT-ELECT JIMMY CARTER

"Early in December 1976, I went to Atlanta and borrowed from Governor George Busbee an office and a couple of rooms in the governor's mansion. From that familiar setting I conducted my final interviews with those I was considering for Cabinet posts."

— President Jimmy Carter
from *Keeping Faith, Memoirs of a President*

During his term as president, Jimmy Carter was our guest at the mansion several times. However, none of these visits was as exciting for the Busbee family and mansion staff as his December 1976 visit, when he was still president-elect. It was thrilling to see history in the making, to watch the parade of Cabinet hopefuls coming and going through the mansion.

President-elect Carter made no announcements to the media during the Cabinet selection process. This, of course, fed the curiosity of reporters and television news crews, who stood in a pack at the mansion gates trying to catch a glimpse of the final contenders as they drove through. The crush of media people made it almost impossible for anyone to enter or leave the mansion grounds.

Knowing that the president-elect faced years of eating fancy gourmet meals, we fed him simple Southern meals during his visit. An avid trout fisherman, he particularly enjoyed this "supper" menu. ■

President-elect Jimmy Carter greets the mansion staff

OFFICIAL WHITE HOUSE PHOTO

SUPPER FOR PRESIDENT-ELECT JIMMY CARTER

MENU

Fried Rainbow Trout

Hushpuppies   Coleslaw

Relish Tray
(bread and butter pickles, green tomato pickles, and banana peppers)

Lemon Cheese Cake

FRIED RAINBOW TROUT

vegetable oil
salt
3 pounds dressed fresh rainbow trout (or trout filets if fish are over ½-pound each)
3 cups plain cornmeal

In deep fat fryer or Dutch oven, heat enough vegetable oil to cover fish. While oil heats, salt fish. Pour cornmeal into paper bag; add fish and shake to coat.

When temperature of oil reaches 375 degrees, quickly drop in fish. Cook for 5 minutes. Remove fish and drain on newspaper covered with paper towels.

Place fish in 200-degree oven to keep warm until all fish have been fried. (Note: After removing fish from hot oil, allow oil to return to 375 degrees before dropping in more fish.)

Yield: 4 servings

HUSHPUPPIES

2 cups plain cornmeal
1 tablespoon all-purpose flour
½ teaspoon baking soda
1 teaspoon baking powder
1 teaspoon salt
3 tablespoons chopped onion
1 egg
1¼ cups buttermilk, divided
vegetable oil used for frying fish

Combine cornmeal, flour, baking soda, baking powder, and salt in bowl. Mix well. Stir in chopped onion. In separate bowl, beat egg; add 1 cup buttermilk and mix well.

In deep fat fryer or Dutch oven, heat vegetable oil to 375 degrees. Add buttermilk mixture to cornmeal mixture, stirring to mix well.

Dip an iced teaspoon into a cup of cold water and scoop up a rounded teaspoonful of batter. Drop batter into hot oil; repeat until all is used. (As batter sits, it will thicken. Stir in ¼ cup buttermilk when batter becomes too thick.)

Cook hushpuppies until golden brown. Remove from oil and drain on newspaper covered with paper towels.

Yield: 4 dozen

COLESLAW

1 head cabbage, shredded or coarsely chopped (8 cups)
1 small carrot, grated
1 tablespoon grated onion
¼ cup sweet relish, with juice
1 cup mayonnaise
½ teaspoon sugar
¼ teaspoon celery seed
¼ teaspoon salt
⅛ teaspoon pepper

Combine first 4 ingredients in large mixing bowl. In separate bowl, combine mayonnaise, sugar, celery seed, salt, and pepper; mix well. Spoon mayonnaise mixture over cabbage mixture. Stir to mix well. Cover and refrigerate until serving time.

Yield: 10 servings

LEMON CHEESE CAKE

1 cup butter, at room temperature
2 cups sugar, divided
1 teaspoon vanilla extract
3 cups sifted all-purpose flour
1 tablespoon baking powder
⅛ teaspoon salt
1 cup whole milk
5 egg whites, at room temperature
Lemon Cheese Filling
7-Minute Icing (see recipe on following page)

Prepare 3 (9-inch) round cake pans: Using pan for pattern, cut 3 circles of wax paper. Grease sides of pans with vegetable shortening and place wax paper in bottom of each pan.

Preheat oven to 350 degrees.

In large bowl of electric mixer, cream butter. Gradually add 1 ¾ cups sugar, blending until mixture is thoroughly creamed. Add vanilla extract and mix. Sift flour, baking powder, and salt together 3 times. Alternately add flour mixture and milk (beginning and ending with flour) to creamed butter and sugar, mixing thoroughly after each addition.

In small bowl of electric mixer, beat egg whites until just stiff enough to form soft, shiny peaks. Gradually beat in remaining ¼ cup sugar. Gently fold beaten egg whites into batter. Pour batter into prepared pans.

Bake for 20 minutes, or until cake tests done. Cool in pans for 5 minutes. Turn out of pans onto wire racks. Remove wax paper immediately; cool.

Spread Lemon Cheese Filling between cooled cake layers. Cover top and sides of cake with 7-Minute Icing.

Yield: 16 servings

LEMON CHEESE FILLING:

½ cup butter
1 cup sugar
6 egg yolks, beaten
grated rind and juice of 2 lemons

Melt butter in top of double boiler. Add sugar, beaten egg yolks, lemon rind, and lemon juice. Cook, stirring constantly, until mixture thickens (about 10 minutes). Cool before spreading on cake layers.

7-MINUTE ICING:

1 egg white
⅛ teaspoon cream of tartar
dash salt
3 tablespoons cold water
¾ cup sugar
½ teaspoon vanilla extract
2 teaspoons light corn syrup

Place first 5 ingredients in top of double boiler over boiling water. (Upper pan should not touch surface of water.) Beat mixture with hand-held electric mixer for 4-5 minutes, or until icing stands in pointed, stiff peaks. Remove from heat.

Pour hot water out of pan and replace with cold water. Place pan of icing over cold water. Add vanilla extract and corn syrup to icing. Beat until icing stands in shiny peaks and is stiff enough to hold shape. Immediately spread on top and sides of cake.

VISITING AMBASSADORS FROM FOREIGN COUNTRIES

Over the years, several of the official representatives of foreign governments to the United States made their way from Washington, D.C., to Georgia. Entertaining ambassadors was an interesting and enjoyable part of George's efforts to build beneficial relationships for Georgia with other countries.

One of our first such visitors was Ambassador Menelas Alexandrakis of Greece. In the years following his visit in 1975, Georgia established close ties with Greece and subsequently opened a port office in Athens.

Soon after the Greek ambassador's visit, we entertained Ambassador Juan de Ollagui of Mexico. Each ambassador and his wife was honored at a black-tie dinner in the state dining room of the mansion.

Lady Ransbotham, wife of the ambassador from Great Britain, was entertained at a luncheon at the governor's mansion in 1976 while Lord Ransbotham was visiting other areas of the state.

The menus for these events consisted primarily of traditional Southern foods. We did not

Ambassador and Mrs. Menelas Alexandrakis of Greece

BILL BIRDSONG

try to imitate our international guests' native foods. One exception was a Greek dessert served at the dinner honoring Ambassador Alexandrakis. Given to us by Greek-American friends, the dessert fit in so well with the rest of the meal that I'm sure the recipe came from *southern* Greece. ∎

BILL BIRDSONG

DINNER HONORING AMBASSADOR AND MRS. ALEXANDRAKIS OF GREECE

MENU

Oysters Mary

Asparagus and Artichoke Salad

Tournedos Monegasques

Green Rice   Small Whole Carrots

Effie's Dinner Rolls

Karidopita

OYSTERS MARY

3 (12-ounce) containers fresh oysters, drained
2 cups oyster crackers
2 hard-boiled eggs
2 raw eggs
1 cup whole milk
½ teaspoon salt
½ teaspoon pepper
1 teaspoon dry mustard
¼ teaspoon worcestershire sauce
4 tablespoons butter, cut into small chunks
paprika

Preheat oven to 350 degrees.

Cut each oyster into 2-3 pieces. Crush crackers. Remove yolks of hard-boiled eggs and crumble; discard whites. Beat raw eggs. Place all ingredients except paprika in large saucepan. Cook over medium heat, stirring frequently until oysters are done and liquid is absorbed (about 10 minutes).

Spoon scant ½ cup of oyster mixture into lightly greased, individual baking shells or ramekins. Sprinkle with paprika. Bake for 15 minutes.

Yield: 8 servings

ASPARAGUS AND ARTICHOKE SALAD

1 cup sliced fresh mushrooms
1 (15-ounce) can white asparagus spears, drained, and cut in half
1 (14-ounce) can artichoke hearts, drained, and cut into halves
Mustard Dressing
lettuce leaves

Place mushrooms, asparagus, and artichoke hearts in glass or plastic dish; pour Mustard Dressing over all. Cover and refrigerate for several hours (no longer than 24 hours).

To serve, remove vegetables with slotted spoon, reserving dressing. Place lettuce leaves on salad plates; arrange vegetables on lettuce and spoon reserved dressing over top.

Yield: 8 servings

MUSTARD DRESSING:

½ cup olive or vegetable oil
1 tablespoon lemon juice
2 tablespoons snipped chives
1 tablespoon Dijon mustard
½ teaspoon salt
½ teaspoon grated lemon peel

Combine all ingredients in jar with tight-fitting lid. Shake well.

Yield: about ½ cup

TOURNEDOS MONEGASQUES

salt and freshly ground pepper
6 tournedos (small slices of filet of beef), 1½ inches thick
½ cup butter, divided
6 thick slices eggplant
2 medium tomatoes
½ cup veal stock or beef bouillon
¼ cup dry white wine
salt and pepper to taste
24 pitted ripe olives

Season tournedos. Sauté in ¼ cup butter over medium-high heat, browning both sides, but allowing beef to remain rare in middle. Remove from pan and keep warm.

Add remaining butter to pan. Sauté eggplant slices over medium heat, browning both sides; cook until soft. Remove eggplant from pan and keep warm.

Peel, seed, and chop tomatoes. Add to pan and cook until soft and mushy. Add stock and wine. Cook and stir until brown solids from pan are released into mixture. Season to taste. Add olives.

Place 1 tournedo on each slice of eggplant. Pour sauce over each serving.

Yield: 6 servings

GREEN RICE

¾ cup thinly sliced green onions with tops
½ cup finely chopped green pepper
2 tablespoons vegetable oil
1 cup regular long-grain white rice
¼ cup snipped fresh parsley
1 teaspoon salt
¼ teaspoon pepper
2 cups chicken broth, boiling

Preheat oven to 350 degrees.

Sauté onions and green pepper in oil until tender, but not brown. Place rice in 2-quart baking dish. Stir in sautéed vegetables, parsley, salt, pepper, and broth.

Cover and bake for 30-35 minutes, or until rice is tender and liquid is absorbed. Toss lightly with a fork before serving.

Yield: 6 servings

SMALL WHOLE CARROTS

1½ pounds small carrots
salt
melted butter

Wash and scrape carrots. Place in saucepan containing 1 inch of salted boiling water. Cover; reduce heat. Cook for 10-20 minutes, just until tender. Serve with melted butter.

Yield: 6 servings

EFFIE'S DINNER ROLLS

(recipe on page 131)

KARIDOPITA

Prior to the dinner for Ambassador and Mrs. Alexandrakis, we received a box of homemade Karidopita from one of our Greek-American dinner guests. Our good friend, Mimi Skandalakis, shares her favorite recipe for this delicious Greek nut cake.

12 eggs, separated
1½ cups sugar
1½ cups zwieback crumbs
1 teaspoon ground cinnamon
¼ teaspoon ground cloves
½ teaspoon salt
2 cups ground walnuts or pecans
2 tablespoons rum
Karidopita Syrup

Preheat oven to 350 degrees.

In small bowl of electric mixer, beat egg whites until stiff; set aside. In large bowl of electric mixer, beat egg yolks and sugar until light and fluffy. Mix together zwieback crumbs, cinnamon, cloves, salt, nuts, and rum in separate bowl.

Fold egg whites into yolk-sugar mixture. Stir egg-sugar mixture into zwieback-spice mixture; mix well. Pour into lightly greased 11 x 13-inch baking pan. Bake for 30-40 minutes, until cake tests done. Cool. Prepare Karidopita Syrup and pour warm syrup over cooled cake. Cut into diamond-shaped pieces.

Yield: 40 (2-inch) pieces

KARIDOPITA SYRUP:

1 cup sugar
1 cup water
1 (4-inch) cinnamon stick
½ cup honey
1 teaspoon lemon juice
1 tablespoon rum

Boil sugar, water, and cinnamon stick until syrup begins to thicken (about 10 minutes), stirring occasionally. Remove from heat. Add honey, lemon juice, and rum. Stir and pour over cake while syrup is warm.

Yield: about 2½ cups

DINNER HONORING AMBASSADOR AND MRS. DE OLLAGUI OF MEXICO

MENU

Mushroom and Shrimp Bisque

Cranberry Soufflé Salad

Ham Steak with Orange-Currant Sauce

French-Style Green Beans   Potatoes au Gratin

Small Corn Muffins

Rum Cream Pie

MUSHROOM AND SHRIMP BISQUE

1 pound fresh mushrooms, washed and sliced
1½ cups water
2 teaspoons salt, divided
¼ cup chopped onion
¼ cup melted butter or margarine
¼ cup all-purpose flour
dash pepper
2½ cups whole milk
½ cup whipping cream
2 cups cooked shrimp, peeled, deveined, and chopped
fresh parsley sprigs

In covered saucepan, cook mushrooms in water with 1 teaspoon salt for 10 minutes. Drain, reserving liquid. Set mushrooms aside.

Sauté onion in butter until tender. Blend in flour, pepper, and remaining salt. Stir in reserved mushroom liquid and milk. Cook over medium heat, stirring constantly, until mixture thickens and reaches boiling point. Remove from heat.

Stir in cream, shrimp, and mushrooms. Serve hot or cold, garnished with fresh parsley sprigs.

Yield: 6 cups

CRANBERRY SOUFFLÉ SALAD

1 envelope unflavored gelatin
2 tablespoons sugar
¼ teaspoon salt
1 cup water
½ cup mayonnaise
2 tablespoons lemon juice
1 teaspoon grated lemon rind
¼ cup chopped walnuts
1 (16-ounce) can whole berry cranberry sauce
1 orange or apple, peeled and diced, or 1 (8½-ounce) can pineapple tidbits
lettuce leaves

Thoroughly mix gelatin, sugar, and salt in small saucepan. Add water; place over low heat, stirring constantly until gelatin is dissolved. Remove from heat.

Stir in mayonnaise, lemon juice, and lemon rind. Blend with hand-held electric mixer. Pour into 8 x 8 x 2-inch freezer-proof pan. Place in freezer for about 15 minutes, or until firm around edges, but soft in center. Remove from freezer and transfer to large mixing bowl.

Beat until fluffy. Fold in walnuts, cranberry sauce, and diced fruit. Turn into 4-cup mold or individual molds. Cover and refrigerate until firm. Unmold onto lettuce leaves. Serve with mayonnaise, if desired.

Yield: 8 servings

HAM STEAK WITH ORANGE-CURRANT SAUCE

6 (½-inch) fully cooked ham slices
2 tablespoons butter
Orange-Currant Sauce

Slash fat around edges of ham slices. Heat butter in skillet. Sauté ham until lightly browned on each side. Serve with Orange-Currant Sauce.

Yield: 6 servings

ORANGE-CURRANT SAUCE:

2 teaspoons dry mustard
1 teaspoon paprika
1 teaspoon ground ginger
¼ teaspoon salt
2 tablespoons lemon juice
juice and grated rind of 2 oranges
2 tablespoons water
½ cup currant jelly

Mix dry mustard, paprika, ginger, and salt. Add fruit juices, rind, and water. Allow to stand 30 minutes.

Combine above mixture with jelly in saucepan. Heat gently; do not boil. Sauce should be served just warm.

Yield: about 1 cup

SMALL CORN MUFFINS

(recipe on page 33)

FRENCH-STYLE GREEN BEANS

2 pounds fresh green beans
2 teaspoons salt
6 tablespoons butter or margarine

Wash beans under cold running water; drain. Trim ends of beans with sharp knife. Cut each bean in half lengthwise.

Place beans in 2 inches of boiling salted water in large saucepan. Cover. Reduce heat and boil gently for 15 minutes, or until tender. Drain beans; toss with butter.

Yield: 8 servings

POTATOES AU GRATIN

6 medium white potatoes
1 teaspoon salt
1 (10¾-ounce) can cream of celery soup
1½ cups whole milk
1 cup grated cheddar cheese
4 tablespoons butter, divided
salt and white pepper to taste

Preheat oven to 350 degrees.

Peel potatoes and cut into ¼-inch slices. Cook in boiling salted water for 8-10 minutes, until just tender. Drain in colander.

In saucepan, combine soup, milk, and cheese. Cook, stirring occasionally, over medium heat until cheese is melted.

Place layer of potatoes in 2½-quart casserole. Dot with 2 tablespoons butter. Sprinkle lightly with salt and white pepper. Pour half of soup mixture over potato layer. Repeat layers, using rest of ingredients.

Bake, uncovered, for 20-30 minutes, until hot and bubbly.

Yield: 8 servings

RUM CREAM PIE

5 eggs, separated
¾ cup sugar
1¼ tablespoons unflavored gelatin
¼ cup cold water
1 cup whipping cream, whipped
¼ cup rum
1 (9-inch) Pie Crust, baked (recipe on page 194)
1 (1-ounce) square sweetened chocolate, shredded
2-3 tablespoons slivered almonds, toasted

In small bowl of electric mixer, beat egg whites until stiff. In large bowl, beat egg yolks for 2 minutes; beat in sugar until light.

Soften gelatin in cold water. Dissolve over hot water. Fold into egg yolk mixture. Gently fold whipped cream into stiffly beaten egg whites. Combine with egg yolk mixture. Mix in rum.

Pour into baked pie crust. Top with shredded chocolate and toasted almonds. Chill until firm. Before serving, garnish with additional whipped cream, if desired.

Yield: 6-8 servings

LUNCHEON HONORING LADY RANSBOTHAM OF GREAT BRITAIN

MENU

Fruit Cup with Ginger Cream Dressing

Rock Cornish Hen Alexandra

Wild Rice Deluxe   Molded Broccoli Salad

Buttermilk Biscuits

Grasshopper Pie

FRUIT CUP WITH GINGER CREAM DRESSING

1 ripe avocado
lemon juice
1 (20-ounce) can pineapple chunks in heavy syrup
1 cup cantaloupe balls
1 cup fresh grapefruit sections, cut into chunks
Ginger Cream Dressing (see recipe on following page)
1 (3-ounce) package lime-flavored gelatin, made according to package directions

Cut avocado into chunks, removing seed and peel. Sprinkle with lemon juice. Drain pineapple, reserving syrup for use in Ginger Cream Dressing. Gently toss avocado and fruit together; refrigerate until chilled through.

With sharp knife, cut gelatin into small cubes. Spoon avocado-fruit mixture into stemmed compotes. Spoon 2 tablespoons Ginger Cream Dressing over each serving. Garnish with cubes of lime gelatin.

Yield: 8 servings

GINGER CREAM DRESSING:

1 cup sour cream
½ teaspoon ground ginger
1-2 tablespoons heavy syrup from pineapple used in fruit cup

Combine all ingredients; mix well. Serve over avocado-fruit mixture.

Yield: about 1 cup

ROCK CORNISH HEN ALEXANDRA

6 tablespoons butter or margarine
2 Rock Cornish hens, split
8 shallots or green onions, cut fine
1 small tomato, peeled and chopped
2 tablespoons finely cut parsley
½ teaspoon dried thyme
½ cup dry white wine
salt and pepper to taste
¾ cup sour cream
paprika

Heat butter in skillet until very hot. Brown hens well all over. Add shallots, tomato, parsley, and thyme, stirring to blend. Add wine; salt and pepper to taste. Cover skillet and cook over low heat for 45 minutes to 1 hour. Turn hens frequently.

Just before serving, add sour cream, mixing with sauce in skillet. Heat, but do not boil. Remove hens to hot plates and pour sauce over each half. Lightly sprinkle each serving with paprika.

Yield: 4 servings

WILD RICE DELUXE

1 cup wild rice
2 cups chicken broth
1 cup orange juice
2 cups sliced fresh mushrooms

Place rice in colander; rinse with cold water. Bring chicken broth and orange juice to boil. Stir in rice. Cover; reduce heat to low. Simmer, stirring occasionally, for 30 minutes.

Stir in mushrooms. Cover and simmer an additional 15-30 minutes, until rice is tender and liquid absorbed.

Yield: 6-8 servings

MOLDED BROCCOLI SALAD

1 envelope unflavored gelatin
2 cups hot beef consommé
2 (10-ounce) packages chopped broccoli, cooked, drained, and mashed
4 hard-boiled eggs, chopped
½ cup mayonnaise
dash Tabasco sauce
dash worcestershire sauce
vegetable oil

Dissolve gelatin in hot consommé. Cool slightly. Add remaining ingredients; mix well. Pour into lightly oiled, individual salad molds. Cover and refrigerate until set.

Yield: 6-8 servings

BUTTERMILK BISCUITS

(recipe on page 48)

GRASSHOPPER PIE

22 chocolate wafers, finely crushed
4 tablespoons butter, melted
22 regular-sized marshmallows
¾ cup whole milk
1 tablespoon green crème de menthe
3 tablespoons white crème de cacao
green food coloring
1 cup whipping cream, whipped
sweet chocolate curls for garnish

Preheat oven to 350 degrees.

Mix crushed wafers with melted butter. Pat into greased 9-inch pie plate. Bake for 8 minutes. Set aside to cool.

Melt marshmallows in milk in top of double boiler over rapidly boiling water; cool. Stir in crème de menthe, crème de cacao, and *1* drop of green food coloring. Let mixture stand until syrupy and thickened.

Fold in whipped cream and pour into crust. Refrigerate for several hours or overnight. Before serving, lightly sprinkle with chocolate curls.

Yield: 6-8 servings

REV. BILLY GRAHAM

There's no better way to bring warmth to a cold winter night than to have Billy Graham and a hundred international evangelists over for a reception. That's just what we did in January of 1976.

Rev. Graham and his ministerial colleagues were attending a meeting in Atlanta, and George and I invited them to the mansion. Some of the evangelists were from countries so small and unfamiliar to us that we had to look them up in the index of our atlas.

The evening was unstructured — no sermons and no speeches. George welcomed the group, Rev. Graham thanked us for our hospitality, and refreshments were served. In spite of the language barriers, the personalities of our guests came through as the evening progressed.

George and Rev. Graham traded stories and decided that, as unlikely as it might seem, politicians and religious leaders have much in common. People do not tend to see the human side of either. For example, we discovered that Rev. Graham possesses a keen sense of humor — a fact that often surprises people. George, too, enjoys a good joke and frequently is taken seriously when he is being less than serious.

As our evening with the evangelists drew to a close, we sang hymns familiar the world over. It was interesting to hear hymns sung in unison in so many different languages. ■

BILL BIRDSONG

RECEPTION FOR BILLY GRAHAM AND INTERNATIONAL EVANGELISTS

MENU

Wassail Coffee

Cheese Wafers Salted Peanuts

Olive Bites

Spinach Balls Shrimp Mold

Puff Shells with Chicken Williamsburg

Peanut Fingers Pecan Tassies

Cheese and Fresh Fruit

Claxton Fruitcake

WASSAIL

6 inches stick cinnamon
16 whole cloves
1 teaspoon whole allspice
3 medium oranges
whole cloves
6 cups cider or apple juice
2 cups cranberry juice cocktail
¼ cup sugar
1 teaspoon Angostura bitters

Break cinnamon in pieces; tie in cheesecloth bag with 16 whole cloves and allspice. Stud oranges with additional whole cloves. In large saucepan, combine cider, cranberry juice cocktail, sugar, bitters, spice bag, and studded whole oranges. Cover; simmer over low heat for 10 minutes.

Remove spice bag and oranges. Pour wassail into warm serving bowl; float studded oranges. Serve hot. (Note: Red food coloring may be added for brighter red.)

Yield: 8-9 cups

CHEESE WAFERS

1 pound sharp cheddar cheese, grated
½ cup butter
2 cups all-purpose flour
¼ teaspoon salt
⅛ teaspoon cayenne pepper

Bring cheese and butter to room temperature. Cream cheese and butter together in large bowl of electric mixer. Add flour, salt, and cayenne pepper. Mix well, using hands if necessary. Form into 1½-inch diameter rolls. Wrap in wax paper and chill until firm.

Preheat oven to 325 degrees.

Slice dough into ¼-inch rounds. Place on ungreased baking sheet and bake for 25 minutes. (Note: Watch carefully. Do not brown.)

Yield: approximately 10 dozen

OLIVE BITES

½ pound sharp cheddar cheese, grated
¼ cup butter
1 cup all-purpose flour
½ teaspoon garlic salt
¼ teaspoon salt
dash cayenne pepper
1 (10-ounce) jar small pimiento-stuffed olives

Bring cheese and butter to room temperature. Preheat oven to 350 degrees.

Cream cheese and butter together in large bowl of electric mixer. Add flour, garlic salt, salt, and cayenne pepper. Mix well. Use hands to form mixture into ball. Knead several times.

Shape pieces of dough around olives, completely encasing olives with thin layer of dough. Place on ungreased baking sheet and bake for 25 minutes, or until light golden.

Yield: approximately 6 dozen

SPINACH BALLS

2 (10-ounce) packages frozen chopped spinach
2½ cups herb seasoned stuffing mix
2 onions, finely chopped
6 eggs, beaten
¾ cup butter or margarine
½ cup grated parmesan cheese
1 teaspoon garlic salt
½ tablespoon dried thyme
½ tablespoon pepper
1 tablespoon monosodium glutamate (Ac'cent)

Preheat oven to 350 degrees.

Cook spinach according to package directions until thawed. Drain completely. Add all other ingredients, mixing thoroughly. Shape into balls, using a teaspoon full of mixture for each ball. (If balls do not hold shape well, add more stuffing mix.) Place on ungreased baking sheet and bake for 20 minutes.

Yield: 5 dozen

SHRIMP MOLD

1 (10¾-ounce) can tomato soup
3 (3-ounce) packages cream cheese
2 tablespoons unflavored gelatin
3 tablespoons cold water
1 cup mayonnaise
2 cups canned shrimp, drained
¼ teaspoon garlic salt
juice of 1 lemon
1 small onion, grated
½ cup finely chopped celery
½ cup finely chopped green pepper
lettuce leaves
fresh dill

Heat soup; dissolve cream cheese in soup, stirring until well blended. Soften gelatin in cold water and dissolve in soup. Let cool. Add mayonnaise to soup mixture, mixing well. Add shrimp, mashing as it is added. Add garlic salt, lemon juice, onion, celery, and green pepper; mix well.

Pour into lightly oiled 4-cup fish mold. Cover with plastic wrap and refrigerate until set (about 3 hours). Unmold onto bed of lettuce and sprinkle with fresh dill.

Yield: As an hors d'oeuvre, serves approximately 24; as a salad course, serves approximately 12-16

PUFF SHELLS WITH CHICKEN WILLIAMSBURG

Preheat oven to 400 degrees.

Double Puff Shell recipe on page 56. Drop by teaspoonfuls 2 inches apart onto greased baking sheets, making about 36 puffs in all. Bake for about 15 minutes, or until golden and puffed.

Remove from oven; cool. Slice off top of each shell with serrated knife. Remove any soft dough inside. Fill with Chicken Williamsburg.

Yield: approximately 36

CHICKEN WILLIAMSBURG:

2 cups chopped cooked chicken
1 cup finely chopped celery
2 hard-boiled eggs, chopped
½ cup mayonnaise
½ (10¾-ounce) can cream soup (mushroom or chicken)
2 tablespoons minced onion
1 tablespoon lemon juice

Preheat oven to 350 degrees.

Combine all ingredients in saucepan. Heat, stirring to mix well. Spoon mixture into puff shells. Bake until hot.

Yield: filling for approximately 48 puffs

PEANUT FINGERS

1 loaf white bread
1 cup peanut butter
1 cup corn oil

Preheat oven to 250 degrees.

Cut crust from bread. Cut each slice of bread into 4 "fingers." Bake crusts and fingers on ungreased baking sheet for 1 hour. In meantime, mix peanut butter and corn oil into paste.

Make crumbs out of crusts. Dip fingers into peanut butter mixture and roll in crumbs. Store in tightly covered container.

Yield: 8-10 dozen

PECAN TASSIES

3 ounces cream cheese, at room temperature
½ cup butter, at room temperature
1 cup all-purpose flour
1 egg
¾ cup dark brown sugar, firmly packed
1 tablespoon melted butter
1 teaspoon vanilla extract
½ cup chopped pecans

In bowl of electric mixer, cream together cream cheese and butter. Add flour; mix well. Press dough evenly around sides and bottom of miniature muffin tins. (This is easier if dough is chilled slightly before using.)

Preheat oven to 350 degrees.

Beat egg. Add brown sugar, melted butter, and vanilla extract. Mix well; stir in chopped pecans.

Spoon 1 tablespoon of pecan filling into each pastry shell. Bake for 20 minutes.

Yield: approximately 2 dozen

SECRETARY OF TRANSPORTATION WILLIAM COLEMAN

One of the most interesting dinner parties we had at the mansion brought together two guests who, twenty years earlier, never would have been at the same table — the nation's second black Cabinet member and one of the nation's most vocal segregationists during the 1960s.

William Coleman was the United States Secretary of Transportation in 1976, the year the department wrote its first National Transportation Policy. In the fall of that year, Secretary Coleman conducted a series of conferences to receive comment on the policy. The first conference was to be held in Atlanta, and we invited Secretary Coleman and his family to be our house guests.

That same year, Alabama Governor George Wallace served on the Transportation Committee of the National Governors Association. He was attending the transportation conference, so we asked him to join us for dinner one evening.

It was this set of circumstances that brought these two men together at our dinner table in September 1976. Even though they had never before met, their paths were intertwined with the history they both represented.

In 1954, a young Bill Coleman was working as a law clerk for Justice Felix Frankfurter. It was during that year that the Supreme Court handed down the landmark decision known as "Brown vs. The Board of Education of Topeka," which

OFFICIAL U.S. DEPT. OF TRANSPORTATION PHOTO

held that "the separate but equal doctrine has no place in the field of public education." As Justice Frankfurter's law clerk, William Coleman played an important role in this historic decision. More than two decades had passed — allowing time for healing and understanding to grow between groups of people whose beliefs and actions had clashed years before.

For Secretary Coleman's daughter, Levita, the evening was cause for apprehension, anxiety, and a feeling of uneasiness. A recent graduate from law school, Levita was an engaging young woman with a world of opportunity before her. But she told me that she could not forget the past. She expected to have an extreme dislike for Governor Wallace. Instead, she found him to be an interesting and enjoyable conversationalist who had mellowed over the years in many of his attitudes.

I think that Levita's reaction to Governor Wallace was influenced greatly by his appearance. He was a physically broken man struggling to overcome the injuries of an assassination attempt.

The experiences of this evening made all of us realize the benefits of dealing person to person, where prejudices and anxieties seem trivial. ∎

DINNER FOR SEC. WILLIAM COLEMAN AND GOV. GEORGE WALLACE

MENU

Soup Supreme

Chicken Virginia

Long Grain and Wild Rice   Oriental Vegetable Saute

Processor Buttermilk Biscuits

Luscious Strawberry Dessert

SOUP SUPREME

2 (12-ounce) containers fresh oysters, poached in their liquor
5 cups half-and-half
1 (4½-ounce) jar creamed spinach baby food
4 tablespoons butter
1 small clove garlic, minced
1 teaspoon monosodium glutamate (Ac'cent)
2 teaspoons A-1 Sauce
½ teaspoon salt
dash black pepper
generous dash cayenne pepper
4 teaspoons cornstarch mixed with 4 teaspoons cold water
⅔ cup whipping cream, whipped

Purée oysters in blender container or food processor bowl. In large saucepan, heat half-and-half just to simmer. Add oyster purée, spinach, butter, garlic, monosodium glutamate, A-1 Sauce, salt, black pepper, and cayenne pepper. Heat to simmer, stirring until smooth. Do not boil.

Add cornstarch mixture. Heat, stirring until soup is slightly thickened. Ladle into serving bowls. Top each serving with a spoonful of whipped cream.

Yield: 8 servings

CHICKEN VIRGINIA

8 boneless chicken breast halves
salt and pepper
¼ cup melted butter
8 thin slices Virginia ham
Grape Sauce
8 whole mushrooms, sautéed

Preheat oven to 350 degrees.

Sprinkle chicken with salt and pepper. Line broiler pan with aluminum foil. Place chicken on foil, skin side down, and brush with butter. Place on upper rack in hot oven. Turn on broiler element and broil for 15 minutes. Turn, brush with butter, and broil 10 more minutes, or until done. To serve, place a piece of chicken on a slice of ham. Pour Grape Sauce over chicken. Garnish each serving with a mushroom.

Yield: 8 servings

GRAPE SAUCE:

3 tablespoons butter
3 tablespoons all-purpose flour
½ teaspoon monosodium glutamate (Ac'cent)
½ teaspoon salt
1½ cups chicken broth
2 tablespoons lemon juice
2 tablespoons sugar
1 cup whole seedless white grapes

Melt butter in saucepan. Blend in flour, monosodium glutamate, and salt. Gradually add chicken broth and cook, stirring constantly, until thickened. Stir in lemon juice and sugar.

Just before serving, add grapes and heat.

Yield: 2½ cups

LONG GRAIN AND WILD RICE

(prepare according to package directions)

ORIENTAL VEGETABLE SAUTÉ

1 (10-ounce) package frozen small green peas
1 (4-ounce) can sliced mushrooms
1 (5-ounce) can water chestnuts
2 tablespoons butter
2 cups diagonally sliced celery
½ cup sliced green onions
1 teaspoon seasoned salt
¼ teaspoon seasoned pepper

Cook peas according to package directions. Drain mushrooms. Drain and slice water chestnuts.

Melt butter in large saucepan. Add mushrooms, water chestnuts, celery, green onions, and seasonings. Sauté over medium-high heat for 1-2 minutes; add peas and sauté an additional minute, or until vegetables are crisp-tender, stirring constantly.

Yield: 6 servings

PROCESSOR BUTTERMILK BISCUITS

2½ cups self-rising flour
½ cup cold butter, cut into 1-inch pieces
¾ cup buttermilk

Preheat oven to 450 degrees.

Position knife blade in bowl of food processor. Add flour and butter. Quickly turn processor on and off 8-10 times, until mixture resembles coarse meal. With processor running, slowly add buttermilk through food chute until dough forms ball, leaving sides of bowl. Turn dough out onto lightly floured board; knead lightly 4-5 times.

Roll dough out to ½-inch thickness. Cut with 2-inch biscuit cutter. Place rounds on ungreased baking sheet. Bake for 8-10 minutes.

Yield: 1½ dozen

LUSCIOUS STRAWBERRY DESSERT

4 cups frozen strawberries, thawed and divided
1 cup sugar
2 tablespoons cornstarch
red food coloring
1½ cups all-purpose flour
½ cup dark brown sugar
1 cup finely chopped pecans
1 cup butter, at room temperature
1 (8-ounce) package cream cheese, at room temperature
1 cup XXXX confectioners' sugar
1 teaspoon vanilla extract
2 cups whipped topping

In saucepan, combine 2 cups strawberries and their juice with sugar and cornstarch. Cook over low heat, stirring frequently, until juices thicken (about 10 minutes). Remove from heat. Stir in remaining strawberries, their juice, and 2 drops of food coloring. Cool; refrigerate.

Preheat oven to 400 degrees.

Mix flour, brown sugar, pecans, and butter. Press into 9 x 13 x 2-inch pan. Bake for 15 minutes. Cool.

Mix cream cheese, confectioners' sugar, and vanilla extract. Add whipped topping. Beat until well blended. Pour over cooled crust. Pour strawberry topping over filling. Cover and refrigerate overnight. Cut into squares.

Yield: 15 servings

BUSBEE FAMILY THANKSGIVING

The Georgia governor's mansion is well suited for so many types of entertaining — from the smallest of dinner parties to the largest of receptions, from highly elegant to downright homey. Every Thanksgiving, we had the occasion to put on a dinner of the large and homey variety.

It gave us a great deal of pleasure to gather our extended family together on this one day each year. George's four brothers and sisters and their families traveled to Atlanta from south Georgia for the day. Our four children always enjoyed seeing cousins that they had grown up with but seldom were able to see as adults. And, of course, with each new year, there were more and more little Busbee cousins at the Thanksgiving dinner.

Like most families, the Busbee family has a traditional Thanksgiving menu. Ours did not change when we moved into the governor's mansion. The kitchen staff used our family recipes to prepare the same meal that I had prepared for the last twenty-five years.

Our family get-togethers were fun, informal, and fairly uneventful . . . with one exception. It was a Thanksgiving that I was truly thankful to make it through! On Thanksgiving morning that year, the cook walked out in a huff as a result of a work schedule disagreement with Mary Dwozan, the mansion manager. Most of the meal had been prepared before the cook made her exit. Only the dressing remained to be made, and the cornbread and biscuits for the dressing had already been baked.

I've made a lot of dressing in my time, but never for forty people. Mary and I stood in the kitchen in total dismay, wondering how to tackle such a large amount of dressing. In walked my then twenty-year-old son, Buz. He marched up to the sink and began to "scrub up," as if for surgery. Soon Buz was presiding over the most enormous mixing bowl any of us had ever seen. He crumbled cornbread and biscuits into the bowl as though he really knew what he was doing (which, of course, he didn't). As Buz mixed, Mary and I poured broth. Buz was literally up to his elbows in dressing.

Together, the three of us finished the dressing and got it into the oven before the rest of the family even knew about our mini-crisis in the kitchen. I'm sure the cook, who never returned to work, would be surprised to learn that we not only had dressing that day, but that it was a huge success. So, Pearline, now you know "the rest of the story." ■

FAMILY THANKSGIVING DINNER

MENU

Roast Turkey with Benny Sauce

Dressing with Giblet Gravy

Mae's Scalloped Oysters

Fresh Pole Beans   Sweet Potato Soufflé

Cranberry Mold

Southern Angel Biscuits

Ambrosia

Chocolate Pound Cake

ROAST TURKEY WITH BENNY SAUCE

12-16 pound turkey
Benny Sauce (recipe on page 193)

If turkey is frozen, remove from freezer and place in refrigerator 2-3 days before roasting time.

Preheat oven to 450 degrees.

Remove bag of giblets from turkey cavity; reserve for giblet gravy. Wash turkey and pat dry. Place turkey, breast side up, in roasting pan. Insert meat thermometer into center of inner thigh muscle, being careful not to touch bone. Saturate a clean loosely-woven cloth with vegetable oil; cover turkey with cloth. Place in oven and immediately reduce heat to 350 degrees.

After first 3½ hours, remove cloth and baste turkey with Benny Sauce. Baste about every 15 minutes during remainder of roasting time. Cook to internal temperature of 180-185 degrees, or 15-20 minutes per pound.

When turkey is done, transfer to serving platter and allow to "rest" for 20-30 minutes. The turkey will still be hot and will be more moist than if carved immediately. Slice and serve with warm Benny Sauce.

Yield: 12-14 servings

DRESSING WITH GIBLET GRAVY

6 cups crumbled cold Cornbread
2 cups crumbled cold Buttermilk Biscuits (recipe on page 48)
½ cup chopped onion
½ cup chopped celery and celery leaves
¼ cup chopped green pepper
6 tablespoons butter
approximately 4 cups turkey or chicken broth
¼ cup Benny Sauce (recipe on page 193)
6 eggs, beaten
paprika
Giblet Gravy

Preheat oven to 400 degrees.

Combine crumbled cornbread and biscuits in large bowl. In skillet, sauté onion, celery, and green pepper in butter until tender. Add broth and sautéed vegetables to bread mixture; mix well. Stir in Benny Sauce and eggs. Mixture should be almost "soupy," to allow for loss of moisture during baking. (If dressing is not cooked immediately, more broth should be added.)

Pour dressing into lightly greased 9 x 13 x 2-inch baking pan. Sprinkle lightly with paprika. Bake for 35-40 minutes. Serve with Giblet Gravy.

Yield: 8-10 servings

CORNBREAD:

1 cup all-purpose flour
1 cup plain cornmeal
4 teaspoons baking powder
¾ teaspoon salt
2 eggs
1 cup whole milk
¼ cup vegetable oil

Preheat oven to 425 degrees.

Stir together flour, cornmeal, baking powder, and salt. Add eggs, milk, and oil. Beat just until smooth. (Do not overbeat.) Turn into greased 9 x 9 x 2-inch baking pan. Bake for 20-25 minutes.

Yield: 8 servings (This makes approximately 6 cups when crumbled.)

GIBLET GRAVY:

3 cups water
1 teaspoon salt
turkey giblets and neck
2 tablespoons cornstarch
¼ cup water
3 hard-boiled eggs

Place water, salt, giblets, and neck in small saucepan. Bring to boil; cover and reduce heat to simmer. When liver is done, remove from saucepan and reserve. Continue to cook neck and other giblets until neck meat can be easily pulled off bone, about 45 minutes. Remove giblets and neck from broth and reserve.

Mix cornstarch and water; add to broth. Heat, stirring, until broth is slightly thickened. Coarsely chop giblets. Pull neck meat off bone. Add giblets and neck meat to gravy. Slice eggs and add to gravy. Cook over medium heat, stirring occasionally, until gravy and giblets are hot.

Yield: 2½ cups

MAE'S SCALLOPED OYSTERS

3 (12-ounce) containers fresh oysters in their liquor
salt and pepper to taste
3 tablespoons butter, divided
2 cups oyster crackers, crushed and divided
1 egg, beaten
½ cup whole milk

Preheat oven to 425 degrees.

In saucepan, warm oysters in their liquor. Do not cook. Drain in colander.

In deep 1½-quart baking dish, layer half of the oysters, salt and pepper, and half of the butter (in bits). Sprinkle with half of the crushed oyster crackers. Layer remaining oysters over crackers; salt and pepper. Mix egg and milk well and pour evenly over oysters. Sprinkle with remaining crackers and dot with remaining butter. Bake, uncovered, for 30 minutes.

Yield: 8-10 servings

FRESH POLE BEANS

1½ pounds fresh pole beans
1 quart water
1 tablespoon salt
1 smoked ham hock

String beans very well and snap into 2-inch pieces. Rinse beans in colander. In large saucepan, bring salted water to boil. Add pole beans and ham hock. Return to boil. Reduce heat; cover and simmer for 40-45 minutes, or until beans are tender.

Yield: 4-6 servings

SWEET POTATO SOUFFLÉ

2 eggs
½ to ¾ cup sugar
3 cups cooked, mashed sweet potatoes
3 tablespoons butter, melted
½ teaspoon salt
½ teaspoon allspice
¼ teaspoon ground cinnamon
dash ground nutmeg
1½ teaspoons vanilla extract
¼ cup whole milk
¾ cup miniature marshmallows

Preheat oven to 375 degrees.

Beat eggs and sugar in small bowl of electric mixer. In large bowl of electric mixer, whip potatoes. Add egg-sugar mixture and mix thoroughly. Add butter, salt, allspice, cinnamon, nutmeg, and vanilla extract; mix well. Gradually add milk and mix well. Pour sweet potato mixture into lightly greased 2-quart casserole. Bake, uncovered, for 25 minutes. Sprinkle with marshmallows and bake an additional 5 minutes, or until marshmallows are golden.

Yield: 6 servings

CRANBERRY MOLD

1 (3-ounce) package lemon-flavored gelatin
1 (3-ounce) package strawberry-flavored gelatin
1 cup boiling water
1 (10-ounce) bottle ginger ale
1 cup chopped celery
1 cup chopped pecans
1 cup crushed pineapple, drained
1 (16-ounce) can whole berry cranberry sauce
lettuce leaves

Dissolve lemon and strawberry gelatin in boiling water. Add ginger ale; cool. Let mixture thicken slightly; add remaining ingredients and mix well. Pour into lightly oiled 6-cup mold. Cover with plastic wrap and refrigerate overnight. Unmold onto lettuce leaves to serve.

Yield: 12 servings

SOUTHERN ANGEL BISCUITS

1 package active dry yeast
2 tablespoons very warm water
5 cups all-purpose flour
1 teaspoon baking soda
3 teaspoons baking powder
2 tablespoons sugar
1½ teaspoons salt
1 cup vegetable shortening
2 cups buttermilk

Preheat oven to 400 degrees.

Dissolve yeast in warm water. Sift all dry ingredients into large bowl. Cut in shortening with pastry blender. Add buttermilk and yeast mixture. Stir until thoroughly moistened. Turn onto floured board and knead for 1-2 minutes. Roll out to ½-inch thickness and cut with 2-inch biscuit cutter. Brush with melted butter, if desired.

Bake on ungreased baking sheet for 12-15 minutes, or until lightly browned.

Yield: 5-6 dozen

AMBROSIA

4 cups fresh orange sections, with juice (membranes and seeds removed)
¾ cup fresh-frozen grated coconut (sugar added), thawed
¼ cup sugar

Place orange sections, their juice, and coconut in large bowl; toss lightly to mix. Stir in sugar and refrigerate until thoroughly chilled. (Note: Amount of sugar needed will vary according to sweetness of oranges used.)

Yield: 8 servings

CHOCOLATE POUND CAKE

½ cup vegetable shortening
1 cup margarine, at room temperature
3 cups sugar
3 cups all-purpose flour
½ cup cocoa
½ teaspoon baking powder
½ teaspoon salt
1 tablespoon vanilla extract
1¼ cups whole milk
6 eggs
Chocolate Pound Cake Icing

Preheat oven to 325 degrees.

In large bowl of electric mixer, cream shortening, margarine, and sugar together. Sift all dry ingredients together. Add vanilla extract to milk.

Add eggs, 1 at a time, to creamed margarine mixture, mixing well. Alternately add flour mixture and milk, mixing well. Pour batter into large, greased tube pan. Bake for 1 hour and 20 minutes, or until cake tests done.

Turn cake onto wire rack to cool. Spread with Chocolate Pound Cake Icing. (This cake is also very good without icing.)

Yield: 16 servings

CHOCOLATE POUND CAKE ICING:

½ cup margarine
2 cups sugar
¼ cup cocoa
⅔ cup whole milk
¼ teaspoon salt
2 teaspoons vanilla extract

Place all ingredients except vanilla extract in saucepan. Cook over medium heat, stirring occasionally, until icing reaches soft ball stage (234 degrees on a candy thermometer). Remove from heat; cool slightly. Add vanilla extract. Beat with spoon until smooth and of spreading consistency. (If icing becomes too stiff for easy spreading, beat in 1 tablespoon of cream.)

SIGNORA MARIA PIA FANFANI

Maria Pia Fanfani, wife of former prime minister of Italy, Amintore Fanfani, was our guest in the fall of 1980. Signora Fanfani was honored at a luncheon at the mansion for her involvement in the Georgia Festival of Arts.

Fletcher Wolfe, director of the Atlanta Boy Choir, founded the Georgia Festival of Arts as a cultural exchange organization for both visual and performing artists. Signora Fanfani has played an active role in the group since its inception in 1977.

She refers to herself as "godmother" of the Atlanta Boy Choir and makes frequent trips to visit the boys at their home on Ponce de Leon Avenue. The flags of Italy and the United States fly side by side there as a symbol of the relationship between this lovely lady and the Atlanta Boy Choir.

A talented photo journalist, Signora Fanfani is highly respected in her own country as an outstanding and gifted artist. She also serves as president of the International Red Cross. Among her benevolent activities are numerous trips to disaster areas throughout the world to assist in the distribution of aid.

The luncheon for Signora Fanfani was planned and prepared by Chef Lee Hopper. ∎

LUNCHEON HONORING SIGNORA FANFANI

MENU

Gazpacho Salad in Brandy Snifters

Chicken Soufflé with Sherry Mushroom Sauce

Sautéed Snow Peas

Herb Muffins

Apricot Moscovite

GAZPACHO SALAD IN BRANDY SNIFTERS

1½ cups shredded lettuce
1 cup diced tomatoes, seeds and juice removed
1 cup diced celery
1 cup sliced radishes
1 cup diced cucumbers
½ cup sliced green onions
Oil and Garlic Dressing
alfalfa sprouts

In each of 4 brandy snifters, place layers of lettuce, tomatoes, celery, radishes, cucumbers, and green onions. Pour 1 tablespoon Oil and Garlic Dressing over each serving. Top with small bunch of alfalfa sprouts.

Yield: 4 servings

OIL AND GARLIC DRESSING:

2 cloves garlic, minced
¼ teaspoon salt
½ teaspoon dried oregano
2 teaspoons Dijon mustard
1 tablespoon lemon juice
½ cup olive oil

Combine all ingredients in jar with tight-fitting lid. Refrigerate. Shake well before serving.

Yield: ½ cup

CHICKEN SOUFFLÉ WITH SHERRY MUSHROOM SAUCE

½ medium onion, chopped
1 tablespoon butter
2 cups chopped, cooked chicken
salt and white pepper to taste
1 tablespoon chopped fresh parsley
¼ cup toasted, chopped pecans
4 eggs, separated
2½ cups Medium White Sauce, divided
Sherry Mushroom Sauce (see recipe on following page)

Preheat oven to 375 degrees.

In skillet, sauté onion in butter over medium-high heat until tender. Stir in chicken, salt, and white pepper. Remove from heat. Stir in parsley and pecans.

In large saucepan over medium heat, warm 1½ cups Medium White Sauce. (Reserve remaining cup of white sauce for Sherry Mushroom Sauce.) Beat egg yolks; rapidly stir into warm white sauce. Stir chicken mixture into white sauce mixture. In small bowl of electric mixer, beat egg whites until stiff, but not dry. Stir 1 spoonful of beaten egg whites into chicken mixture, then fold in remainder.

Pour mixture into ungreased 8 x 8-inch baking dish. Bake, uncovered, for 25-30 minutes, or until set. Spoon Sherry Mushroom Sauce over each serving.

Yield: 4-6 servings

MEDIUM WHITE SAUCE:

5 tablespoons butter
5 tablespoons all-purpose flour
½ teaspoon salt
dash white pepper
2½ cups whole milk

Melt butter in heavy saucepan. Blend in flour,

salt, and white pepper. Add milk all at once. Cook and stir over medium heat until mixture is thickened and bubbly. Cook and stir for 1-2 more minutes.

Yield: 2½ cups

SHERRY MUSHROOM SAUCE:

2 tablespoons butter
1 cup sliced, fresh mushrooms
1 cup Medium White Sauce
¼ cup dry sherry

Melt butter in small saucepan. Sauté mushrooms in butter until tender. Heat white sauce in separate saucepan. Add mushrooms to white sauce. Stir in sherry just before serving.

Yield: approximately 1½ cups

SAUTÉED SNOW PEAS

½ pound fresh snow peas
½ teaspoon salt
1 tablespoon butter
dash white pepper

String both sides of snow peas; wash in colander. Bring 2 cups salted water to boil. Drop in snow peas; cook for 25-30 seconds. Drain and plunge peas into cold water.

Melt butter in skillet. Sauté snow peas in butter over medium-high heat until hot through. Stir in white pepper and serve.

Yield: 4 servings

HERB MUFFINS

1¾ cups sifted all-purpose flour
¾ teaspoon salt
1 teaspoon Italian herb seasoning
2 teaspoons baking powder
2 eggs
2-4 tablespoons butter, melted
¾ cup whole milk

Preheat oven to 400 degrees.

Sift dry ingredients together into mixing bowl. In separate bowl, beat eggs; stir in butter and milk. Pour liquid ingredients into dry ingredients. Mix quickly with a fork. Grease 3 muffin tins with vegetable shortening and fill ⅔ full. Bake for 20-25 minutes.

Yield: 1½ dozen

APRICOT MOSCOVITE

6 ounces dried apricots
strip of lemon rind
3 egg yolks
¾ cup plus 2 tablespoons sugar
2 cups whole milk
¼ teaspoon vanilla extract
juice of ½ lemon
2-3 tablespoons cold water
1 envelope unflavored gelatin
½ cup whipping cream
whipped cream for topping (optional)

Wash apricots. Soak overnight in water to cover. Gently stew apricots with lemon rind in covered saucepan until plump and tender. Remove from heat. Cool and drain. Process apricots with metal blade in bowl of food processor until smooth. Return puréed apricots to saucepan.

Blend egg yolks and sugar in food processor. Scald milk and cool. Pour scalded milk into processor bowl. Blend with egg-sugar mixture.

Pour mixture into saucepan with apricot purée. Mix well. Bring to simmer, stirring constantly. Reduce heat to low. Cook, stirring, until slightly thickened (15-20 minutes). Stir in vanilla extract.

Mix lemon juice and cold water. Sprinkle gelatin over lemon water. Stir gelatin mixture into hot apricot custard. Set aside to cool. In small bowl of electric mixer, whip cream until thickened, but not stiff.

When apricot custard reaches room temperature, pour half of custard into a bowl on ice. Stir as custard chills. When it begins to thicken, add remainder of custard and the half-whipped cream. Gently blend mixture by hand. Turn into individual stemmed glasses. Cover and refrigerate until thoroughly chilled. Top each serving with whipped cream, if desired.

Yield: 8 servings

DR. HENRY KISSINGER

By June of 1975, I had reached a point where nothing surprised me. It had become a family joke that my husband would often come home from the office and say, "Guess who's coming to dinner?" Occasionally, he said, "Guess who's coming to breakfast?" The staff was very understanding about accommodating last minute changes in meal plans.

I was surprised but also thrilled when George one day announced that the Secretary of State, Dr. Henry Kissinger, would be coming to the mansion for breakfast. On this occasion, we had more than a week's notice, which gave us plenty of time to prepare.

Our breakfast was set for June 24, 1975. In addition to Dr. Kissinger, our guests would include Peter White, President of the Southern Center for International Studies; Dean Rusk, former Secretary of State; and Mrs. Rusk.

The weather was delightful that week. We decided to serve breakfast on the back porch overlooking the mansion grounds. For several days prior to the occasion, we went to the porch each morning at eight o'clock to check the location of the sun. Our guests wouldn't be able to get scrambled eggs balanced on a fork if they were blinded by the morning sun.

The Secret Service paid several advance visits before the day of the breakfast. I had expected them to patrol the grounds along with the mansion security force, but I was surprised when they asked to see the exact route through the house that Dr. Kissinger would take. I didn't think there would be any trouble lurking behind the schefflera in the foyer; however, they were taking no chances.

JEFF T. BUSBEE

Our honored guest arrived in a long, black limousine with United States flags flying. Secret Service men, with ear plug wires snaking their way to hidden radios, were hanging on all sides of the car.

Dr. Kissinger and the other guests were brought into the drawing room for juice. Shortly after their arrival, I slipped out of the room to check on the status of breakfast. As I passed by the elevator, off stepped three young ladies who were supposed to be in class at that moment — at the University of Georgia seventy miles away. Our youngest daughter and her roommates had shown up, unannounced and uninvited.

The girls were all aflutter. They had gotten up at 5 A.M. for the drive from Athens "just to see Secretary Kissinger come through the mansion gates." They were upstairs with their faces pressed against the windows when Dr. Kissinger arrived.

They had gotten all dressed up just to get a

JEFF T. BUSBEE

peek at our guest, so I took them in and introduced them. Dr. Kissinger was delighted by the girls' unexpected appearance. In spite of his reputation as a "super ego," he was genuinely flattered that they had gotten up so early to see him.

When Dr. Kissinger learned that they had cut classes on his account, he wrote and signed an excuse for each one. Needless to say, those excuses wound up in the girls' scrapbooks instead of on their professors' desks. ■

BREAKFAST HONORING SECRETARY OF STATE HENRY KISSINGER

M E N U

Orange Juice / Cranberry Juice

Sliced Georgia Peaches and Cream

Scrambled Eggs   Baked Grits

*Breakfast Meat Platter
(bacon, ham, and sausage)*

Southern Angel Biscuits

Assorted Jellies and Preserves

M E N U

SLICED GEORGIA PEACHES AND CREAM

8 large, fresh Georgia peaches, chilled
¼ cup sugar
¼ teaspoon ground ginger
2 cups heavy cream

Peel and slice peaches. Portion into 8 chilled compotes. Mix sugar and ginger. Sprinkle sugar mixture over peaches. Pour ¼ cup cream over each serving of peaches.

Yield: 8 servings

SCRAMBLED EGGS

(recipe on page 48)

BAKED GRITS

1 cup regular dry grits
3½ cups water
1½ teaspoons salt
½ cup butter or margarine
1 pound sharp cheddar cheese, grated
1 cup whole milk
4 eggs, beaten

Preheat oven to 325 degrees.

Gradually stir grits into briskly boiling salted water. Return to boil; reduce heat to low. Cover and cook for 15-20 minutes, or until grits are thickened. Stir frequently while cooking.

Add butter, cheese, milk, and eggs. Stir grits until butter and cheese are melted. Pour into greased 2½-quart casserole. Bake, uncovered, for about 1 hour.

Yield: 10-12 servings

SOUTHERN ANGEL BISCUITS

(recipe on page 99)

BILL BIRDSONG

WESTERN BUFFET FOR THE OFFICE OF PLANNING AND BUDGET

The Office of Planning and Budget, a part of the governor's office, works with the governor on the preparation of the annual state budget and assists in writing programs for state services.

Some might call the work of OPB dull, but the Western buffet we hosted for this lively group was anything but boring. The intricacies of the state budget were forgotten as soon as our guests arrived. Greeted at the front door by Marshal Matt Dillon and Miss Kitty (yours truly), of "Gunsmoke" fame, they fell right into the swing of things — with a little help from the country and western band.

The OPB cowboys and cowgirls enjoyed seeing their boss make a spectacle of himself as much as they enjoyed the Georgia barbecue. They all knew that Lt. Governor Zell Miller, the state's No. 1 country music lover, would have been right at home in a cowboy hat and boots that night, but they seemed a bit surprised to see the governor dancing around the mansion ballroom wearing a holster and chaps. ■

BILL BIRDSONG

WESTERN BUFFET

MENU

Barbecued Chicken

Baked Beans

Corn on the Cob

Sliced Tomatoes, Onions, Cucumbers, and Green Peppers Marinated in Italian Dressing

Assorted Hard Rolls

Heavenly Hash Brownies

BARBECUED CHICKEN

¼ cup finely chopped onion
1 clove garlic, minced
2 tablespoons vegetable oil
¾ cup ketchup
⅓ cup white vinegar
1 teaspoon lemon juice
1 tablespoon worcestershire sauce
1 tablespoon dark brown sugar
1 teaspoon dry mustard
½ teaspoon salt
¼ teaspoon pepper
¼ teaspoon Tabasco sauce
2 (2½ to 3-pound) broiler-fryer chickens
vegetable oil

In small saucepan over medium-high heat, cook onion and garlic in vegetable oil until tender. Stir in ketchup, vinegar, lemon juice, worcestershire sauce, brown sugar, dry mustard, salt, pepper, and Tabasco sauce. Reduce heat. Simmer, covered, for 30 minutes, stirring occasionally.

Quarter chickens and brush with vegetable oil. Place chicken pieces skin side up over medium-hot coals. Grill chicken for about 25 minutes. Turn and grill for 15 more minutes. Brush both sides of chicken with sauce and grill an additional 5-10 minutes a side, until chicken is done. During last cooking period, brush frequently with sauce.

Yield: 8 servings

BAKED BEANS

8 slices bacon
1 cup chopped onion
4 (16-ounce) cans pork and beans in tomato sauce
¼ cup dark brown sugar
2 tablespoons worcestershire sauce
2 teaspoons prepared mustard

Preheat oven to 325 degrees.

Cook bacon in skillet over medium heat until crisp; drain, reserving 4 tablespoons drippings. Crumble bacon; set aside. Cook chopped onion in reserved drippings until tender.

In large bowl, combine bacon, onion, pork and beans, brown sugar, worcestershire sauce, and mustard; mix well.

Pour mixture into 3-quart casserole. Bake, uncovered, for 1½ hours.

Yield: 12 servings

CORN ON THE COB

**6 ears fresh corn
salt and pepper
butter or margarine**

Remove husks from corn. Under running water, remove silk with vegetable brush.

Drop corn into boiling salted water. Cook for 6-8 minutes, or until tender. Do not overcook. Serve with salt, pepper, and butter.

Yield: 6 servings

HEAVENLY HASH BROWNIES

**4 eggs, beaten
2 cups sugar
1½ cups all-purpose flour
1 teaspoon vanilla extract
1 cup margarine
⅓ cup cocoa
1½ cups pecans, chopped
1 (6¼-ounce) bag miniature marshmallows
Chocolate Frosting**

Preheat oven to 350 degrees.

In large bowl, combine eggs, sugar, flour, and vanilla extract. Melt margarine in small saucepan; add cocoa and mix well. Add margarine and cocoa mixture to egg mixture and beat well. Stir in nuts.

Pour into greased 9 x 13-inch baking pan. Bake for 25-30 minutes. In meantime, make Chocolate Frosting. As soon as brownies are removed from oven, sprinkle evenly with marshmallows and return pan to oven until marshmallows are slightly melted. Pour Chocolate Frosting over marshmallows, gently spreading to cover. Cool before cutting.

Yield: 4 dozen

CHOCOLATE FROSTING:

**½ cup margarine, melted
⅓ cup whole milk
3 tablespoons cocoa
1 (16-ounce) box XXXX confectioners' sugar
1 teaspoon vanilla extract**

Combine margarine, milk, and cocoa; beat in confectioners' sugar and vanilla extract.

VICE PREMIER DENG XIAOPING

On December 15, 1978, President Jimmy Carter and His Excellency, Deng Xiaoping, Vice Premier of the State Council of the People's Republic of China, announced the agreement for normalization of relations between the United States and the People's Republic of China. Normalization became official on January 1, 1979. Two weeks later, we began preparing for a visit from the Vice Premier, his wife, Madame Zhou Lin, and a sizable Chinese delegation.

Vice Premier Deng and Madame Zhuo flew into Dobbins Air Force Base, just outside Atlanta, on the morning of February 1, 1979. Georgia was the second stop on their tour of the United States, which began in Washington, D.C.

The Vice Premier was the guest of honor at a dinner held in the mansion ballroom on the evening of his arrival.

Our guest had expressed an interest in meeting governors from other states interested in trade with China, so George invited seventeen of his fellow governors to the dinner. Before the rest of our guests arrived, the governors group met in the state dining room to discuss trade with the world's most populous country. After Vice Premier Deng arrived, he met with the governors before going downstairs for dinner.

In a matter of minutes, George and I came to know the Vice Premier and his wife as very open and engaging people. Vice Premier Deng's keen

Madame Zhuo Lin and Vice Premier Deng Xiaoping

GARY WOMACK

sense of humor made him a delightful conversationalist. Even communication through an interpreter did not dim his sparkle and enthusiasm. At less than five feet tall, he was quite a contrast to our son, Jeff, whose 6'4"-inch frame towered over him in the receiving line.

The dinner went without a hitch until toasting time. As is customary, George was to stand before the dessert was served and offer a toast to our honored guest. The world press was gathered at the end of the ballroom patiently awaiting the one photo opportunity of the evening. As George and Vice Premier Deng stood up, so did the other two hundred people in the room — making it impossible for the television crews and news photographers to see the Vice Premier. Groans from the media people prompted George to ask everyone but our guest of honor to remain seated while he "replayed" the toast.

The large number of guests and the short time we had to prepare required the dinner for Vice Premier Deng to be catered. The State Department had provided a brief on our honored guests' food preferences, which was consulted as we planned the menu.

We selected veal as the entree. We did not know until later that the Vice Premier had been served veal at lunch *and* dinner in Washington on the previous day. George asked Vice Premier Deng about his impression of the United States after spending two days here. He answered with a twinkle in his eye, "In the U.S., they serve veal with every meal."

Since the "veal meal" was catered, only the menu is included here. ■

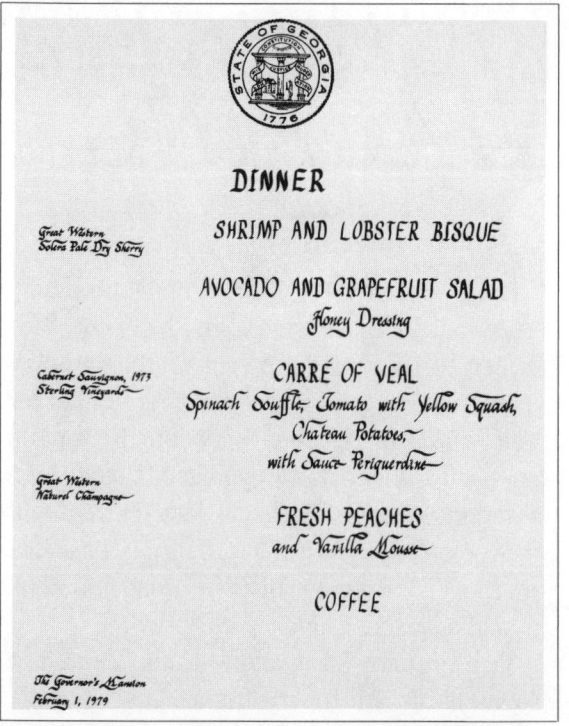

GARY WOMACK

JOAN MONDALE: "JOAN OF ART"

In 1978, Joan Mondale, wife of the Vice President of the United States, traveled to Atlanta as part of her personal campaign to heighten awareness of the arts. Mrs. Mondale's schedule included a meeting with Robert Shaw, music director of the Atlanta Symphony Orchestra; a tour of the High Museum of Art; and a visit to the Nexus Contemporary Art Center.

Traveling with Mrs. Mondale was Bess Abell, her assistant and daughter of former Kentucky governor, Earl Clements. Ms. Abell had also served as social secretary to Lady Bird Johnson during the Johnson presidency.

Mrs. Mondale arrived on the morning of March 2 to be our house guest for one night. All of the good that she accomplished promoting the arts during her official itinerary in Atlanta takes a back seat to her contribution to preserving a precious piece of art at the governor's mansion.

As I showed Mrs. Mondale to the presidential suite, a sudden gust of March wind blasted through an open window and slammed shut the door to the room. A nineteenth-century porcelain urn, filled with magnolia foliage, crashed onto the marble floor. The remnants of the priceless urn lay at our feet. We were stunned.

Mrs. Mondale regained her composure, rushed to open her cosmetic case, and drew out two small powder brushes, one for each of us. Within minutes of her arrival at the mansion, we were on our hands and knees carefully sweeping up tiny shards of antique porcelain. Every sliver was recovered and the vase was later restored by an expert.

After such a "smashing" start, we went on to have a quiet and pleasantly uneventful lunch with our guest. ∎

George presents Joan Mondale with original paintings by Georgia artist Rena Divine

LUNCHEON FOR JOAN MONDALE

Watercress Soup

Chicken Tetrazzini

Orange-Glazed Carrots   Green Pea Timbales

Southern Angel Biscuits

Irish Mist

WATERCRESS SOUP

2 (10¾-ounce) cans cream of asparagus soup
½ cup fresh watercress, cut up
2 soup cans of whole milk
¼ teaspoon dried basil

Place soup and watercress in blender container. Cover and blend at low speed. Pour soup mixture into medium saucepan; add milk and basil. Cook, stirring frequently, over medium heat until smooth and creamy. Serve hot or cold.

Yield: 6 servings

CHICKEN TETRAZZINI

1 (12-ounce) package medium egg noodles
1 (10¾-ounce) can cream of chicken soup
1½ cups chicken stock
4 cups coarsely chopped cooked chicken
1 (8-ounce) carton sour cream
4 tablespoons Durkee Famous Sauce
1 (2-ounce) jar diced pimientos, drained
1 (4-ounce) can sliced mushrooms, drained
¼ cup grated parmesan cheese

Preheat oven to 425 degrees.

Cook noodles according to package directions. Do not overcook. Drain noodles in colander.

In large saucepan, combine soup and chicken stock. Cook, stirring frequently, over medium heat until smooth. Add chicken, sour cream, Durkee Famous Sauce, pimientos, mushrooms, and parmesan cheese. Mix well. Fold in cooked noodles.

Turn mixture into lightly greased 3½-quart baking dish. Bake, uncovered, for about 30 minutes, or until hot and bubbly.

Yield: 10 servings

ORANGE-GLAZED CARROTS

6 medium carrots
¼ cup water
1 tablespoon sugar
1 teaspoon cornstarch
¼ teaspoon salt
¼-½ teaspoon ground ginger
¼ cup orange juice
2 tablespoons butter or margarine

Diagonally slice carrots into 1-inch pieces. Cook, covered, in boiling water for 15 minutes, or until barely tender.

Mix sugar, cornstarch, salt, ginger, orange juice, and butter; pour over carrots. Cook over low heat, stirring occasionally, for 8 minutes.

Yield: 4 servings

GREEN PEA TIMBALES

1½ cups green pea purée
2 tablespoons melted butter
3 eggs, well beaten
salt and pepper

Preheat oven to 300 degrees.

Blend all ingredients well and pour scant ½ cup of mixture into 6 greased individual molds. Set molds in pan of hot water. Bake for 35-40 minutes, until set.

Use sharp knife to loosen edges of timbales from molds. Unmold onto serving plate.

Yield: 6 servings

SOUTHERN ANGEL BISCUITS

(recipe on page 99)

IRISH MIST

1 envelope unflavored gelatin
3 tablespoons cold water
8 egg yolks
2 cups whole milk
1 cup sugar
½ teaspoon vanilla extract
¼ cup Irish Mist liqueur
1 pint whipping cream
½ cup finely chopped toasted almonds

Dissolve gelatin in cold water. Beat egg yolks. In large heavy saucepan, combine egg yolks, milk, and sugar. Cook over medium heat, stirring constantly, until mixture coats a spoon and is thickened. Stir in gelatin mixture, vanilla extract, and Irish Mist. Cool to room temperature.

Whip cream and fold into cooled mixture. Pour into stemmed sherbert glasses. Cover and refrigerate overnight.

Sprinkle with almonds before serving.

Yield: 12 servings

BREAKFAST FOR JOAN MONDALE

MENU

Fresh Fruit Cup

Eggs Benedict

Fig Preserves

EGGS BENEDICT

4 English muffins, split, toasted, and buttered
8 slices Canadian bacon, broiled or pan-fried
8 Poached Eggs
¾ cup Hollandaise Sauce

Top each muffin half with 1 slice of bacon, 1 poached egg, and about 1 tablespoon of Hollandaise Sauce. Serve immediately.

Yield: 4 servings

POACHED EGGS:

vegetable oil
8 eggs

Lightly oil large heavy skillet. Fill skillet with 2-3 inches of water. Heat water to boiling over medium-high heat. Reduce heat to keep water simmering.

Break eggs, 1 at a time, into a dish. Slip each egg into water, holding dish close to water's surface. Simmer 3-5 minutes, depending on desired doneness. When done, lift eggs with slotted pancake turner or spoon onto absorbant paper.

Yield: 4 servings

HOLLANDAISE SAUCE:

3 egg yolks
2 tablespoons lemon juice
¼ teaspoon salt
⅛ teaspoon paprika
dash cayenne pepper
½ cup butter, chilled and cut into small chunks, divided

In saucepan, beat together egg yolks, lemon juice, and seasonings. Add half of butter. Cook over low heat, stirring rapidly, until butter melts. Add remaining butter, stirring constantly, until butter melts and sauce thickens. Use immediately or cover and refrigerate.

(Note: To prepare in blender, measure all ingredients except butter into blender container. Melt butter and add to other ingredients. Blend at low speed for 15-20 seconds, or until sauce thickens. Heat before serving.)

Yield: ¾ cup

SHARKY'S MACHINE PREMIERE RECEPTION

A lighthearted conversation with a cameraman during the filming of a public service announcement in 1981 led to my cameo appearance in a movie with cinema heartthrob Burt Reynolds. I had wisecracked about going into the movies after George went out of office, since I had so much experience making public service announcements.

The cameraman took my comment more seriously than I intended. Several months later, he called the mansion to let me know that extras were being hired at Stone Mountain for the filming of *Sharky's Machine*.

I thought it would be exciting and interesting to see how movies are made — from the vantage point of an extra. My secretary, Pat Reid, and I, accompanied by the ever-present state trooper, went to Stone Mountain and signed up as extras for a garden party scene. For two days we stood in the broiling sun (in the same clothes both days) and pretended to be enjoying a garden party. I had one line. I said it over and over as they filmed and filmed.

The attention to detail was amazing. Massive flower arrangements wilted quickly in the hot sun. Every few minutes they were sprayed with water in an effort to keep them looking fresh. Helicopters equipped with cameras flew overhead, filming the scene from the air.

As it turned out, most of the two days' filming ended up on the cutting room floor. My one line never made it into the movie. In fact, if you blinked at the wrong time while watching *Sharky's Machine*, you probably didn't see me.

Franklin Garrett accepts the film on behalf of the Atlanta Historical Society

GARY WOMACK

Jan and Jerry Reed pose as George directs the photographer

GARY WOMACK

Although I was not "discovered," I have seldom had two more interesting days. The experience gave me a new respect for the hard-working people, both actors and crew, who make movies.

Months after the filming, the premiere of *Sharky's Machine* was held at the Fox Theatre in Atlanta. After the premiere, George and I hosted a reception for the producers and cast at the governor's mansion. The guest list was pure Hollywood "glitz," and more than 150 people attended. Among our guests were the actors who played the leading roles in the movie — Burt Reynolds, Earl Holliman, Rachel Ward, Vittorio Gassman, and Brian Keith. Burt's friends — Lois Nettleton, Jim Nabors, and Miss Lillian Carter — were also there.

Our then-new chef, Holly Wulfing, was given carte blanche to do her very best food presentation that evening. Holly graduated from the Culinary Institute of America and joined the mansion staff in 1981. She did a magnificent job of adding continental flair to our traditional Southern hospitality.

Holly shares with us the recipes used for this elegant reception. ■

GARY WOMACK

Above, *Sharky's Machine* author Bill Diehl and Ed Spivia, director of the Film Division/Georgia Department of Industry and Trade, celebrate with Burt Reynolds. Below, Rachel Ward and George ham it up

GARY WOMACK

SHARKY'S MACHINE RECEPTION

MENU

COLD HORS D'OEUVRES

Roast Contrefilet of Beef with Dipping Sauce

Kiwi and Prosciutto

Duck Gallantine with Cumberland Sauce

Marinated Baby Shrimp

Stuffed Trout

HOT HORS D'OEUVRES

Oysters Burton

Coulibiac

Phyllo-Wrapped Lobster

Chicken Champagnoise

Mini Beef Wellington

DESSERTS

Chocolate Truffles

Pralines

Almond Lace Cookies

Chocolate-Dipped Strawberries

Mini Chocolate Éclairs

ROAST CONTREFILET OF BEEF WITH DIPPING SAUCE

whole strip loin of beef
2 cloves garlic
salt and pepper
Dipping Sauce

Preheat oven to 350 degrees.

Trim strip loin of excess fat cover and silverskin. Rub meat with garlic; season with salt and pepper. Roast for approximately 1½ hours, or until meat thermometer registers 140 degrees (for medium-rare beef). Remove from oven to cool. Refrigerate. Slice thinly before serving. Serve with Dipping Sauce.

Yield: 14-16 servings

DIPPING SAUCE:

1 cup sour cream
1 tablespoon prepared mustard
2 tablespoons horseradish

Combine all ingredients and chill.

Yield: 1 cup

KIWI AND PROSCIUTTO

½ pound prosciutto, sliced paper-thin
12 kiwi fruit, quartered lengthwise

Wrap kiwi quarters with slices of prosciutto. Refrigerate until serving time.

Yield: 4 dozen

DUCK GALLANTINE WITH CUMBERLAND SAUCE

(begin 48 hours before serving time)

1 (3-4 pound) duck
kosher salt
crushed peppercorns
3-4 bay leaves
1 ounce brandy
6 ounces lean pork, diced
6 ounces chicken, diced
Liver Gratin Forcemeat (see recipe on following page)
1 tablespoon tomato paste
3-4 chicken livers, diced
salt to taste
⅓ teaspoon white pepper
⅓ teaspoon pâté spices (Epice Marie)
Cumberland Sauce (see recipe on following page)

Bone duck leaving skin intact. Reserve lean meat from legs. Lay duck out flat, skin side down. Slice off pieces of breast meat and evenly distribute over skin. Transfer to wet, double-strength cheesecloth on a tray. Sprinkle with kosher salt, crushed peppercorns, bay leaves, and brandy. Cover with plastic wrap and refrigerate for 24 hours.

Preheat oven to 325 degrees.

Finely grind diced pork, chicken, and lean meat from duck legs. Add to prepared Liver Gratin Forcemeat, working on a bowl of ice. Add tomato paste, diced chicken livers, salt, white pepper, and pâté spices. Mix well. Remove bay leaves from duck. Spread forcemeat mixture over duck. Roll in cheesecloth; tie at 2-inch intervals. Roll in parchment paper; tie at 2-inch intervals.

Roast on a rack for 15-20 minutes per pound, or until meat thermometer registers 160 degrees. Cool. Refrigerate. Slice and serve with Cumberland Sauce.

Yield: approximately 16 servings

LIVER GRATIN FORCEMEAT:

4 ounces pork fat, chopped
8 ounces chicken livers
1 shallot, finely chopped
¼ cup chopped fresh mushrooms
1½ teaspoons salt
¼ teaspoon pepper
¼ teaspoon pâté spices
¼ teaspoon dried thyme

Render out pork fat; discard pieces. Sauté chicken livers in hot fat until medium-rare; remove from fat. Sauté shallot and mushrooms in same skillet. Add salt, pepper, pâté spices, and thyme. Combine all ingredients; allow to cool. Purée mixture and force through sieve or strainer. Refrigerate for several hours.

CUMBERLAND SAUCE:

1 (14-ounce) jar red currant jelly
zest of 2 oranges
juice of 2 oranges
½ cup port wine

Combine all ingredients in saucepan. Bring to boil; reduce heat and simmer 3-5 minutes. Cool. Serve with Duck Gallantine.

Yield: approximately 1½ cups

MARINATED BABY SHRIMP

(begin 24 hours before serving time)

2½ pounds small raw shrimp, peeled and deveined
2 medium onions
2 lemons
1 (3-ounce) jar capers
1 cup vegetable oil
¾ cup cider vinegar
¼ teaspoon Tabasco sauce
½ teaspoon worcestershire sauce
1 teaspoon dried oregano
salt and pepper to taste

Drop shrimp into large pot of boiling salted water. Return to boil. Drain shrimp and set aside to cool.

Thinly slice onions and lemons. In flat plastic container, layer shrimp, onions, capers, and lemons. Repeat layering, using all ingredients. Pour oil and vinegar over shrimp; add seasonings and refrigerate. Marinate for 24 hours, turning mixture twice. Serve with crackers.

Yield: 12-16 servings

STUFFED TROUT

4 tablespoons butter
3 stalks celery, chopped
1 medium onion, chopped
1 pound crab claw meat
½ pound small shrimp, peeled and chopped
½ cup dry white wine
1 teaspoon dried thyme
1 teaspoon salt
½ teaspoon pepper
½ cup chopped fresh parsley
1 cup bread crumbs (may need more)
6 (8-ounce) trout, boned
Poaching Liquid
Dill Sauce

Melt butter in skillet. Sauté celery and onion until transparent. Add crab meat and shrimp and cook until shrimp turn pink. Add wine, thyme, salt, pepper, and parsley, stirring to mix. Add bread crumbs and mix well. (Mixture should be crumbly, but hold together when squeezed in hand.)

Stuff the cavity of each fish with bread crumb mixture. (They should be full enough so that each cavity has 1 inch of stuffing showing.) Wrap each fish in double-strength cheesecloth. Tie at 1-inch intervals.

In Dutch oven, bring Poaching Liquid to boil. Lower trout into boiling liquid and simmer for 20 minutes. Remove fish; cool and refrigerate. Untie and unwrap fish. Slice and serve with Dill Sauce.

Yield: 48 slices

POACHING LIQUID:

1 (750 ml) bottle dry white wine
1 quart water
2 green onions, chopped
3 bay leaves

Combine all ingredients in Dutch oven.

DILL SAUCE:

1 cup sour cream
½ cup mayonnaise
juice of ½ lemon
¼ cup chopped fresh dill
½ teaspoon curry powder
½ teaspoon salt

Combine all ingredients in small bowl. Chill until serving time.

Yield: approximately 1½ cups

OYSTERS BURTON

1 pound bacon
3 (12-ounce) containers select oysters
vegetable oil for frying
all-purpose flour
egg wash (2 eggs beaten with ½ cup whole milk)
bread crumbs (about 2 cups)
tartar sauce or rémoulade sauce

Preheat oven to 400 degrees.

Place bacon on broiler pan and precook for 5 minutes. (Bacon should still be pliable.) Wrap each oyster with ½ slice of bacon; secure with toothpick.

Heat oil in large heavy skillet. Dredge oysters lightly in flour. Dip in egg wash and roll in crumbs. When temperature of oil reaches 350 degrees, fry oysters until golden. Drain on paper towels. Serve with tartar sauce or rémoulade sauce.

Yield: 4 dozen

COULIBIAC

Coulibiac is classically prepared in a brioche dough. This recipe has been adapted to use puff pastry dough. Since it makes two whole coulibiac, which would serve about 50 people, you might want to freeze one before baking.

1 cup butter
1½ pounds fresh mushrooms, washed and sliced
12 green onions, chopped
½ cup Madeira wine
1 teaspoon allspice
1½ teaspoons ground cinnamon
½ teaspoon ground cloves
½ teaspoon ground nutmeg
1 tablespoon salt
1 teaspoon pepper
1 (4-5 pound) salmon, fileted
4 (10 x 15-inch) sheets frozen puff pastry, thawed
½ cup kasha (coarsely ground buckwheat), cooked according to package directions
½ cup chopped fresh parsley
6 hard-boiled eggs (with yolks and whites chopped separately)
egg wash (2 eggs beaten with ½ cup whole milk)

Melt butter in Dutch oven. Add mushrooms, onions, wine, spices, salt, and pepper. Simmer gently until mushrooms are done. Add fileted salmon, cooking in batches if necessary. Simmer salmon for 10 minutes and remove to cool.

Preheat oven to 350 degrees.

Place 1 sheet of puff pastry on baking sheet. Cut pastry into fish shape, using as much of dough as possible. Spread about ¼ of kasha over surface of dough, leaving 1-inch border around entire edge. Place half of fish on kasha. Sprinkle more kasha on fish. Spoon half of mushroom sauce over kasha. Sprinkle with parsley, egg yolks, and egg whites.

Place second piece of puff pastry over "fish." Press down edges to meet edges of bottom dough; press firmly to secure. Trim excess dough. Using small end of plain pastry tube, cut an "eye" in the fish; use opposite end to indent "scales" on rest of fish.

Repeat procedure for second coulibiac. (Freeze if desired.) Brush coulibiac with egg wash. Bake for 45 minutes to 1 hour, until golden. Slice to serve.

Yield: 2 coulibiac

PHYLLO-WRAPPED LOBSTER

½ cup butter, melted and divided
1 tablespoon flour
salt and pepper
¾ cup whole milk
1 egg yolk
18 ounces cooked lobster
2 tablespoons chopped fresh parsley
¼ cup dry sherry
1 cup grated Swiss cheese
1 pound phyllo dough

Heat 1 tablespoon butter in large saucepan over medium heat. Blend in flour, salt, and pepper. Stir in milk. Cook until thickened, stirring constantly. Add small amount of hot mixture to egg yolk; mix and add back to saucepan. Stir in lobster, parsley, sherry, and cheese. Cool and refrigerate.

Preheat oven to 400 degrees.

Cut phyllo in half and stack. Brush top sheet of dough with butter. Fold top sheet into thirds, bringing long sides toward middle. (Dough should now be shaped like a long rectangle.) Place 1 tablespoon of lobster mixture on lower half of dough. Fold dough like a flag. Lightly brush entire surface with butter. Repeat until all sheets of phyllo dough are used. Bake for 10-15 minutes, until golden.

Yield: 4 dozen

CHICKEN CHAMPAGNOISE

5 pounds white meat chicken, in chunks
flour seasoned with salt and pepper
butter
2 medium onions, diced
4 cloves garlic, minced
2 cups champagne
1 pint whipping cream

Preheat oven to 350 degrees.

Lightly dredge chicken in flour. In Dutch oven, melt 4 tablespoons butter. Sear chicken, in batches, adding more butter as needed. After all chicken has been seared, add 2 more tablespoons butter to Dutch oven. Sauté onion and garlic until transparent. Drain off excess butter.

Add champagne. Reduce by ⅓. Add cream and chicken; mix well. Cover and bake for 20 minutes. Adjust seasonings before serving.

Yield: 24 servings

MINI BEEF WELLINGTON

1½ pounds mushrooms, washed and finely chopped
3 shallots, finely chopped
1 cup dry sherry
1½ teaspoons salt
½ teaspoon pepper
1 (5 to 6-pound) whole beef tenderloin, trimmed
vegetable oil
3½ pounds puff pastry (thawed, if frozen)
1 (2¾-ounce) can liver pâté
egg wash (2 eggs beaten with ½ cup whole milk)

Combine mushrooms, shallots, sherry, salt, and pepper in saucepan. Bring to boil. Reduce heat and simmer until all liquid is absorbed, about 45 minutes. Cool.

Preheat oven to 425 degrees.

Cut beef into 1-inch cubes. Sear beef in small amount of hot oil, cooking just long enough to seal in juices. (This should be done in small batches.) Cool.

Using a 3 or 3½-inch biscuit cutter, cut puff pastry into circles. Spread each beef cube with ¼ teaspoon pâté and ½ teaspoon mushroom mixture. Place on circle of dough, stretching dough to seal. Pinch to seal tightly. Place sealed side down on baking sheets. Brush with egg wash. Bake for 10-15 minutes, until golden.

Yield: 5-6 dozen

CHOCOLATE TRUFFLES

1 pint whipping cream
5 tablespoons sugar
4 tablespoons butter
2 pounds semi-sweet chocolate, melted
2 ounces liqueur (Grand Marnier or Amaretto)
cocoa

In large saucepan, boil together cream, sugar, and butter. Stir in chocolate. Remove from heat. Cool and refrigerate until firm.

In large bowl of electric mixer, beat chilled mixture until light and fluffy. Add liqueur; mix well. Refrigerate until firm.

Scoop chocolate mixture with very small scoop or pipe with plain tip from a pastry bag. (Scoops should be bite-sized.) Chill until firm. Roll in cocoa. Chill until serving time.

Yield: 6-8 dozen

PRALINES

1 cup granulated sugar
1 cup dark brown sugar
⅛ teaspoon salt
½ cup evaporated milk
1 teaspoon vanilla extract
1 tablespoon butter
2 cups pecan halves

Combine both sugars, salt, and evaporated milk in large saucepan. Bring to boil. Reduce heat and cook until soft ball stage (234 degrees on a candy thermometer), stirring occasionally. Remove from heat. Stir in vanilla extract, butter, and pecan halves. Drop by tablespoonfuls onto waxed paper. (Work quickly to avoid premature hardening.)

Yield: 1½ dozen

ALMOND LACE COOKIES

1¾ cups finely ground blanched almonds
1¼ cups sugar
1¼ cups butter
4 tablespoons all-purpose flour
5 tablespoons whole milk

Preheat oven to 350 degrees.

Place all ingredients in skillet. Cook over low heat, stirring, until butter is melted and ingredients are blended. Keep mixture warm.

Drop by heaping teaspoonfuls onto greased baking sheets, about 2 inches apart. Bake until golden, about 5 minutes. Remove from pan, loosening gradually with metal spatula. Roll each cookie over handle of wooden spoon to shape into cylinder. Remove from spoon when cool.

Yield: 6-8 dozen

CHOCOLATE-DIPPED STRAWBERRIES

1 (12-ounce) package semi-sweet chocolate chips
2 pints fresh strawberries, washed and dried

Melt chocolate in top of double boiler. Dip ends of strawberries in chocolate. Place on wax paper to set. Refrigerate until serving time.

Yield: 2-3 dozen

MINI CHOCOLATE ÉCLAIRS

½ cup vegetable shortening
1 cup water
pinch salt
1 cup minus 3 tablespoons all-purpose flour
4 large eggs
Chantilly Cream
Chocolate Glaze

Preheat oven to 400 degrees.

In saucepan, bring shortening and water to boil. Remove from heat. Add salt and flour, stirring until dough comes away from sides of pan (adding a little more flour if necessary). Add eggs 1 at a time, stirring well between additions.

Fill plain-tipped pastry bag with mixture. Pipe small "tubes" about the size of a thumb onto parchment lined baking sheet. Bake until éclairs are golden and there is a hollow sound when they are tapped (20-35 minutes). Cool. Fill éclairs with Chantilly Cream either by slicing horizontally and piping filling into cavity or by using a bismark-tipped pastry bag and filling éclair from the end.

Using small spatula, spread tops of éclairs with warm Chocolate Glaze. If glaze is too thin, cool briefly before spreading. If glaze is too thick, add a few drops of hot water. Refrigerate until serving time.

Yield: 3 dozen

CHANTILLY CREAM:

1 cup whole milk
3 egg yolks
⅓ cup sugar
2 tablespoons cornstarch
1 teaspoon vanilla extract
½ cup whipping cream, whipped

In small saucepan, heat milk just to boiling; remove from heat. Beat egg yolks and sugar together in separate saucepan; stir in cornstarch. Slowly add scalded milk to yolk mixture, mixing quickly to avoid cooking yolks. Return mixture to medium-low heat. Cook until thickened, stirring constantly. Remove from heat. Stir in vanilla extract. Cool. Fold whipped cream into cooled mixture.

CHOCOLATE GLAZE:

2½ ounces unsweetened chocolate
½ cup sugar
3½ tablespoons water

Melt chocolate in top of double boiler. Add sugar and water. Mix well. Place over direct heat, stirring until mixture comes to boil. Remove from heat. Beat with wire whip for a few seconds, until slightly thickened.

PRIME MINISTER NOUIRA OF TUNISIA

As part of a tour of the United States, Prime Minister Hedi Nouira of Tunisia and his wife made a stop in Georgia in the spring of 1975. They were our special guests at a luncheon at the governor's mansion.

Traveling with the Prime Minister were several of his top aides; the Tunisian Ambassador to the United States, Ali Hedda; the United States Ambassador to Tunisia, Talcott Seelye; and their wives. The State Department's Deputy Chief of Protocol, Ambassador Stuart Rockwell, and his wife also attended the luncheon.

Ambassador and Mrs. Rockwell were our only English-speaking guests that day. For the first time, George and I had to depend on interpreters to talk to our guests. It takes twice as long to get something said. I learned to pity diplomats who spend their professional lives talking through someone else.

In preparation for the luncheon, George and I read briefing papers supplied by the State Department, which helped us speak knowledgeably with our guests about their country. The Prime Minister was interested in the South, and Georgia, in particular. His questions pointed out a common misconception many foreign guests have on their first visit to the South. Agriculture is often assumed to be the sole basis of our economy. The tremendous industrial development in the South, and particularly in Georgia, is always a dramatic surprise.

After a news conference and reception the following day, Prime Minister Nouira and his party left for Sea Island to recharge their batteries for a few days before resuming their U.S. tour. ■

LUNCHEON FOR PRIME MINISTER NOUIRA OF TUNISIA

MENU

Vichyssoise

Chicken Parisienne

Minted Carrots and Peas   Yellow Rice

Effie's Dinner Rolls

Key Lime Pie

VICHYSSOISE

4 leeks (white part), finely sliced
¼ cup finely chopped onion
¼ cup butter
5 medium potatoes, cut in quarters
1 carrot, sliced
1 quart chicken broth
1 teaspoon salt
3 cups whole milk
2 cups heavy cream
chopped chives

Sauté leeks and onion in butter. Add potatoes, carrot, chicken broth, and salt. Bring to rapid boil. Cover; reduce heat. Simmer until potatoes and carrot are soft. Drain, reserving liquid. Mash and rub vegetables through strainer or process in food processor until smooth. Heat reserved liquid, puréed vegetables, and milk for 10-15 minutes. Do not boil.

Season to taste. Cool. Add cream and chill. Serve in chilled cups. Garnish with chives.

Yield: 16-18 servings

CHICKEN PARISIENNE

2 large or 3 medium chicken breasts, split (boneless, if desired)
1 (10¾-ounce) can cream of mushroom soup
1 cup sour cream
1 (4-ounce) can sliced mushrooms, with liquid
½ cup dry sherry
paprika

Preheat oven to 350 degrees.

Place chicken breasts, skin side up, in oblong baking dish. Combine soup, sour cream, mushrooms with liquid, and sherry. Mix well and pour over chicken. Sprinkle generously with paprika.

Cover and bake for 1 to 1¼ hours, or until tender.

Yield: 4-6 servings

MINTED CARROTS AND PEAS

8 small carrots
3 cups fresh or frozen green peas
¼ cup butter
3 tablespoons chopped fresh mint leaves
salt to taste

Cook whole carrots in small amount of boiling salted water, covered, for 15 minutes, or until tender. Cook peas in boiling salted water until tender. Drain vegetables.

Melt butter in skillet, browning slightly. Add vegetables and mint. Salt to taste; toss lightly. Serve immediately.

Yield: 6-8 servings

YELLOW RICE

(prepare according to package directions)

EFFIE'S DINNER ROLLS

2 packages active dry yeast
½ cup warm water
¾ cup vegetable oil
2 cups cold water
2 eggs, beaten
¾ cup sugar
2 teaspoons salt
8 cups sifted all-purpose flour
¼ cup butter
flour (as needed for rolling dough)

Dissolve yeast in ½ cup warm water. Pour yeast mixture, vegetable oil, cold water, beaten eggs, sugar, and salt in large bowl of electric mixer; beat well. Gradually add flour, beating after each addition. When dough becomes too stiff to be mixed with electric mixer, beat last additions of flour in by hand; mix well. (Dough will be *very* sticky.) Transfer to bowl with tight-fitting lid. Cover; refrigerate overnight.

Flour hands well. Pinch off half of dough. Return remaining dough to refrigerator. Melt butter. Sift about ¾ cup flour onto board. Flour hands again. Place dough on floured board; work in just enough flour to make it possible to roll out dough. Roll dough to ¼-inch thickness; cut with 2-inch biscuit cutter. Slightly stretch each round of dough from center. Dip 1 half of each round in melted butter; fold top half of dough over buttered half. Place on ungreased, heavy baking sheet 2 inches apart. Allow to rise for 2 hours.

Preheat oven to 475 degrees.

Bake for 6-8 minutes. Watch carefully. (Note: Remainder of dough can be refrigerated for up to 1 week.)

Yield: 8 dozen (entire recipe)

KEY LIME PIE

4 eggs, separated
1 cup sugar, divided
⅔ cup Key lime juice
½ teaspoon salt
1 tablespoon unflavored gelatin
½ cup water
1 Key lime rind, finely grated
1 (9-inch) graham cracker crust
1 cup whipping cream
2-3 tablespoons XXXX confectioners' sugar

Beat egg yolks; add ½ cup sugar, lime juice, and salt. Cook in double boiler until mixture coats a spoon. Remove from heat.

Dissolve gelatin in water. Add to egg and sugar mixture. Add rind and mix well. Chill, until mixture begins to thicken. Beat egg whites with remaining sugar until they stand in soft peaks. Fold whites into chilled mixture.

Pour into graham cracker crust. Chill. Just before serving, whip cream and fold in confectioners' sugar; spread over pie.

Yield: 6 servings

GEORGE BUSBEE

VAN CLIBURN

In the spring of 1976, a citizens group called Atlanta Landmarks, Inc., was engaged in a difficult struggle to save the historic Fox Theatre from the wrecking ball. More than two million dollars was needed for an emergency mortgage payment.

Nationally known artists performed benefit concerts in Atlanta that year to aid the "Save the Fox" effort. One of the first such artists was the world-famous virtuoso, Van Cliburn. A child prodigy, Van had captured the attention of the entire world at age twenty-four, when he won the International Tchaikovsky Competition in Moscow in 1958. In the years that followed, he won many more honors and enjoyed a busy international concert schedule.

Van Cliburn accepted our invitation to spend the night at the mansion after his concert. His mother was traveling with him and was also our guest. In addition to the usual preparation for overnight visitors, the grand piano in the ballroom was tuned before Van arrived. He did not feel the need to practice, however, so we were not treated to a "private" Van Cliburn performance.

The concert was on the night before Easter Sunday, so we asked Van, his mother, and a Cliburn cousin who lives in Atlanta to join us for church the next morning. Before church, we enjoyed a light brunch together in the family dining room. ■

EASTER BRUNCH FOR VAN CLIBURN

MENU

Slice of Honeydew Melon

Beth's Blueberry Muffins

Cheese Soufflé

Crisp Bacon

BETH'S BLUEBERRY MUFFINS

1½ cups all-purpose flour
½ cup sugar
2 teaspoons baking powder
½ teaspoon salt
1 egg, beaten
¼ cup vegetable oil
½ cup whole milk
1 cup blueberries (fresh or frozen)
¼ cup water
1 tablespoon sugar

Preheat oven to 400 degrees.

In bowl, sift together first 4 ingredients. Add beaten egg, oil, and milk; stir until well blended. Bring blueberries, water, and 1 tablespoon sugar to boil in saucepan. Drain blueberries, discarding liquid.

Add blueberries to batter, stirring to mix. Spoon into lightly greased muffin tins. Bake for about 20 minutes.

Yield: 1 dozen

CHEESE SOUFFLÉ

butter
grated parmesan cheese
⅓ cup butter
⅓ cup all-purpose flour
1 tablespoon grated onion
½ teaspoon dry mustard
1½ cups whole milk
1 cup (4 ounces) grated cheddar cheese
6 eggs, separated
¼ teaspoon cream of tartar

Preheat oven to 350 degrees.

Butter sides and bottom of 2½-quart soufflé dish or casserole. Dust with parmesan cheese. In large saucepan, melt ⅓ cup butter; blend in flour, onion, and mustard. Cook over medium-high heat, stirring constantly, until mixture is smooth and bubbly. Stir in milk all at once. Cook, stirring constantly, until mixture boils and thickens. Remove from heat. Stir in cheddar cheese until melted.

In small bowl of electric mixer, beat egg yolks at high speed until thick and lemon colored, about 5 minutes. Blend small amount of hot cheese mixture into yolks. Stir yolk mixture into cheese mixture.

Wash and dry beaters. In large bowl of electric mixer, beat egg whites and cream of tartar at high speed, until stiff but not dry, just until whites no longer slip when bowl is tilted. Gently, but thoroughly, fold yolk mixture into whites. Carefully pour into prepared dish. For a "top hat," hold a spoon upright and circle mixture to make a ring about 1 inch from side of dish and 1 inch deep.

Bake until soufflé is puffy, delicately brown, and shakes slightly when oven rack is gently moved back and forth (35 to 40 minutes). Serve immediately.

Yield: 6 servings

GOVERNOR'S STAFF FAMILY CHRISTMAS PARTY

Our annual Christmas party for the governor's staff and their families was held about a week before Christmas each year. More than fifty children, dressed in their holiday best, came to the mansion with their parents, who always had as much fun as the children. The spontaneous excitement and enthusiasm of the children was catching.

Each year we had different entertainment for the youngsters — magicians, mimes, puppeteers, or storytellers. Of course, Santa Claus made an annual appearance. Over the course of

BILL BIRDSONG

BILL BIRDSONG

the evening, he heard the requests of each child, as well as those of a few adults.

The staff always outdid itself for the annual Christmas party. The mansion, beautifully decorated throughout, was filled with the sights and smells of Christmas. Poinsettias were clustered attractively in the ballroom. There was a "kiddie corner" for the children, filled with goodies for the young at heart — a gingerbread house, Snoopy cookies, clown pops, Christmas cookies, and punch.

After each party, the gingerbread house and remaining children's goodies were delivered to Egleston Hospital, where they were enjoyed by children who would be spending Christmas in the hospital. Poinsettias used at the party were taken to Our Lady of Perpetual Help, a home for the terminally ill. ∎

BILL BIRDSONG

CHRISTMAS PARTY

MENU

Eggnog   Wassail

Sliced Roast Beef and Turkey / Party Bread

Chicken Salad in Toast Cups

Shrimp Mold

Sausage Balls

Boursin Cheese   Pecan Cheese Ball   London Cheese Roll

Fresh Fruit

Toasted Pecans

Fruitcake Cookies   Brown Sugar Cookies

Haystacks   Bourbon Balls

Mrs. Baker's Fudge   Pecan Crescents

EGGNOG

12 eggs, separated
1 cup sugar
1 cup bourbon
¼ cup rum
¼ cup brandy
1 quart half-and-half
¼ cup XXXX confectioners' sugar
1 pint whipping cream
1 teaspoon vanilla extract
ground nutmeg

In large bowl of electric mixer, beat egg yolks until lemon colored. Gradually add sugar. With mixer running, slowly add bourbon, rum, and brandy; add half-and-half. Cover and refrigerate overnight.

Just before serving, beat egg whites with electric mixer until stiff, gradually adding confectioners' sugar. Fold into egg yolk mixture. Whip cream; add vanilla extract and fold into egg mixture.

Pour eggnog into chilled punch bowl. Sprinkle with nutmeg.

Yield: 12-16 servings

WASSAIL

(recipe on page 88)

CHICKEN SALAD IN TOAST CUPS

⅔-1 cup mayonnaise
2 tablespoons cider vinegar
1 teaspoon salt
4-5 cups cut-up cooked chicken
1 cup chopped celery
1 cup finely chopped green pepper
2 teaspoons grated onion
Toast Cups

In large bowl, mix mayonnaise, vinegar, and salt with fork. Add chicken, celery, green pepper, and onion. Toss well; cover and refrigerate for several hours. Right before serving, spoon into Toast Cups.

Yield: filling for 7-8 dozen Toast Cups

TOAST CUPS:

1 loaf thin-sliced bread
melted butter

Preheat oven to 375 degrees.

Trim crusts from bread. Cut each slice into 4 squares. Brush with melted butter. Press bread squares into miniature muffin tins with fingers.

Bake for 8 minutes, or until golden. Remove from tins.

Yield: approximately 7 dozen

SHRIMP MOLD

(recipe on page 89)

SAUSAGE BALLS

2 cups Bisquick
1 pound hot sausage
1 cup grated sharp cheddar cheese

Preheat oven to 350 degrees.

In large bowl, mix all ingredients together with hands. Shape mixture into small balls the size of a nickel. (Do not make any larger because Bisquick will rise, compensating for shrinkage of sausage.) Place sausage balls on jellyroll pan and bake for 12-15 minutes, or until brown. (Note: These may be frozen and reheated before serving.)

Yield: 9 dozen

BOURSIN CHEESE

16 ounces cream cheese, at room
    temperature
1 cup butter, at room temperature
2 cloves garlic, crushed
1 teaspoon dried oregano
¼ teaspoon dried thyme
¼ teaspoon dried basil
¼ teaspoon ground marjoram
¼ teaspoon dried dill
cracked black pepper (optional)

In bowl of electric mixer, blend all ingredients except pepper together. Shape into ball. Roll in cracked black pepper, if desired. Refrigerate for at least 24 hours before serving. Serve with crackers. (Note: This may be frozen.)

Yield: 20 servings

PECAN CHEESE BALL

16 ounces sharp cheddar cheese, grated, at
    room temperature
8 ounces cream cheese, at room temperature
½ medium onion, finely chopped
1 (2-ounce) jar pimiento-stuffed olives, finely
    chopped
1 teaspoon worcestershire sauce
1 cup finely chopped pecans
cayenne pepper to taste
1 tablespoon finely chopped fresh parsley
chopped pecans
chopped fresh parsley

In large bowl of electric mixer, mix cheddar and cream cheese together very well. Add onion, olives, worcestershire sauce, 1 cup chopped pecans, and cayenne pepper; mix until smooth. Mix in 1 tablespoon parsley and let stand for 15 minutes.

Shape cheese mixture into ball and roll in equal parts of chopped pecans and parsley. Refrigerate until serving time. Serve with crackers. (Note: Cheese ball may be frozen.)

Yield: 20 servings

LONDON CHEESE ROLL

11 ounces cream cheese (1 8-ounce and 1
    3-ounce package), at room temperature
4 ounces blue cheese, at room temperature
1 cup thinly sliced ripe olives
2 cups coarsely chopped walnuts or pecans,
    divided

In large bowl of electric mixer, blend cheeses. Stir in olives and 1 cup of nuts. Spread remaining nuts on sheet of wax paper. Lightly flour hands. Shape cheese mixture into 2 rolls, each about 1½ inches in diameter. Roll in nuts until well coated. Wrap in wax paper and refrigerate overnight. Serve with crackers or melba rounds. (Note: Cheese rolls freeze well.)

Yield: 12 servings

TOASTED PECANS

(recipe on page 67)

FRUITCAKE COOKIES

1½ cups dark brown sugar
½ cup butter, at room temperature
4 eggs
3 cups all-purpose flour
1½ teaspoons ground cinnamon
½ teaspoon ground nutmeg
1½ teaspoons allspice
3 tablespoons buttermilk
½ cup peach brandy
1 teaspoon baking soda
flour to dredge fruit
6 cups chopped pecans
1 pound candied pineapple, chopped
1 pound candied cherries, chopped

Preheat oven to 250 degrees.

In large bowl of electric mixer, cream sugar and butter. Add eggs 1 at a time, beating after each addition. In separate bowl, mix flour and spices. Combine buttermilk and brandy. Alternately add flour mixture and buttermilk mixture to creamed butter and sugar.

Combine soda with enough extra flour to dredge chopped pecans and fruit. Dredge pecans and fruit and add to batter. Mix thoroughly with spoon. (Batter will be very thick.) Drop by teaspoonfuls onto well-greased baking sheets. Bake for 35-40 minutes. Remove to wire racks to cool. (Note: These will keep in cookie tins for 1 month.)

Yield: 8 dozen

BROWN SUGAR COOKIES

7 cups all-purpose flour
1 tablespoon baking soda
1 tablespoon cream of tartar
1 cup butter, at room temperature
4 cups dark brown sugar
4 eggs
1 tablespoon vanilla extract

Mix dry ingredients. In large bowl of electric mixer, cream butter and brown sugar. Add eggs 1 at a time; add vanilla extract. Gradually add dry ingredients. Cover and refrigerate for 1-2 hours.

Form dough into rolls, about 1¼ inches in diameter. Wrap in wax paper and refrigerate for several hours until firm.

Preheat oven to 350 degrees.

Slice dough into ¼-inch rounds and place on greased baking sheets. Bake for 8 minutes. Remove cookies from baking sheet as soon as they are done. Cool on wire racks.

Yield: 22 dozen

HAYSTACKS

(microwave recipe)

1 (6-ounce) package butterscotch morsels
½ cup smooth peanut butter
½ cup salted cocktail peanuts
2 cups chow mein noodles

Place butterscotch morsels and peanut butter in 2-quart microwave-proof bowl. Cover with plastic wrap. Microwave on medium power for 3-5 minutes, or until most of chips are shiny or soft: blend well with spoon.

Gently stir in peanuts and chow mein noodles. Drop mixture by forkfuls onto wax paper. Cool until set. Store in covered container.

Yield: 2½ dozen

BOURBON BALLS

1 cup XXXX confectioners' sugar
2 tablespoons cocoa
¼ cup bourbon
2 tablespoons light corn syrup
2 cups crushed vanilla wafers
1 cup finely chopped pecans or walnuts
XXXX confectioners' sugar

Sift confectioners' sugar and cocoa together into medium bowl. Combine bourbon and syrup; stir into sugar mixture. Mix well. Add crushed wafers and nuts; mix well.

Roll mixture into small balls, about ¾ inch in diameter. Drop each ball into confectioners' sugar; roll to coat. Allow balls to dry for several hours. Store in airtight container. (Note: Bourbon balls freeze well.)

Yield: 3 dozen

MRS. BAKER'S FUDGE

4½ cups sugar
1 (12-ounce) can evaporated milk
1 cup margarine
3 (12-ounce) packages semi-sweet chocolate chips
1 (7-ounce) jar marshmallow creme
1½ teaspoons vanilla extract
2 cups chopped pecans

Place sugar, evaporated milk, and margarine in large, heavy saucepan. Cook over medium heat, stirring constantly, until mixture reaches soft ball stage (234 degrees on a candy thermometer).

Place chocolate chips and marshmallow creme in large mixing bowl; pour hot mixture over all. Stir until chocolate chips and marshmallow creme are melted and mixture is smooth.

Add vanilla extract and pecans; beat to thoroughly mix. Pour into 2 buttered 9 x 9 x 2-inch pans. Cool and cut into 1-inch squares.

Yield: 13 dozen

PECAN CRESCENTS

½ cup butter or margarine, at room temperature
½ cup vegetable shortening
⅓ cup sugar
2 teaspoons water
2 teaspoons vanilla extract
2 cups all-purpose flour
½ cup finely chopped pecans
XXXX confectioners' sugar

In large bowl of electric mixer, cream butter, shortening, and sugar together. Add water and vanilla extract. Gradually add flour and pecans; mix well. Cover and refrigerate for 3-4 hours.

Preheat oven to 325 degrees.

Form dough into long rolls, about ½ inch in diameter. Cut rolls into 3-inch lengths and shape into crescents. Bake on ungreased baking sheets for 15 minutes. Do *not* brown.

Remove from oven and allow to cool slightly. Roll crescents in confectioners' sugar. Cool completely. Store in covered container.

Yield: 4 dozen

HER MAJESTY, QUEEN BEATRIX OF THE NETHERLANDS

In June 1982, a royal tour of the United States brought Queen Beatrix of The Netherlands and her husband, Prince Claus, to Atlanta. Queen Beatrix had ascended to the throne as the sixth monarch of her country after the abdication of her mother, Queen Juliana, in 1980. The Netherlands is the largest foreign investor in Georgia, hence Queen Beatrix's decision to include Atlanta on her itinerary.

Queen Beatrix had expressed an interest in meeting the heads of Georgia's major energy/power companies and some of Atlanta's political and business leaders. A luncheon was given in her honor at the governor's mansion so that she could meet many of these people.

Queen Beatrix and Prince Claus arrived at the mansion in a motorcade of limousines, accompanied by Mayor and Mrs. Andrew Young and Mr. and Mrs. Cecil M. Phillips. As the other forty guests arrived, they were taken to the drawing room to await the traditional official toast. Fortunately, George was able to toast "Her Majesty, Queen Beatrix of The Netherlands," instead of using her full title of typical regal length — Beatrix Wilhelmina Armgard, Queen of The Netherlands, Princess of Orange-Nassau, Princess of Lippe-Biesterfeld.

Queen Beatrix and Prince Claus arrive at the mansion

GARY WOMACK

Taking advantage of the beautiful summer weather, we opened the doors to the mansion gardens and seated our guests on the porches and in both dining rooms. The elegant luncheon menu was planned and prepared by Chef Holly Wulfing. ■

LUNCHEON IN HONOR OF QUEEN BEATRIX OF THE NETHERLANDS

MENU

Chilled Cucumber Soup

Chicken Duxelles

Sautéed Zucchini and Yellow Squash

Buttered Noodles With Poppy Seeds

Southern Angel Biscuits

Peach Melba Crêpes

CHILLED CUCUMBER SOUP

2 medium cucumbers
1 cup water
1 small onion, sliced
¼ teaspoon salt
⅛ teaspoon white pepper
2 cups chicken stock (or broth), divided
¼ cup all-purpose flour
1 small bay leaf
1 cup whipping cream (or sour cream)
1 tablespoon chopped fresh dill

Peel, seed, and chop cucumbers. Place in medium saucepan. Add water, onion, salt, and white pepper. Cook over medium heat until cucumber is very soft. Purée cooked mixture in bowl of food processor or in electric blender.

Combine ½ cup chicken stock and flour; stir until smooth. Add mixture to remaining stock. Combine cucumber purée, stock mixture, and bay leaf in saucepan. Simmer over low heat for 2-3 minutes. Strain, cool, and refrigerate.

Just before serving, stir in cream and dill. Adjust seasonings. (Note: Soup should be served very cold.)

Yield: 6 servings

CHICKEN DUXELLES

2 cups chicken stock (or broth)
4 tablespoons Roux
3 whole chicken breasts, skinned, boned, and split
3 cups Mushroom Duxelles
all-purpose flour for dredging
salt and pepper
½ cup clarified butter
¼ cup dry sherry
½ cup whipping cream

Preheat oven to 350 degrees.

In medium saucepan, heat chicken stock to boiling. Whisk in Roux to thicken; set aside. Pound chicken and cut each piece in half. Place ¼ cup Mushroom Duxelles in center of each piece of chicken. Roll chicken to enclose duxelles. Season flour with salt and pepper. Roll each piece of chicken in flour. In large skillet, sear chicken in clarified butter. Place in 2-quart casserole. Bake, uncovered, for 15 minutes.

Drain excess grease from skillet; deglaze pan with sherry. Cook over medium-high heat until sherry is reduced by half. Add thickened chicken stock and cream. Bring to boil; reduce heat. Reduce sauce until thick enough to coat a spoon. Add chicken to sauce. Simmer 2-3 minutes. Spoon sauce over chicken before serving.

Yield: 6 servings

ROUX:

2 tablespoons butter
2 tablespoons all-purpose flour

Combine butter and flour in saucepan. Cook over low heat, stirring constantly, until lightly browned (about 5 minutes).

MUSHROOM DUXELLES:

1 pound fresh mushrooms, washed and finely chopped
2 shallots, finely chopped
⅔ cup dry sherry
1 teaspoon salt
¼ teaspoon pepper

Combine all ingredients in saucepan. Bring to boil. Reduce heat and simmer for 30-40 minutes, until all liquid is absorbed. Cool.

SAUTÉED ZUCCHINI AND YELLOW SQUASH

⅓ cup clarified butter
2 medium zucchini squash, sliced in half, then sliced into "half moons"
2 medium yellow squash, sliced in half, then sliced into "half moons"
1 clove garlic, finely chopped
salt and pepper to taste
½ teaspoon dried basil
½ teaspoon dried oregano

Heat butter in large skillet. Add squash and garlic. Sauté over medium-high heat, stirring constantly, for 4-5 minutes. Stir in seasonings. Cook an additional 1-2 minutes, until squash is barely tender.

Yield: 6 servings

BUTTERED NOODLES WITH POPPY SEEDS

½ cup butter
2 cups cooked egg noodles
1 teaspoon poppy seeds
salt and pepper to taste

Melt butter in medium skillet. Stir in noodles, poppy seeds, salt, and pepper. Cook over medium heat, stirring frequently, until heated through.

Yield: 4-6 servings

SOUTHERN ANGEL BISCUITS

(recipe on page 99)

PEACH MELBA CRÊPES

1 (10-ounce) package frozen raspberries
¼ cup currant jelly
2 tablespoons butter
¼ teaspoon almond extract
1 (16-ounce) can peach slices, drained
1 pint vanilla ice cream
6 Crêpes
½ cup whipping cream, whipped with 1 tablespoon sugar
¼ cup slivered almonds, toasted

Thaw raspberries; force through sieve. In medium saucepan, combine raspberry purée, currant jelly, butter, and almond extract. Bring to boil over moderate heat. Stir in peaches; cool.

Spoon about ⅓ cup of ice cream into center of each Crêpe; fold sides over. Spoon peaches and sauce over each Crêpe. Pipe whipped cream over each serving. Sprinkle with toasted almonds.

Yield: 6 servings

CRÊPES:

4 eggs
¼ teaspoon salt
2 cups all-purpose flour
2¼ cups whole milk
¼ cup melted butter

Combine all ingredients in blender; blend 1 minute. Scrape down sides and blend an additional 15 seconds. Cover and refrigerate for at least 1 hour. Brush 6-inch nonstick pan with butter. Heat pan over medium-high heat. Add 2-3 tablespoons crêpe batter. Quickly swirl pan to cover bottom with batter. When batter loses glossy look, turn crêpe with spatula. Cook for a few seconds and remove. (Note: Crêpes can be frozen for use at a later time.)

Yield: approximately 2 dozen

FAMILY FAVORITES

Everyone who cooks (and eats) has a few favorite recipes. Many of these recipes have been passed from generation to generation through our families. The Busbee family's favorite recipes blend two regions of the South — north Louisiana and south Georgia.

The food that I enjoyed as I grew up in north Louisiana was similar to yet different from that of the Busbee family in south Georgia. It was only after I "married into" a Georgia family that I realized the influence my Cajun and Creole neighbors had on my taste buds. Families in both regions might have had pots of black-eyed peas and ham hocks simmering on the stove, but the pot in Ruston, Louisiana, always had a pod or two of hot red pepper in it.

Like all families, we have our share of good cooks who put a "pinch of this and a dash of that" in their best recipes. The following recipes have been painstakingly gathered, tested, and "cleaned up" in an effort to make them foolproof for those of you who don't have Aunt Lil's phone number.

APPETIZERS

SWEET'N SOUR RUMAKI

6 slices bacon
1 (8-ounce) can water chestnuts, drained
1 cup ketchup
½ cup dark brown sugar

Preheat oven to 350 degrees.

Cut each slice of bacon into 3 pieces. Wrap each water chestnut with piece of bacon and secure with toothpick. Place bacon-wrapped water chestnuts in baking pan, with toothpicks pointing up. Bake, uncovered, for 35-45 minutes, until bacon is done.

Carefully pour off grease. Combine ketchup and brown sugar, mixing well. Pour over water chestnuts. Bake an additional 30 minutes, basting often with sauce. Serve warm.

Yield: 1-1½ dozen

GARLIC CHEESE ROLL

16 ounces sharp cheddar cheese, grated, at room temperature
3 (3-ounce) packages cream cheese, at room temperature
3 cloves garlic, minced
1 teaspoon sugar
1 teaspoon lemon juice
dash salt
dash cayenne pepper
paprika

Combine all ingredients except paprika in large bowl of electric mixer. Mix well. Shape into rolls 1½ inches in diameter. Roll in paprika. Wrap in wax paper and refrigerate for several hours. Serve with crackers.

Yield: approximately 4 cups of cheese spread

MELANIE'S CHEESE RING

You often have to coax people to try this cheese ring *with* the strawberry preserves. Once they try it, they find the unusual combination delicious.

16 ounces sharp cheddar cheese, grated, at room temperature
1 medium onion, grated
¾ cup mayonnaise
1 cup chopped pecans
dash salt
dash black pepper
dash cayenne pepper
1 (12-ounce) jar strawberry preserves

Mix all ingredients except preserves. (Use hands to thoroughly mix.) On large round plate, shape cheese mixture into ring, leaving room around it for crackers. Spoon strawberry preserves into center of ring. Refrigerate for several hours.

About 15 minutes before serving, remove cheese ring from refrigerator. Serve with saltine crackers.

Yield: 4 cups of cheese spread

SHERRY CHEESE PÂTÉ

2 (3-ounce) packages cream cheese, at room temperature
1 cup grated cheddar cheese, at room temperature
½ teaspoon curry powder
¼ teaspoon salt
4 teaspoons dry sherry
1 (8-ounce) jar chopped chutney
4-5 green onions, finely sliced

Combine cream cheese, cheddar cheese, curry powder, salt, and sherry; mix thoroughly. Spread into small shallow dish, shaping to ½-inch thickness. Chill 30 minutes or until firm.

Spread chutney over cheese mixture. Sprinkle with green onions. Serve with sesame or wheat crackers.

Yield: 8 servings

DESTIN DIP

1 (6½-ounce) can minced clams
2 (3-ounce) packages cream cheese, at room temperature
dash garlic salt
dash white pepper

Drain clams, reserving 1 tablespoon clam juice. In small bowl of electric mixer, cream softened cream cheese. Add garlic salt and white pepper; mix well. Add reserved clam juice; mix well. Stir in clams with a spoon. Cover and refrigerate for several hours to meld flavors. Bring to room temperature before serving. Serve with chips or crackers.

Yield: ¾ cup

CRAB-STUFFED MUSHROOMS

1 pound pasteurized crab meat
2 dozen large mushrooms (1½ inches in diameter)
1 tablespoon all-purpose flour
½ teaspoon salt
¼ teaspoon celery salt
¼ teaspoon white pepper
dash cayenne pepper
¼ cup butter or margarine, melted
½ cup light cream
1 tablespoon dry sherry
1 tablespoon chopped fresh parsley
2 tablespoons grated parmesan cheese
paprika

Preheat oven to 350 degrees.

Remove any remaining shell from crab meat. Wash mushrooms in cold water and dry; remove stems and mince, reserving 2 tablespoons.

In medium saucepan, blend flour and seasonings into butter. Gradually add cream. Cook over medium heat, stirring constantly, until thick and smooth. Add reserved minced mushroom stems, sherry, and parsley; mix well. Stir in crab meat. Stuff mushroom caps with crab meat mixture. Sprinkle with parmesan cheese and paprika. Place on well-greased baking sheet. Bake for 15-20 minutes, until lightly browned.

Yield: 2 dozen

RENA'S SHRIMP SPREAD

2 (4½-ounce) cans deveined medium shrimp
1 (8-ounce) package cream cheese, at room temperature
2 tablespoons mayonnaise
1 tablespoon grated onion
1 teaspoon white wine vinegar
2 teaspoons Dijon mustard
1 teaspoon celery seed
2-3 drops Tabasco sauce

Drain 1 can of shrimp; place in food processor bowl fitted with metal blade. Add cream cheese, mayonnaise, onion, vinegar, mustard, celery seed, and Tabasco sauce. Blend until smooth and of spreading consistency.

Drain second can of shrimp; add to puréed mixture. Mix well with a spoon. Serve with crackers.

Yield: 1¼ cups

MARINATED CHICKEN DRUMMETTES

1¾ cups soy sauce
½ cup sugar
1 clove garlic, crushed
1 teaspoon grated fresh ginger root
½ teaspoon monosodium glutamate (Ac'cent)
5 pounds chicken drummettes

Combine first 5 ingredients in bowl; mix well. Place drummettes in lightly greased 9½ x 15½-inch baking dish. Pour marinade over chicken. Cover and refrigerate overnight (or for at least 3 hours).

Preheat oven to 275 degrees.

Turn drummettes in sauce before baking. Cover and bake for 1 hour. Remove cover and bake an additional 30 minutes, basting occasionally.

Yield: 18-20 servings

CHICKEN TURNOVERS

1 (8-ounce) package cream cheese, at room temperature
½ cup butter or margarine, at room temperature
2 cups all-purpose flour, sifted
½ teaspoon salt
2 tablespoons butter or margarine
1 medium onion, chopped
4 ounces fresh mushrooms, chopped
1½ cups coarsely ground chicken
1 tablespoon soy sauce
1 tablespoon dry sherry
½ teaspoon curry powder
½ teaspoon sugar
2-3 tablespoons heavy cream

Combine cream cheese, ½ cup butter, flour, and salt. Blend with hands until mixture holds together. Form dough into ball. Wrap in wax paper and chill overnight (or for at least 4 hours).

Preheat oven to 400 degrees.

Heat 2 tablespoons butter in large skillet. Sauté onion and mushrooms until onion is transparent. Remove with slotted spoon to large bowl. Add chicken to skillet. Cook, stirring, over medium heat for 1-2 minutes.

Add soy sauce, sherry, curry powder, and sugar to skillet. Cook over medium-low heat, stirring to mix well, for 2-3 minutes. Pour mixture into bowl with onion and mushrooms. Mix well. Add enough cream to moisten mixture. Allow to cool.

On lightly floured board, roll dough as thinly as possible, about ⅛-inch thick. Cut into rounds with 3-inch biscuit cutter. Place scant teaspoon of filling on 1 side of each round. Moisten edge of dough with water; fold dough over. Moisten top edge of dough with water; press edge with fork to seal. Prick top of dough with fork. Bake on ungreased baking sheets for 15 minutes, or until lightly browned.

Yield: 3-4 dozen

SALADS

RASPBERRY CREAM MOLDS

1 (10-ounce) package frozen raspberries, thawed
1 (8½-ounce) can crushed pineapple, in heavy syrup
1½ teaspoons unflavored gelatin
¼ cup cold water
1 (3-ounce) package raspberry-flavored gelatin
1 cup boiling water
1 teaspoon lemon juice
dash salt
1 cup sour cream
¼ cup chopped pecans
lettuce leaves

Drain raspberries, reserving syrup; chop coarsely. Drain pineapple, reserving syrup. Soften unflavored gelatin in cold water. Dissolve raspberry gelatin in boiling water; pour into bowl. Add softened, unflavored gelatin, stirring to dissolve. Add reserved fruit syrup, lemon juice, and salt. Refrigerate until slightly thickened.

Fold in sour cream, pecans, and fruit. Pour into lightly oiled individual salad molds. Cover with plastic wrap and refrigerate until firm. Unmold onto lettuce leaves.

Yield: 6 servings

YUM-YUM SALAD

juice of 1 lemon
1 (20-ounce) can crushed pineapple, in its own juice
1 cup sugar
2 envelopes unflavored gelatin
⅓ cup cold water
1 (8-ounce) jar maraschino cherries, drained and divided
¼ teaspoon salt
1 cup grated cheddar cheese
½ pint whipping cream, whipped
lettuce leaves

Combine lemon juice, pineapple and its juice, and sugar in saucepan. Bring to boil over medium-high heat, stirring to dissolve sugar. Remove from heat and set aside. Dissolve gelatin in cold water; add to hot mixture. Cool completely.

Cut cherries into quarters, reserving 10 whole cherries for garnish. Add cherries, salt, and cheese to cooled pineapple mixture; mix well. Fold in whipped cream. Spoon mixture into lightly oiled individual salad molds. Cover each with plastic wrap and refrigerate several hours or overnight. To serve, unmold onto lettuce leaves and garnish each serving with cherry.

Yield: 10 servings

SUNDERLAND SALAD

1 (8-ounce) can pineapple tidbits, in their own juice
3 tablespoons lemon juice
1 envelope unflavored gelatin
1 (3-ounce) package cream cheese, at room temperature
⅓ cup mayonnaise
1 cup miniature marshmallows
1 cup sliced bananas
1 (11-ounce) can mandarin orange sections, drained
½ cup drained maraschino cherries, halved
½ cup coarsely chopped walnuts
1 cup heavy cream, whipped (or commercial whipped topping)
lettuce or watercress

Drain pineapple, reserving juice. Pour lemon juice into measuring cup and add enough reserved pineapple juice to make ½ cup; pour into small saucepan. Sprinkle gelatin over liquid in pan. Let stand 5 minutes to soften. Cook over low heat, stirring constantly, until gelatin is dissolved. Remove from heat.

In large bowl, beat cream cheese and mayonnaise with wooden spoon until smooth. Add drained pineapple tidbits, marshmallows, bananas, orange sections, cherries, walnuts, and gelatin mixture. (For a less sweet salad, cut down on amount of cherries used.) Mix well. Refrigerate for 20 minutes, or until mixture mounds slightly when dropped from a spoon. Gently fold in whipped cream.

Turn into 9 x 5 x 3-inch loaf pan lined with wax paper. Freeze until firm (at least 4 hours). To serve, turn out of pan and cut into slices. Serve on beds of lettuce or watercress.

Yield: 12 servings

MILLION-DOLLAR MARINATED SALAD

3 cloves garlic, minced
1 tablespoon salt
1 teaspoon pepper
¾ cup chopped fresh parsley
1½ teaspoons dried thyme
2 cups vegetable oil
¾ cup white wine vinegar
½ pound fresh shrimp, cooked, peeled, and deveined
1 (8-ounce) can bamboo shoots, drained
1 (14-ounce) can artichoke hearts, drained and quartered
1 (14-ounce) can hearts of palm, drained and cut into bite-sized pieces
8 ounces fresh mushrooms, sliced
1 pint of cherry tomatoes, washed
lettuce leaves

Mix garlic, salt, pepper, parsley, thyme, vegetable oil, and vinegar in bowl; set aside. In large bowl, combine shrimp, bamboo shoots, artichoke hearts, hearts of palm, mushrooms, and tomatoes. Pour dressing over shrimp mixture; toss to mix. Cover and refrigerate overnight. Serve on individual beds of lettuce.

Yield: 8-10 servings

SALMON SALAD MOLD

1 (15½-ounce) can salmon, drained
1 (10¾-ounce) can tomato soup
1 (8-ounce) package cream cheese, at room temperature
2 envelopes unflavored gelatin
½ cup cold water
2 tablespoons finely chopped onion
2 teaspoons horseradish
¼ teaspoon worcestershire sauce
1 cup chopped celery
1 cup mayonnaise
lettuce leaves

Pick any remaining bones out of salmon and break up meat with a fork. Place salmon, soup, and cream cheese in top of double boiler. Cook over medium heat, stirring until cheese melts. In meantime, dissolve gelatin in water. When salmon, soup, and cream cheese are thoroughly blended, add gelatin and mix well. Add onion, horseradish, and worcestershire sauce; mix well. Stir in celery and mayonnaise.

Pour mixture into lightly oiled 5-cup mold. Cover with plastic wrap and refrigerate until firm. Turn out onto lettuce leaves to serve.

Yield: 12 servings

SHRIMP SALAD PIQUANT

2 teaspoons lemon juice
½ cup chopped green onions, including tops
½ cup chopped celery
1 clove garlic, minced
1 teaspoon salt
3 tablespoons horseradish mustard
1 tablespoon paprika
½ teaspoon cayenne pepper
3 tablespoons ketchup
⅔ cup white wine vinegar
1 cup vegetable oil
3 pounds fresh shrimp, cooked, peeled, and deveined
lettuce leaves
2 hard-boiled eggs, finely chopped

Purée first 9 ingredients in blender or food processor. Add vinegar and oil; mix well.

Pour mixture over shrimp. Cover and refrigerate for 3 hours. Drain and place shrimp on beds of lettuce. Sprinkle chopped egg over each serving.

Yield: 8 servings

HOT CHICKEN SALAD

2 cups coarsely chopped cooked chicken
2 cups chopped celery
1 cup mayonnaise
1 teaspoon salt
½ cup slivered almonds
2 tablespoons minced onion
1 tablespoon lemon juice
½ cup grated sharp cheddar cheese
1 cup crushed potato or corn chips

Preheat oven to 400 degrees.

Mix all ingredients except cheese and chips in large bowl. Spoon into 2-quart baking dish. Sprinkle with cheese; top with crushed chips. Bake, uncovered, for 30 minutes, or until hot and bubbly.

Yield: 6 servings

ORIENTAL CHICKEN SALAD

3 tablespoons soy sauce
1 teaspoon prepared mustard
1 tablespoon vegetable oil
1 tablespoon mayonnaise
2½ cups cooked chicken, cut into thin strips
3 cups cooked long-grain white rice
1 cup sliced green onions, including tops
1 small head lettuce, shredded
1 (3-ounce) can chow mein noodles

In large bowl, blend soy sauce, mustard, vegetable oil, and mayonnaise. Stir in chicken. Cover and refrigerate for 1 hour.

Stir in rice and green onions. Cover and refrigerate until serving time. Spoon onto beds of shredded lettuce. Top each serving with generous sprinkle of chow mein noodles.

Yield: 8 servings

COLD ARTICHOKE RICE SALAD

An excellent accompaniment to fried or barbecued chicken, this salad is great for summer get-togethers. It can be made the day before, which is nice if you're feeding a crowd and don't want to spend the day of the party in the kitchen.

2½ cups water
1 (8-ounce) package chicken flavor Rice-A-Roni
4 green onions, thinly sliced
½ green pepper, chopped
12 pimiento-stuffed olives, sliced
2 (6-ounce) jars marinated artichoke hearts
¾ teaspoon curry powder
⅓ cup mayonnaise

In medium saucepan, heat water to boiling. Stir in Rice-A-Roni rice-vermicelli mixture and chicken flavor packet. Return to boil, reduce heat, and cover. Simmer for 15 minutes, or until rice is tender and liquid is absorbed. (Do not overcook!) Transfer rice to large bowl to cool.

Add onions, green pepper, and olives to cooled rice. Drain artichoke hearts, reserving marinade. Slice artichoke hearts and add to rice mixture. Combine marinade, curry powder, and mayonnaise. Pour over rice mixture and stir gently to mix well. Cover and refrigerate until serving time.

Yield: 6-8 servings

SOUPS AND STEWS

SPANISH BEAN SOUP

½ pound dried garbanzo beans
1 ham bone
1 beef bone
1 cup chopped onion
1 pound potatoes, peeled and cubed
2 teaspoons paprika
salt to taste
1 pound chorizo (Spanish sausage), cooked and cut into ¼-inch slices

Soak garbanzo beans overnight in enough salted water to cover beans. Drain beans and place in Dutch oven with 2 quarts water. Add ham and beef bones. Bring to boil; reduce heat to low. Cover and simmer for 45 minutes, or until beans are tender and meat loosens from bones. Remove bones; allow to cool enough to remove meat from bones. Coarsely chop meat and discard bones.

Return meat to Dutch oven. Add onion, potatoes, paprika, salt, and chorizo. Bring to boil; reduce heat and cover. Cook for 15-20 minutes.

Yield: 8-10 servings

RED BEAN SOUP

3 tablespoons olive oil
1 cup chopped onion
1 cup chopped carrot
2 cloves garlic, minced
6 cups water
1½ cups dried red kidney beans, washed and picked over
1 meaty ham hock
2 (16-ounce) can tomatoes, drained
1 tablespoon tomato paste
salt and pepper to taste
2 tablespoons unsalted butter, cut into bits and softened
3-4 green onions, minced

Heat oil in Dutch oven. Add onion, carrot, and garlic. Cook over medium-low heat, stirring, for 5 minutes. Add water, beans, and ham hock. Bring water to boil. Reduce heat and simmer, partially covered, for 45 minutes, or until beans are barely tender.

Add tomatoes, tomato paste, salt, and pepper. Cover and simmer for 45 minutes, or until beans are very soft. Break up tomatoes with a fork. Remove ham hock and discard.

Purée mixture in bowl of food processor. Return to Dutch oven and bring to simmer. Remove from heat; stir in butter. Ladle soup into heated bowls. Top each serving with green onions.

Yield: 6-8 servings

SAPELO ISLAND FISH CHOWDER

3 medium onions, minced
3 tablespoons bacon drippings
2-3 pounds fresh firm-fleshed fish (such as flounder or bass), cleaned
3 cups boiling water
1 (8-ounce) bottle clam juice
4 teaspoons salt
5 medium white potatoes, peeled and cut into small cubes
Tabasco sauce to taste
1 (12-ounce) can evaporated milk
whole milk (2-4 cups, depending on thickness desired)

In skillet over medium-high heat, sauté onions in bacon drippings until tender. In Dutch oven, cook fish in boiling water until done, but not mushy; remove fish and set aside to cool. Remove bones and skin from fish and discard; set aside meat.

Strain fish liquor; add onions, clam juice, and salt. Boil potatoes in fish liquor until well done. Add fish meat, Tabasco sauce, evaporated milk, and whole milk. Heat to just under boiling, stirring occasionally.

Yield: 10 servings

CHEDDAR CHOWDER

3 cups water
3 chicken bouillon cubes
4 medium potatoes, peeled and cubed
1 medium onion, sliced
1 cup grated carrots
½ cup diced green pepper
⅓ cup butter or margarine
⅓ cup all-purpose flour
3½ cups whole milk
4 cups (16 ounces) grated sharp cheddar cheese
1 (2-ounce) jar diced pimiento, drained
¼ teaspoon Tabasco sauce

Bring water to boil in Dutch oven; add bouillon cubes. Add vegetables; bring to boil. Reduce heat; cover and simmer 12 minutes or until vegetables are tender.

Melt butter in large heavy saucepan. Blend in flour and cook 1 minute over medium heat, stirring constantly. Gradually add milk. Cook over medium heat until thickened, stirring constantly. Add cheese and stir until melted.

Stir cheese mixture, pimiento, and Tabasco sauce into vegetable mixture. Cook over medium heat, stirring frequently, until hot. Do not boil.

Yield: 8-10 servings

GERMAN SAUSAGE CHOWDER

1 pound fully cooked smoked bratwurst or knockwurst
2 medium potatoes, peeled and diced
½ cup chopped onion
1½ teaspoons salt
dash pepper
2 cups water
4 cups shredded cabbage
3 cups whole milk, divided
3 tablespoons all-purpose flour
1 cup grated Swiss cheese
snipped fresh parsley

Cut bratwurst into ½-inch pieces. In Dutch oven, combine bratwurst, potatoes, onion, salt, pepper, and water. Bring to boil; reduce heat. Cover and simmer for 20 minutes or until potatoes are almost tender. (Do not overcook, or potatoes will become mushy before rest of ingredients are cooked.)

Stir in cabbage. Cover and simmer for 10 more minutes, or until vegetables are tender. Stir in 2½ cups milk. Blend remaining milk with flour; stir into soup. Cook and stir soup until thickened and bubbly.

Stir in grated cheese; heat until melted. Garnish with snipped parsley.

Yield: 8 servings

OLD-FASHIONED BEEF STEW

4 pounds boneless beef round or shoulder roast
1 cup vegetable oil
2 medium onions, chopped
4 stalks celery, sliced
8 medium carrots, scraped and cut into 1-inch pieces
1 large clove garlic, minced
1 teaspoon salt
1 teaspoon celery salt
1 teaspoon dried basil
½ teaspoon dried oregano
1 tablespoon paprika
¾ cup all-purpose flour
2 cups burgundy wine
2 cups water
4 cups beef bouillon
1 bay leaf and 12 peppercorns tied in cheesecloth bag
1 (16-ounce) can tomatoes
4 medium potatoes, peeled and cut into chunks
1 (16-ounce) jar small onions, drained

Cut meat into 1½-inch cubes. Heat oil in Dutch oven. Over medium-high heat, brown meat well on all sides, stirring frequently. Add chopped onions, celery, carrots, garlic, salt, and celery salt. Cook over medium heat for 10 minutes, stirring frequently.

Reduce heat to low. Mix basil, oregano, paprika, and flour. Slowly shake mixture into pot, stirring to blend well. Stir in wine, water, and bouillon. Bring to gentle boil. Add bay leaf and peppercorns. Stir in tomatoes. Bring to boil. Reduce heat; cover and simmer for 1½ hours, stirring occasionally.

Add potatoes and small onions. Bring to boil; cover and reduce heat. Cook 40 minutes, or until potatoes are done, stirring occasionally.

Yield: 12 servings

SEAFOOD

GRILLED SWORDFISH

Even those who "don't eat fish" frequently discover that they like swordfish. A firm and meaty fish, swordfish has a very delicate flavor.

½ cup melted butter
¼ cup lemon juice
½ teaspoon worcestershire sauce
2 teaspoons salt
¼ teaspoon pepper
dash Tabasco sauce
2 pounds swordfish steaks

Combine all ingredients except fish. Baste swordfish on both sides with butter mixture.

Place fish on grill, 4 inches from medium-hot coals. Cook for 8 minutes. Baste and turn fish. Baste with remaining sauce. Cook 7-10 minutes longer, until fish flakes easily with fork.

Yield: 4-6 servings

TUNA CASSEROLE

2 (10¾-ounce) cans cream of mushroom soup
1¾ cups grated medium cheddar cheese, divided
1 (12½-ounce) can chunk light tuna, drained
3 cups cooked long-grain white rice
1 (17-ounce) can LeSueur early peas, drained
salt and pepper to taste

Preheat oven to 350 degrees.

In large saucepan, heat soup and 1 cup of cheese until cheese is melted, stirring to mix. Add tuna and rice; mix well. Gently stir in peas. Salt and pepper to taste. Mix well.

Pour mixture into lightly greased 2½-quart baking dish. Sprinkle with remaining cheese. Bake, uncovered, for 30-35 minutes, or until hot and bubbly.

Yield: 8 servings

SHRIMP CREOLE

1 quart water
3-4 slices fresh lemon
4 whole black peppercorns
2 pounds fresh shrimp, peeled and deveined
4 slices bacon
2 tablespoons butter or margarine
1½ cups chopped onion
1½ cups chopped green pepper
1 cup sliced celery
¼ cup chopped fresh parsley
1 clove garlic, minced
1 (28-ounce) can tomatoes
1 (6-ounce) can tomato paste
2 teaspoons sugar
2 teaspoons lemon juice
1 teaspoon worcestershire sauce
1 teaspoon salt
¼ teaspoon black pepper
¼-½ teaspoon cayenne pepper
¼ teaspoon dried basil
½ teaspoon dried thyme
1 bay leaf
1½ cups long-grain white rice
½ teaspoon gumbo filé powder

In large saucepan, bring water to boil. Add lemon slices, peppercorns, and shrimp. Return to boil; reduce heat and simmer, uncovered, for 2 minutes. Drain shrimp, reserving 1 cup of cooking liquid. Remove lemons and peppercorns; discard.

In same saucepan over medium heat, cook bacon until crisp; remove to paper towel to drain. Crumble and set aside. To bacon drippings, add butter, onion, green pepper, celery, parsley, and garlic. Cook, stirring frequently, for 5 minutes, or until vegetables are tender.

Stir in reserved shrimp liquid, bacon, tomatoes, tomato paste, sugar, lemon juice, worcestershire sauce, salt, black pepper, cayenne pepper, basil, thyme, and bay leaf. Bring mixture to boil; reduce heat to low. Cover and simmer for 30 minutes. In meantime, cook rice according to package directions.

Just before serving, stir filé powder and boiled shrimp into mixture in saucepan. Bring to boil; reduce heat to low. Simmer for about 5 minutes, or until shrimp are heated through. Serve over hot, cooked rice.

Yield: 8 servings

SUNBELT SHRIMP AND RICE

1½ tablespoons butter
1 tablespoon all-purpose flour
½ teaspoon salt
1 teaspoon curry powder
½ teaspoon worcestershire sauce
3-4 drops Tabasco sauce
1½ cups whole milk
2 cups (8 ounces) grated sharp cheddar cheese, divided
2 cups cooked shrimp, peeled and deveined
3 cups cooked long-grain white rice
paprika

Preheat oven to 350 degrees.

Melt butter in large saucepan. Stir in flour, salt, curry powder, worcestershire sauce, and Tabasco sauce; blend well. Add milk and cook over medium heat, stirring constantly, until thickened. Stir in 1 cup of cheese. Cook, stirring constantly, until cheese is melted.

Stir shrimp and rice into cheese sauce. Pour mixture into greased 2½-quart baking dish. Top with remaining cheese. Sprinkle lightly with paprika. Bake, uncovered, for 20 minutes, or until cheese melts.

Yield: 6 servings

NEW ORLEANS CASSEROLE

3 tablespoons vegetable oil
½ cup chopped green pepper
1 cup chopped onion
1 clove garlic, minced
1 pound sweet Italian sausage, sliced
1 cup cubed ham
2 cups regular long-grain white rice
1 (28-ounce) can tomatoes
3 cups chicken bouillon
¼ cup brandy
1 teaspoon salt
⅛ teaspoon pepper
5 drops Tabasco sauce
¼ teaspoon dried basil
¼ teaspoon dried thyme
1 pound cooked shrimp, peeled and deveined

Heat oil in large skillet. Sauté green pepper, onion, and garlic in oil until tender. Add sausage and ham; stir and cook over medium heat until sausage is done. Add rice and cook, stirring, until rice is pale gold. Stir in tomatoes, bouillon, brandy, and seasonings. Bring to boil; reduce heat and cover. Simmer for 15 minutes. Stir in shrimp. Cover and cook for about 5 minutes, until shrimp are hot.

Yield: 12 servings

SHRIMP WITH GREEN NOODLES

1 (8-ounce) package medium spinach noodles
2 pounds medium shrimp, peeled and deveined
½ cup butter, clarified
salt and pepper to taste
1 (10¾-ounce) can cream of mushroom soup
¾ cup mayonnaise
1 cup sour cream
1 tablespoon chopped chives
4 tablespoons dry sherry
½ teaspoon Dijon mustard
½ cup grated sharp cheddar cheese

Cook noodles for 2 minutes less than directed on package; drain. Line lightly greased 12 x 7½-inch baking dish with noodles.

Preheat oven to 350 degrees.

In large skillet, sauté shrimp in clarified butter until pink and tender, about 5 minutes. Cover noodles with shrimp. Salt and pepper to taste.

In medium bowl, combine soup, mayonnaise, sour cream, and chives; mix well. Stir in sherry and mustard, mixing well. Pour sauce evenly over shrimp. Sprinkle with cheese. Bake, uncovered, for 25-30 minutes, or until hot and bubbly.

Yield: 6-8 servings

CHARLES DURANT'S CHANNEL BASS

1 (2 to 3-pound) bass
salt and pepper to taste
½ cup butter
lemon juice
dry white wine

Preheat oven to 450 degrees.

Filet fish and cut into 2 to 3-inch squares. Salt and pepper each piece of fish.

Place butter in 9 x 13-inch baking dish in oven. Leave in oven until butter is browned. (This gives the fish its distinctive flavor.) Place fish skin side up in sizzling hot butter. Bake, uncovered, for 10-15 minutes.

Turn fish and baste with browned butter. Sprinkle each piece with lemon juice and wine. Bake for an additional 5 minutes, or until fish flakes easily with a fork. Place fish under broiler to lightly brown. Baste with sauce and serve.

Yield: 4-6 servings

RED SNAPPER LOUISIANA

1 cup chopped green onion
1 cup chopped green pepper
1 cup chopped fresh mushrooms
1 clove garlic, crushed
2 tablespoons olive oil
2 (14½-ounce) cans tomatoes, drained
4 drops Tabasco sauce
1 (4-pound) fresh red snapper, cleaned and butterflied
1 cup dry white wine, divided
salt and pepper to taste

In large skillet over medium-high heat, cook onion, green pepper, mushrooms, and garlic in olive oil until tender. Add tomatoes, breaking them up with spoon; add Tabasco sauce. Cook over medium-low heat, stirring occasionally, for 30 minutes. In meantime, preheat oven to 350 degrees.

Place fish in lightly buttered 15½ x 9½-inch baking dish. Open fish and pour half of wine over bottom half. Salt and pepper lightly. Spoon half of cooked sauce over bottom half of fish. Close fish and pour remaining wine over top. Salt and pepper lightly. Spoon remaining sauce over fish. Bake, uncovered, for about 30 minutes, or until fish flakes easily with a fork.

Yield: 8 servings

JOAN'S SEAFOOD GUMBO

¾ cup vegetable oil
1 cup all-purpose flour
1 large onion, chopped
4 stalks celery, sliced
1 (16-ounce) can tomatoes
4 cloves garlic, minced
½ cup chopped fresh parsley
1 teaspoon dried thyme
1 teaspoon cayenne pepper
1 bay leaf
2 (14½-ounce) cans chicken broth
2 pounds fresh shrimp, peeled and deveined
1 pound crab claw meat
2 cups long-grain white rice
2-3 dozen raw oysters, shucked
1½ teaspoons salt
½ teaspoon black pepper
chopped fresh parsley
sliced green onions
gumbo filé powder

Heat oil in Dutch oven. (Do not use nonstick type.) Stir in flour and cook over medium-low heat for 10-15 minutes, stirring constantly, until roux is color of a copper penny. Stir in onion and celery; cook for 10 minutes. Add next 6 ingredients. Cook for 10 minutes, stirring occasionally. Stir in chicken broth. Bring to boil; cover and reduce heat. Simmer for 30 minutes, stirring occasionally.

Add shrimp and crab meat. Cover and simmer for 15 minutes. In meantime, cook rice according to package directions. Add oysters to Dutch oven. Cover and simmer an additional 15 minutes. Stir in salt and black pepper. Remove bay leaf.

Ladle gumbo into soup bowls over hot, cooked rice. Sprinkle each serving with parsley, green onions, and filé powder.

Yield: 12 servings

SOUTHERN GUMBO

½ cup diced bacon
1 large green pepper, chopped
2 large onions, chopped
2 green onions, sliced
2 cloves garlic, minced
4-5 tablespoons all-purpose flour
5 cups water, divided
2 cups cubed cooked ham
2½ teaspoons salt
2 tablespoons chopped fresh parsley
½ teaspoon dried thyme
1 (28-ounce) can tomatoes
2 bay leaves
2 (16-ounce) packages frozen cut okra
2 cups long-grain white rice
2 pounds fresh shrimp, cooked, peeled, and deveined
1 (12-ounce) package frozen crab meat, thawed
1 tablespoon gumbo filé powder
5 drops Tabasco sauce

In Dutch oven, sauté bacon over medium-high heat until crisp. Remove bacon to paper towel to drain; crumble and set aside. Sauté green pepper, onions, and garlic in bacon drippings until tender. Add flour and cook over medium-low heat, stirring constantly, until flour is golden brown. Gradually add 2½ cups of water, stirring constantly. Stir in ham and remaining water. Add salt, parsley, thyme, tomatoes, and bay leaves. Bring to boil; reduce heat. Cover and simmer, stirring occasionally, for 30 minutes.

Stir in frozen okra. Cover and cook over low heat for 1 hour. In meantime, cook rice according to package directions. Add shrimp and crab meat to Dutch oven. Cook only until shrimp and crab meat are hot.

Just before serving, remove bay leaves from gumbo; stir in filé powder and Tabasco sauce. Ladle gumbo into soup bowls over hot, cooked rice. Sprinkle bacon over each serving.

Yield: 12 servings

MEATS

PEPPER STEAK

1 (1-pound) round or flank steak
1 teaspoon salt
⅛ teaspoon pepper
2 tablespoons vegetable oil
2 tablespoons minced onion
1 clove garlic, minced
2 green peppers, diced
1 cup beef bouillon
1 cup drained canned tomatoes or 3 fresh tomatoes, quartered
1 cup long-grain white rice
1½ tablespoons cornstarch
2 teaspoons soy sauce
¼ cup water

Cut meat across the grain into 2-inch strips; sprinkle with salt and pepper. Heat oil in large skillet over medium-high heat. Cook steak, onion, and garlic until meat is brown. Add green peppers and bouillon. Bring to boil. Cover; reduce heat and simmer for 30 minutes.

Add tomatoes; cover and simmer for 15 minutes. Meanwhile, cook rice according to package directions. Combine cornstarch, soy sauce, and water; add to meat mixture. Cook for 5 minutes, stirring constantly. Serve over hot, cooked rice.

Yield: 4 servings

BEEF BURGUNDY

2 pounds round steak or london broil
2 teaspoons salt
¼ teaspoon freshly ground pepper
2 tablespoons vegetable oil
1 medium onion, chopped
1 cup sour cream
½ cup burgundy wine
1 cup grated medium cheddar cheese
1 clove garlic, minced
¼ teaspoon dried thyme
¼ teaspoon ground marjoram
¼ teaspoon dried basil
1½ cups long-grain white rice
1 (10¾-ounce) can cream of mushroom soup

Preheat oven to 325 degrees.

Cut meat into 1½-inch cubes; season with salt and pepper. Heat oil in large skillet. Over medium-high heat, brown meat on all sides. Stir in onion and cook until tender. Transfer to 3-quart casserole. Add sour cream, wine, cheese, garlic, and herbs; mix well. Cover and bake for 2 hours, or until meat is tender.

Cook rice according to package directions. Add soup to meat mixture; stir to mix well. Cover and bake an additional 20 minutes. Serve over hot, cooked rice.

Yield: 6-8 servings

MARINATED FLANK STEAK

½ cup soy sauce
¼ cup vegetable oil
2 tablespoons water
2 teaspoons dark brown sugar
2 cloves garlic, minced
½ teaspoon grated fresh ginger root
¼ teaspoon black pepper
1 (2 to 3-pound) flank steak

In small bowl, combine all ingredients except steak; mix well. Place flank steak in glass baking dish; pour marinade over steak. Cover and refrigerate for 4 hours, turning once.

Grill steak over medium coals, or broil in oven about 6 inches from heat, for 5 minutes on each side (or to desired doneness). Baste occasionally with marinade during cooking.

To serve, slice thinly across grain.

Yield: 4-6 servings

FILET MIGNON ALFONSE

4 (6-ounce) beef filets
salt and pepper to taste
1 tablespoon butter or margarine
¼ cup chopped onion
¼ cup diced bacon
1½ cups sliced fresh mushrooms
4 artichoke bottoms
salt and pepper to taste
¼ cup beef gravy
2 tablespoons burgundy wine

Season filets with salt and pepper. Broil or grill to desired doneness and keep warm. Melt butter in medium skillet. Cook onion and bacon in butter over medium-high heat for about 5 minutes, stirring frequently. Add mushrooms and artichoke bottoms. Season with salt and pepper. Stir in gravy and wine. Cover, reduce heat, and simmer for 10 minutes.

Place filets on plates. Top each filet with artichoke bottom and spoonful of mushroom mixture.

Yield: 4 servings

SOUTHERN SIRLOIN TIP ROAST

1 (8-ounce) bottle Italian salad dressing
1 (3-pound) sirloin tip roast
salt and pepper to taste
1 (10¾-ounce) can cream of mushroom soup
1 package Lipton onion soup mix
¾ cup water

Pour salad dressing over roast. Cover and refrigerate for 1-2 hours.

Preheat oven to 350 degrees.

Remove roast from dressing; discard dressing. Salt and pepper meat; place in 3-quart roaster.

Combine mushroom soup, onion soup mix, and water; pour over meat. Cover and bake for 3 hours, basting occasionally with sauce.

Yield: 6-8 servings

BARBECUED POT ROAST AND DUMPLINGS

2 tablespoons flour
1 (4-pound) beef round roast
3 tablespoons vegetable oil
1 (16-ounce) can tomatoes
2 cups water
2 cloves garlic, crushed
1 tablespoon salt
½ teaspoon pepper
2 medium onions, sliced
¼ cup white wine vinegar
¼ cup lemon juice
¼ cup ketchup
2 tablespoons dark brown sugar
1 tablespoon worcestershire sauce
1 teaspoon prepared mustard
¼ teaspoon paprika
Dumplings

Rub flour on meat. Heat oil in Dutch oven; brown roast on all sides. Place rack under meat. Add tomatoes, water, garlic, salt, and pepper. Bring to boil. Cover, reduce heat, and simmer for 2 hours.

Combine remaining ingredients except Dumplings. Pour over meat. Cover and simmer for 1½ hours, or until meat is tender. Transfer roast to oven-proof platter. Keep warm in oven while Dumplings cook.

Yield: 8 servings

DUMPLINGS:

¾ cup sifted all-purpose flour
½ cup plain cornmeal
1½ teaspoons baking powder
½ teaspoon salt
½ cup whole milk
2 tablespoons vegetable oil

Sift together flour, cornmeal, baking powder, and salt. Bring sauce in Dutch oven to boil. Stir milk and vegetable oil into sifted dry ingredients. Drop by large teaspoonfuls into boiling sauce. Cook, uncovered, over medium heat for 10 minutes. Cover and cook for an additional 10 minutes. Serve immediately with sliced barbecued pot roast and sauce.

Yield: approximately 16

BEEF BONAPARTE

2 pounds lean ground beef
1 (14½-ounce) can tomatoes
1 (8-ounce) can tomato sauce
1 clove garlic, minced
2 teaspoons sugar
2 teaspoons salt
2-3 drops Tabasco sauce
⅛ teaspoon cracked black pepper
1 bay leaf
1 (5-ounce) bag fine egg noodles
1 (3-ounce) package cream cheese, at room temperature
6 green onions, chopped
1 (8-ounce) carton sour cream
1 cup grated cheddar cheese
6 ounces mozzarella cheese, sliced

Brown ground beef in large heavy skillet; drain off fat. Stir in tomatoes, tomato sauce, garlic, sugar, salt, Tabasco sauce, pepper, and bay leaf. Bring to boil; reduce heat. Simmer, uncovered, stirring occasionally, for 10 minutes.

Preheat oven to 350 degrees.

Cook noodles according to package directions; drain well. In large bowl, combine hot noodles with cream cheese, green onions, and sour cream. Lightly grease an 8 x 12½-inch baking dish. Spread noodle mixture in bottom of dish. Top with meat mixture. Sprinkle cheddar cheese over meat. Bake, covered, for 25 minutes. Uncover and place slices of mozzarella over cheddar cheese layer. Bake for an additional 10 minutes, or until cheese melts.

Yield: 8 servings

QUICK BEEF STROGANOFF

Served with a tossed salad and French bread, this is a quick and easy meal.

2 (4-ounce) cans mushrooms, stems and pieces, drained
1 medium onion, diced
1 clove garlic, minced
2 tablespoons butter
2 pounds lean ground beef
salt and pepper to taste
1 cup sour cream
1 (10¾-ounce) can cheddar cheese soup
⅓ cup whole milk
3 cups hot, cooked rice

In large skillet over medium-high heat, sauté mushrooms, onion, and garlic in butter. Add meat, salt, and pepper. Cook, stirring occasionally, until beef is browned; drain off fat.

Add sour cream; mix well. Add soup and milk; mix well. Simmer until hot and bubbly. Serve over hot, cooked rice.

Yield: 6 servings

GRILLED PORK LOIN

1 (5-pound) boneless pork loin roast, rolled and tied
6 tablespoons Dijon mustard
½ cup water
¼ cup vegetable oil
2 tablespoons soy sauce

Pierce pork several times with long-tined fork. Place in shallow baking dish. Combine mustard, water, oil, and soy sauce. Mix well and pour over roast. Cover and let stand at room temperature for 1 hour.

Remove meat from marinade, reserving marinade. Insert spit rod through center of roast. Insert meat thermometer near center of roast, avoiding rod.

Cook on rotisserie over drip pan, with medium-hot coals on either side of pan. Grill for 1½ hours. Brush with marinade, and grill another 1 to 1½ hours, until meat thermometer registers 170 degrees for well-done. During last cooking period, baste several times with marinade. Heat remaining marinade and serve with roast.

Yield: 8-10 servings

EVA JO'S FRUITED PORK LOIN

1 tablespoon all-purpose flour
1 teaspoon salt
1 teaspoon dry mustard
¼ teaspoon pepper
1 (3½ to 4-pound) boneless pork loin roast
2 cups drained, cooked, and sieved quince fruit or pears
¼ cup dark brown sugar
¼ teaspoon ground cinnamon
¼ teaspoon ground cloves
spiced crab apples or Seckel pears

Preheat oven to 325 degrees.

Combine flour, salt, mustard, and pepper; rub roast with flour mixture. Place roast fat side up in open roasting pan. (Do not add water.) Roast, uncovered, until meat thermometer registers 185 degrees (approximately 35-40 minutes per pound).

In meantime, combine sieved fruit, brown sugar, cinnamon, and cloves; mix well. After pork has roasted 1½ to 2 hours, remove from oven and spread with fruit mixture. Return to oven for remaining cooking time. Baste frequently with pan juices.

Remove pork loin to serving platter. Garnish with spiced crab apples or Seckel pears.

Yield: 6-8 servings

OVEN-BARBECUED PORK CHOPS

This is a good "make-ahead" main dish. If refrigerated before baking, allow dish to reach room temperature before baking.

6 (¾-inch thick) center-cut pork chops
salt and pepper to taste
1-2 tablespoons vegetable oil
6 onion slices
6 lemon slices
½ cup ketchup
1 cup water
¼ cup cider vinegar
2 heaping tablespoons dark brown sugar

Preheat oven to 350 degrees.

Season pork chops with salt and pepper. Heat oil in large skillet. Brown pork chops on both sides; place in 9 x 13 x 2-inch baking dish. Top each pork chop with slice of onion and slice of lemon.

In small bowl, mix ketchup, water, vinegar, and brown sugar; pour over pork chops. Cover tightly with aluminum foil. Bake for 1 to 1½ hours, until tender. Spoon sauce over chops before serving.

Yield: 6 servings

SWEDISH PORK CHOPS

4 (½-inch thick) pork chops
½ teaspoon powdered ginger
2 tablespoons all-purpose flour
1 teaspoon salt
½ teaspoon white pepper
3 tablespoons butter
½ pound pitted, dried prunes
1½ cups boiling water
1 tablespoon port wine
¼ cup heavy cream

Rub chops with ginger. Mix flour, salt, and pepper; turn chops in mixture to coat well. Melt butter in large skillet. Brown pork chops on both sides. Cover and cook over medium-low heat until tender, about 35-45 minutes. Remove from skillet and keep warm.

In meantime, cook prunes in water until they become plump and tender, about 10 minutes. Drain, reserving 2 tablespoons cooking liquid.

Add prunes and port wine to skillet in which pork chops were cooked. In small saucepan, heat cream to lukewarm; pour into skillet, stirring constantly. Add reserved prune liquid and pork chops. Cover and cook over low heat for 5 minutes.

Yield: 4 servings

HAM JAMBALAYA

5 slices bacon
1½ cups regular long-grain white rice
1 medium onion, chopped
1 green pepper, chopped
1 clove garlic, minced
1 (16-ounce) can tomatoes
1 (14½-ounce) can chicken broth
1 bay leaf
½ teaspoon salt
½ teaspoon dried thyme
2½ cups cubed cooked ham
1 pound fresh shrimp, boiled, peeled, and deveined
3-4 drops Tabasco sauce

Fry bacon in large skillet until crisp; drain on paper towel. Crumble bacon and set aside.

In same skillet over medium heat, cook rice, onion, green pepper, and garlic in bacon drippings until rice is lightly browned, stirring frequently. Stir in tomatoes and their liquid. Stir in chicken broth, bay leaf, salt, and thyme. Cover and simmer for 15 minutes. (Do not overcook rice. Add water if additional liquid is needed.)

Stir in ham, shrimp, and Tabasco sauce. Cover and cook until rice is tender (about 5 minutes). Before serving, stir well and sprinkle with bacon.

Yield: 8 servings

EARLINE'S HAM BALLS

1 pound trimmed ham, ground
1 pound trimmed fresh pork, ground
2 eggs, beaten
2 cups bread crumbs
¾ cup whole milk
Sauce for Ham Balls

Preheat oven to 375 degrees.

Combine all ingredients except Sauce in large bowl. Mix well. Using hands, form mixture into egg-shaped balls 2½ inches long. Place in lightly greased 9½ x 15½-inch baking dish. Pour sauce over ham balls. Bake, uncovered, for 1½ hours.

Yield: 8 servings

SAUCE FOR HAM BALLS:

1¼ cups dark or light brown sugar
2 cups water
2 tablespoons prepared mustard
¼ cup white wine vinegar
1½ teaspoons salt

Place all ingredients in small saucepan. Mix and heat just to dissolve sugar. Cool slightly. Pour over ham balls before baking.

VEAL WITH PEPPERS

3 pounds boneless veal, cut into 1½-inch cubes
2 teaspoons salt
½ teaspoon pepper
2 tablespoons vegetable oil, divided
1 cup dry white wine
2 tablespoons butter, divided
2 large onions, sliced
2 cups sliced fresh mushrooms
2 cloves garlic, minced
2 (16-ounce) cans tomatoes, drained and coarsely chopped
2 tablespoons cornstarch
¼ cup cold water
2 cups long-grain white rice
2 large green peppers, cut into rings
2 small red peppers, cut into rings
¼ cup chopped fresh parsley

Sprinkle veal cubes with salt and pepper. Heat half of oil in large skillet. Brown half of veal in hot oil; transfer to Dutch oven with slotted spoon. Repeat with remaining veal.

Add wine to skillet. Stir and bring to boil; pour over veal. In same skillet, melt 1 tablespoon butter over medium heat. Cook onions until barely tender; add to Dutch oven. Saute mushrooms and garlic in remaining butter; set aside. Add tomatoes to Dutch oven. Bring to boil. Reduce heat. Cover and simmer for 1 hour.

Combine cornstarch and water; stir into hot veal mixture. In meantime, cock rice according to package directions. Add peppers and reserved mushroom mixture to veal mixture. Cover and simmer until veal and peppers are tender, about 15 minutes. Serve over hot, cooked rice. Sprinkle parsley over each serving.

Yield: 8 servings

ROAST LEG OF LAMB WITH MINT SAUCE

1 (5-pound) leg of lamb
Mint Sauce

Remove lamb from refrigerator 1 hour before roasting time. Preheat oven to 450 degrees. Place meat, fat side up, on rack in uncovered pan. Immediately reduce heat to 325 degrees.

For well-done meat, roast 30 minutes to the pound, or until meat thermometer registers 175 degrees. For slightly rare meat, roast to an internal temperature of 160 degrees. Serve with Mint Sauce.

Yield: 6-8 servings

MINT SAUCE:

½ cup apple-mint jelly
½ cup white wine vinegar
2 tablespoons dark brown sugar
½ teaspoon dry mustard
1 teaspoon lemon juice
2 drops green food coloring
2 teaspoons cornstarch

In small saucepan over medium heat, combine apple-mint jelly, wine vinegar, brown sugar, mustard, and lemon juice. Stir and heat until jelly melts and sugar dissolves. Add food coloring and cornstarch; mix thoroughly. Continue cooking, stirring constantly, until mixture thickens. Serve with sliced lamb.

Yield: 1 cup

POULTRY

DURKEE'S CHICKEN

This chicken is delicious served with plain white rice. The recipe makes enough sauce to serve over both the chicken and the rice.

½ cup butter or margarine
½ cup white vinegar
salt and pepper to taste
1 (3-pound) chicken, cut into serving pieces
¾ cup Durkee Famous Sauce
2 tablespoons mayonnaise
2 tablespoons prepared mustard
1 cup water
1 tablespoon all-purpose flour
¼ cup water

In small saucepan, melt butter. Add vinegar, salt, and pepper. Heat to boiling; remove from heat. Broil chicken pieces skin side down, about 6 inches from heat, for 20 minutes. Baste frequently with butter mixture. Turn chicken and broil an additional 10 minutes, or until done.

In meantime, mix Durkee Famous Sauce, mayonnaise, mustard, and 1 cup of water in saucepan. Cook, stirring frequently, over medium heat until smooth and bubbly. Mix flour and ¼ cup water; add to Durkee mixture. Heat, stirring, until thickened.

Place chicken in 2½-quart casserole. Pour Durkee mixture over chicken. Cover and place in warm oven until ready to serve.

Yield: 6 servings

CHICKEN WITH TARRAGON

2 whole chicken breasts, boned and split
salt and pepper to taste
1 tablespoon butter
1 tablespoon finely chopped green onion
½ teaspoon dried tarragon
½ cup dry white wine

Sprinkle chicken with salt and pepper. Melt butter in skillet over medium heat. Place chicken in skillet skin side up. Cover and cook over medium-low heat for 10 minutes. Turn, cover, and cook an additional 5 minutes. Remove chicken and set aside.

Add green onion to skillet and cook briefly. Stir in tarragon and wine. Return chicken to skillet. Cover and cook over medium-low heat for 10 minutes. Uncover and continue cooking, basting often, for 5 more minutes, or until chicken is very tender.

Yield: 4 servings

BEEFY CHICKEN

1 (2½-ounce) jar dried beef, in wafer-thin slices
6 slices lean bacon
3 whole chicken breasts, skinned, boned, and split
¼ teaspoon pepper
½ pound fresh mushrooms, sliced (or 8-ounce can sliced mushrooms, drained)
1 tablespoon butter or margarine
1 (10¾-ounce) can cream of mushroom soup
2 tablespoons dry sherry

Preheat oven to 300 degrees.

Cover bottom of 12 x 7½ x 2-inch baking dish with beef slices. Wrap a slice of bacon around each piece of chicken; sprinkle with pepper. (Do not add salt because beef is very salty.) Arrange chicken over beef.

In small skillet, sauté mushrooms in butter over medium-high heat for 2-3 minutes; spread mushrooms over chicken. Combine soup and sherry in small bowl; mix until smooth. Pour soup mixture over chicken and mushrooms.

Cover tightly with aluminum foil. Bake for 2 hours. Uncover. Increase oven temperature to 350 degrees. Bake for an additional 20-30 minutes. During last baking period, spoon sauce over chicken several times.

Yield: 6 servings

CHICKEN-ARTICHOKE BAKE

1 (3-pound) chicken, cut into serving pieces
1 onion, chopped
6 tablespoons butter, divided
salt and pepper
½ pound fresh mushrooms, sliced (or 8-ounce can sliced mushrooms, drained)
2 tablespoons all-purpose flour
1 cup chicken broth or bouillon
¼ cup dry white wine
1 (14-ounce) can artichoke hearts, drained

Preheat oven to 375 degrees.

In large skillet, brown chicken and onion in 4 tablespoons of butter. Salt and pepper to taste. Remove chicken and onions to 2½-quart casserole. Add remaining 2 tablespoons of butter to skillet. Over medium-high heat, sauté mushrooms for 2-3 minutes.

Sprinkle flour over mushrooms. Stir in chicken broth and wine. Simmer for 5 minutes, stirring constantly, until thickened and smooth. Arrange artichoke hearts among chicken pieces; pour mushroom sauce over all. Cover and bake for 40 minutes, or until done.

Yield: 6 servings

SOUR CREAM MARINATED CHICKEN

1 cup sour cream
2 tablespoons lemon juice
2 teaspoons worcestershire sauce
1 teaspoon paprika
1½ teaspoons celery salt
½ teaspoon salt
½ teaspoon pepper
¼ teaspoon garlic powder
3 whole chicken breasts, skinned, boned, and split
½ cup margarine
2-3 cups dry bread crumbs

Combine sour cream, lemon juice, worcestershire sauce, and seasonings in bowl; mix well. Place chicken in bowl, spooning mixture over each piece. Cover and refrigerate overnight, turning once or twice.

Preheat oven to 350 degrees.

Melt margarine in 7½ x 12-inch baking dish. Remove chicken from marinade. Roll in bread crumbs; place in dish. Bake, uncovered, for 1 hour. (Do not turn while baking.) Remove chicken from dish and drain on heavy paper bag.

Yield: 6 servings

CHICKEN LIVERS STROGANOFF

¾ pound chicken livers
1 (4-ounce) can sliced mushrooms, drained
¼ cup chopped onion
¾ cup vermouth
½ teaspoon dried rosemary, crushed
¼ teaspoon dried thyme
1 teaspoon salt
1 (8-ounce) package medium egg noodles
¾ cup sour cream

Combine first 7 ingredients in medium saucepan. Bring to boil. Cover, reduce heat, and simmer for 20 minutes. In meantime, cook noodles according to package directions.

Stir sour cream into chicken liver mixture. Cook over medium heat, stirring constantly, until heated through. Serve over hot, cooked noodles.

Yield: 4 servings

SOUTH GEORGIA CHICKEN CASSEROLE

½ cup all-purpose flour
½ teaspoon salt
⅛ teaspoon pepper
1 (3-pound) chicken, cut into serving pieces
4 tablespoons butter, divided
1 (4-ounce) can mushrooms, stems and pieces
3 tablespoons lemon juice
3 tablespoons worcestershire sauce
1 bay leaf
½ cup water

Preheat oven to 350 degrees.

Combine flour, salt, and pepper. Roll chicken in flour mixture to coat well. Reserve remaining flour.

Melt 2 tablespoons butter in 12 x 7½-inch baking dish. Arrange chicken in dish; dot with small chunks of remaining butter. Sprinkle reserved flour over chicken. Add mushrooms and their liquid. Sprinkle lemon juice and worcestershire sauce over chicken; add bay leaf. Pour water over all.

Cover tightly with aluminum foil. Bake for 1 hour, or until chicken is tender. Baste with sauce once or twice during baking.

Yield: 6 servings

CHICKEN SPAGHETTI

½ cup vegetable oil
1½ cups chopped onion
1 clove garlic, minced
½ cup all-purpose flour
2 (28-ounce) cans tomatoes
2 (6-ounce) cans tomato paste
1 cup chopped celery
½ cup chopped green pepper
½ large lemon, sliced and seeded
6 cups cooked boneless chicken, torn into large pieces
1 (4-ounce) can sliced mushrooms, drained
1 teaspoon salt
⅛ teaspoon cayenne pepper
16 ounces thin spaghetti
3 hard-boiled eggs, chopped

Heat oil in Dutch oven. Sauté onion and garlic over medium-high heat until tender, but not brown. Add flour and mix well. Stir in tomatoes and tomato paste; break up tomatoes with spoon. Add celery and green pepper.

Cut lemon slices into eighths; add to tomato mixture. Bring to boil; reduce heat to simmer. Cook, uncovered, for 30 minutes, stirring occasionally.

Add chicken, mushrooms, salt, and cayenne pepper to tomato mixture and simmer for 15 minutes. In meantime, cook spaghetti according to package directions; drain. Just before serving, stir spaghetti and chopped eggs into tomato mixture.

Yield: 12 servings

CURRIED CHICKEN

Curried Chicken can be prepared ahead of time and reheated just before serving. Add a salad and crusty bread, and you have a delightful meal.

½ cup chopped onion
5 tablespoons butter or margarine
6 tablespoons all-purpose flour
2-3 teaspoons curry powder
1¼ teaspoons salt
¼ teaspoon powdered ginger
1¼ teaspoons sugar
1 cup boiling water
1 cup chicken broth
2 cups whole milk
2 cups long-grain white rice
4 cups cubed, cooked chicken
1 teaspoon lemon juice
Condiments (see list below)

Cook onion in butter in top of large double boiler until tender. Stir in flour and seasonings. Add water, broth, and milk. Cook, stirring frequently, until smooth.

In meantime, cook rice according to package directions. Add chicken and lemon juice to mixture in double boiler, and cook until chicken is heated through. Serve curried chicken over hot, cooked rice with your choice of the following condiments:

> chopped green olives, chopped pecans or peanuts, shredded coconut, chopped onions, chopped celery, crumbled cooked bacon, chopped hard-boiled eggs, chutney

Yield: 6-8 servings

VEGETABLES

SUE'S MARINATED VEGETABLES

1 (16-ounce) can French-style green beans
1 (17-ounce) can LeSueur early peas
1 (14-ounce) can fancy Chinese vegetables
1 (6-ounce) can sliced water chestnuts
1½ cups thinly sliced celery
3 medium onions, thinly sliced
¼ cup sugar
¾ cup cider vinegar
1 teaspoon salt
pepper to taste

Drain canned vegetables; discard liquids. Combine all ingredients in large bowl. Mix well. Cover and refrigerate for several hours or overnight. (Note: This will keep in refrigerator for several weeks.)

Yield: 12-14 servings

GREEN BEANS HORSERADISH

A different and easy way to prepare green beans, this dish is good served hot or cold.

2 (16-ounce) cans whole green beans
2 slices bacon
1 large onion, sliced
1 cup mayonnaise
2 hard-boiled eggs, chopped
1 heaping tablespoon horseradish
juice of 1 lemon
1 teaspoon worcestershire sauce
garlic salt, celery salt, and onion salt to taste
dash pepper
½ teaspoon dried parsley flakes

Drain liquid from beans into saucepan; add bacon and onion. Cook over medium heat until onion is almost tender. Add beans and cook for 5 minutes.

In meantime, in a small bowl, blend mayonnaise with remaining ingredients. Set aside at room temperature.

Drain liquid from beans and onion; remove bacon and discard. Add mayonnaise mixture to beans and onion. Toss lightly to mix.

Yield: 6 servings

SUNDAY VEGETABLE CASSEROLE

1 (12½ to 15-ounce) can asparagus spears, drained
1 (10¾-ounce) can cream of mushroom soup
½ cup grated sharp cheddar cheese
1 (17-ounce) can LeSueur early peas, drained
2-3 tablespoons slivered almonds

Preheat oven to 350 degrees.

Arrange asparagus in bottom of shallow 6½ x 10-inch baking dish. In medium bowl, combine soup and cheese; mix well. Gently stir in peas. Spoon mixture evenly over asparagus. Top with slivered almonds.

Bake, uncovered, for 25-30 minutes.

Yield: 6 servings

CARROTS WITH WALNUTS

1½ pounds carrots, cut into 3-inch julienne strips
1 tablespoon sliced green onion
2 tablespoons butter or margarine, melted
1 (3-ounce) package walnuts, coarsely chopped
snipped fresh parsley

Place carrots and green onion in steamer rack over boiling water. Steam for 8-10 minutes, or until just tender. (Carrots can be cooked in boiling salted water for 10 minutes, if desired.)

Remove carrots to serving bowl. Add butter and walnuts. Lightly toss to mix. Sprinkle with parsley and serve.

Yield: 6 servings

CREOLE SQUASH

2 slices bacon
2½ cups sliced zucchini squash
¼ cup chopped onion
¼ cup chopped green pepper
¼ cup chopped celery
½ cup sliced fresh mushrooms
2 cups canned tomatoes, drained
¼ teaspoon salt
⅛ teaspoon cayenne pepper
⅓ cup fine bread crumbs

Preheat oven to 350 degrees.

Fry bacon in large skillet until crisp; remove to paper towel. In bacon drippings, sauté zucchini, onion, green pepper, celery, and mushrooms until almost tender, stirring frequently. Add tomatoes, salt, and cayenne pepper; stir in bread crumbs.

Pour mixture into lightly greased 1½-quart casserole. Crumble bacon and sprinkle on top of zucchini mixture. Bake, uncovered, for 20 minutes, or until hot and bubbly.

Yield: 4 servings

BUTTERNUT BAKE

2 pounds butternut squash
4 tablespoons margarine, melted
2 tablespoons honey
1 teaspoon sugar
½ teaspoon salt
ground nutmeg

Preheat oven to 400 degrees.

Cut squash in half; scoop out seeds and discard. Peel and cut squash into 1-inch cubes. Place squash in bowl; drizzle with margarine and honey. Sprinkle with sugar and salt. Toss to coat.

Spoon squash into 1½-quart baking dish. Sprinkle lightly with nutmeg. Cover and bake for 1 hour, or until tender.

Yield: 6 servings

MRS. PATRICK'S EGGPLANT

2 medium eggplant, peeled and cubed
1 cup sharp cheddar cheese cubes, divided
1 cup cracker crumbs, divided
1 (2-ounce) jar diced pimientos, divided
1 (5-ounce) can evaporated milk

Preheat oven to 425 degrees.

Cook eggplant in 4 cups of boiling salted water until tender; drain in colander. In 1½-quart baking dish, layer half of the eggplant, cheese, cracker crumbs, and pimientos. Repeat layers. Pour evaporated milk over all. Bake, uncovered, for 15-20 minutes, or until hot and bubbly.

Yield: 8 servings

SPINACH WITH SOUR CREAM

1 (10-ounce) package frozen chopped spinach
1 tablespoon grated onion
2 eggs
1 cup grated parmesan cheese
1 tablespoon all-purpose flour
½ cup sour cream
¼ teaspoon salt
dash pepper
2 tablespoons butter, melted

Preheat oven to 350 degrees.

Cook spinach and onion in small amount of boiling water until spinach is thawed. Drain in colander or strainer; mash with back of spoon to remove *all* excess moisture.

In medium bowl, beat eggs. Add remaining ingredients and mix well. Stir in spinach and onion, mixing well. Pour mixture into greased 1-quart casserole. Bake, uncovered, for 25-30 minutes, or until center is set. Do not overcook.

Yield: 4 servings

BROCCOLI CASSEROLE

2 (10-ounce) packages frozen chopped broccoli
1 (10¾-ounce) can cream of mushroom soup
½ cup mayonnaise
3 eggs, well beaten
¼ cup finely chopped onion
2 cups grated sharp cheddar cheese
¼ teaspoon salt
⅛ teaspoon pepper
cracker crumbs

Preheat oven to 350 degrees.

Cook broccoli according to package directions; drain and mash in colander. In large bowl, combine all ingredients except cracker crumbs; mix well. Pour into lightly greased 2-quart baking dish. Sprinkle with cracker crumbs. Bake, uncovered, for 50 minutes to 1 hour, until center is set.

Yield: 8 servings

DOT'S POTATOES DELUXE

1 (32-ounce) bag frozen hash brown potatoes
6 tablespoons butter
1 (10¾-ounce) can cream of chicken soup
1 cup chopped onion
1 cup grated cheddar cheese
1 (8-ounce) carton sour cream
½ teaspoon salt
¼ teaspoon pepper
½ cup bread crumbs or crushed corn flakes
2 tablespoons butter, melted

Preheat oven to 375 degrees.

In large skillet, cook potatoes in butter until thawed, stirring frequently. In large bowl, combine soup, onion, cheese, sour cream, salt, and pepper. Add potatoes and mix well. Pour into greased 12 x 7½-inch baking dish. Bake, uncovered, for 40 minutes.

Sprinkle potatoes with bread crumbs or crushed corn flakes. Drizzle with melted butter and bake an additional 15 minutes, or until top is lightly browned.

Yield: 8-10 servings

BROOKE'S SWEET POTATOES

2 (29-ounce) cans sweet potatoes, drained
½ cup butter, at room temperature
2 tablespoons sugar
1 teaspoon vanilla extract
5 tablespoons margarine, at room temperature
1 cup light brown sugar
3 tablespoons all-purpose flour
¾ teaspoon ground cinnamon
⅔ cup chopped pecans

Preheat oven to 350 degrees.

In large bowl of electric mixer, whip potatoes until smooth. Add butter, sugar, and vanilla extract. Mix well. Spoon into lightly greased 12 x 7½-inch baking dish.

In small bowl, mash margarine with fork. Stir in brown sugar, flour, and cinnamon; add pecans and mix well. Sprinkle over potato mixture. Bake, uncovered, for 20 minutes.

Yield: 10 servings

ZAPPED VIDALIA ONIONS

(microwave recipe)

4 Vidalia onions, 3-4 inches in diameter
4 beef bouillon cubes
garlic salt
2-3 tablespoons butter
bread crumbs
grated parmesan cheese
paprika

Peel and cut root end off of each onion; remove ¾ inch of core from each. Place 1 beef bouillon cube in indentation of each onion. Sprinkle with garlic salt. Press ½ tablespoon of butter over each bouillon cube.

Place onions in 9-inch glass dish. Cover with plastic wrap, venting at 1 corner. Cook in microwave oven on high power for 12-14 minutes, or until tender. Do not overcook. Let stand for 5 minutes.

Remove plastic wrap and sprinkle onions with bread crumbs, parmesan cheese, and paprika. Broil in conventional oven until lightly browned.

Yield: 4 servings

SIDE DISHES

ANNE'S RICE

½ cup margarine
1½ cups regular long-grain white rice
1 (10½-ounce) can beef consommé
1 (10½-ounce) can beef broth
1 teaspoon salt
½ package (3 tablespoons) Lipton onion soup mix
1 (4-ounce) can sliced mushrooms, drained

Preheat oven to 350 degrees.

Melt margarine in skillet. Cook rice in margarine over medium-high heat for 3-4 minutes, stirring constantly, until lightly browned. Spoon rice into 2-quart casserole. Stir in all other ingredients. Cover and bake for 30-40 minutes, until rice is done and liquid is absorbed.

Yield: 8 servings

RICE CHANTILLY

3 cups cooked long-grain white rice
1 cup grated sharp cheddar cheese, divided
2 dashes cayenne pepper
1 teaspoon salt
½ cup sour cream

Preheat oven to 350 degrees.

Combine rice, ½ cup cheese, cayenne pepper, salt, and sour cream. Mix well and pour into lightly greased 1½-quart baking dish. Top with remaining ½ cup cheese.

Bake, uncovered, for 20 minutes.

Yield: 4-6 servings

CARLTON'S FRIED RICE

2 medium onions
4 slices lean bacon
4 eggs
¾ teaspoon salt
3-4 tablespoons vegetable oil
3 cups cooked white rice
4 tablespoons butter
1 (10-ounce) package frozen green peas
soy sauce

Thinly slice onions. Cut bacon crosswise into ½-inch wide pieces. Beat eggs and salt in small bowl for 10 seconds. Heat oil in large heavy skillet over medium heat; add onions and bacon. Stir-fry for 2-3 minutes. Pour beaten eggs into skillet, allowing them to flow evenly over entire pan. When eggs are about to set, turn and scramble lightly. Stir in cooked rice. Remove from heat.

In small saucepan, melt butter over medium heat. Stir in peas and cook until thawed. Add peas and butter to rice mixture. Cover and cook over medium-low heat until hot through. Stir frequently to avoid scorching. (If necessary, add small amount of water.) Serve with soy sauce.

Yield: 6 servings

RED HOT RICE

3 slices bacon, diced
1 cup chopped onion
⅓ cup tomato paste
2¼ cups water
1½ teaspoons salt
¼ teaspoon pepper
½ teaspoon sugar
1 cup regular long-grain white rice

Cook bacon in large skillet until crisp; remove with slotted spoon and drain on paper towel. Cook onion in bacon drippings until golden. Add tomato paste, water, salt, pepper, and sugar. Bring to boil, stirring to mix. Reduce heat and simmer for 5 minutes. Stir in rice. Bring to boil; cover and reduce heat. Simmer for 20 minutes.

Stir bacon into rice. Cover and continue to cook for 15-20 minutes, or until rice is tender and liquid is absorbed.

Yield: 6 servings

YUMMY RICE CASSEROLE

An easy side dish to prepare ahead, this casserole can be refrigerated for up to 2 days before baking. If rice is cold, bake an extra 5-10 minutes.

1 cup regular long-grain white rice
1 egg
1 cup grated sharp cheddar cheese
¼ cup vegetable oil
½ cup chopped fresh parsley
1 cup chopped onion
1 (10¾-ounce) can cream of celery soup
2 tablespoons grated parmesan cheese
2 tablespoons bread crumbs
1 teaspoon butter or margarine

Cook rice according to package directions.

Preheat oven to 350 degrees.

In large bowl, beat egg. Add cheese, oil, parsley, onion, and soup. Mix well. Add cooked rice and mix well.

Spoon mixture into lightly greased 2-quart casserole. Sprinkle with parmesan cheese and bread crumbs. Dot with butter. Bake, uncovered, for 40 minutes.

Yield: 6-8 servings

SHARON'S BROCCOLI-RICE CASSEROLE

1 cup chopped onion
1 cup chopped celery
1 tablespoon vegetable oil
2 (10-ounce) packages frozen chopped broccoli
1 (10¾-ounce) can cream of mushroom soup
1 (5-ounce) can evaporated milk
2 cups grated sharp cheddar cheese
3 cups cooked long-grain white rice
½ teaspoon salt
¼ teaspoon pepper
¼ teaspoon worcestershire sauce
2 tablespoons butter, melted

Preheat oven to 350 degrees.

In skillet over medium-high heat, sauté onion and celery in oil for 4-5 minutes; set aside. Cook broccoli according to package directions; drain *well* in colander.

In medium saucepan, combine soup, evaporated milk, and cheese. Cook over medium heat, stirring occasionally, until cheese melts.

Combine sautéed onion and celery, soup mixture, rice, and seasonings. Mix well. Pour into 9 x 13 x 2-inch baking dish. Drizzle with melted butter. Bake, uncovered, for 30 minutes.

Yield: 12 servings

THE BEST MACARONI AND CHEESE

2 tablespoons butter or margarine
2 tablespoons all-purpose flour
1 teaspoon salt
⅛ teaspoon white pepper
1 teaspoon dry mustard
2½ cups whole milk
2 cups grated sharp cheddar cheese, divided
8 ounces elbow macaroni
paprika

In medium saucepan, melt butter. Stir in flour, salt, pepper, and dry mustard. Add milk. Cook over medium heat, stirring constantly, until sauce begins to thicken and is smooth. Add 1½ cups cheese. Heat until melted, stirring frequently.

Preheat oven to 375 degrees.

Meanwhile, cook macaroni according to package directions; drain. Combine with sauce; mix well. Pour into lightly greased 2-quart casserole. Sprinkle with remaining cheese and paprika.

Bake, uncovered, for 20-25 minutes, or until hot and bubbly.

Yield: 6 servings

GARLIC CHEESE GRITS

1 cup regular dry grits
4 cups water
½ teaspoon salt
1 (6-ounce) roll Kraft process cheese food with garlic
½ cup butter or margarine, cut into small chunks
1 teaspoon worcestershire sauce
1 egg, beaten

Slowly stir grits into briskly boiling salted water. Return to boil; reduce heat to low. Cover and cook for 15-20 minutes, stirring frequently.

Preheat oven to 300 degrees.

Cut cheese into small chunks; stir into grits. (If cheese roll with garlic is unavailable, use 1½ cups grated sharp cheddar cheese and 1 clove garlic, crushed.) Continue cooking over low heat. Stir in butter and worcestershire sauce. Add beaten egg; stir rapidly to mix. Stir until cheese and butter are melted. Pour into greased 2-quart casserole. Bake, uncovered, for 1 hour.

Yield: 8 servings

PINEAPPLE DELIGHT

A *delicious* accompaniment to ham or turkey, Pineapple Delight is the perfect dish to jazz up your traditional Thanksgiving or Christmas dinner.

1 (20-ounce) can pineapple chunks, in their own juice
3 tablespoons all-purpose flour
½ cup sugar
1 cup grated sharp cheddar cheese
¼ cup butter, melted
½ cup crushed Ritz crackers

Preheat oven to 350 degrees.

Drain pineapple, reserving 3 tablespoons juice. In medium bowl, combine flour and sugar. Slowly stir in reserved pineapple juice. Add pineapple chunks and cheese; mix well. Pour into lightly greased 1-quart casserole.

Mix butter and cracker crumbs in small bowl. Sprinkle over pineapple mixture. Bake, uncovered, for 20-30 minutes, until hot and bubbly.

Yield: 4-6 servings

SWEETS

GREAT CHOCOLATE CHIP COOKIES

½ cup butter, at room temperature
½ cup vegetable shortening
1 cup granulated sugar
½ cup dark brown sugar
2 teaspoons vanilla extract
2 eggs
2 cups all-purpose flour
1 teaspoon baking soda
1 teaspoon salt
1 (12-ounce) package semi-sweet chocolate chips
1 cup chopped pecans

Preheat oven to 375 degrees.

In large bowl of electric mixer, cream together butter, shortening, granulated sugar, and brown sugar. Add vanilla extract and eggs; beat until light and fluffy. Gradually add flour, baking soda, and salt; blend well.

Stir in chocolate chips and pecans. Mix well with spoon. Drop by teaspoonfuls onto ungreased baking sheets. Bake for 8-10 minutes. Remove cookies to wire racks to cool.

Yield: 7-8 dozen

JACKIE WIGGINS'S OATMEAL COOKIES

1½ cups dark or light brown sugar
1 cup granulated sugar
1 cup margarine, at room temperature
2 eggs
1 teaspoon vanilla extract
2 cups all-purpose flour
½ teaspoon salt
½ teaspoon baking soda
1 teaspoon baking powder
2 cups uncooked oatmeal
1 cup corn flakes
2 cups raisins or chopped pecans

Preheat oven to 350 degrees.

In large bowl of electric mixer, blend together brown sugar, granulated sugar, margarine, eggs, and vanilla extract.

Sift together flour, salt, baking soda, and baking powder. Gradually add to sugar mixture. Stir in oatmeal, corn flakes, and raisins or pecans. Drop by teaspoonfuls onto ungreased baking sheets. Bake for 10 minutes. Remove to wire racks to cool.

Yield: 8 dozen

HELLO DOLLIES

½ cup butter or margarine
1½ cups graham cracker crumbs
1 cup shredded, sweetened coconut
1 cup chopped pecans
1 (6-ounce) package semi-sweet chocolate chips
1 (14-ounce) can sweetened condensed milk

Preheat oven to 325 degrees.

Place butter in 9 x 13-inch glass baking dish and melt in oven. Sprinkle graham cracker crumbs over butter; press lightly with hands.

Sprinkle coconut, pecans, and chocolate chips into dish in layers. Do not stir. Pour condensed milk over all. Bake, uncovered, for 25-30 minutes, until edges are lightly browned. Cool and refrigerate until firm; cut into squares. Store loosely covered at room temperature.

Yield: 2 dozen

LIZZIES

½ cup butter, at room temperature
1½ cups dark brown sugar
4 eggs
1 cup bourbon
3 tablespoons whole milk
5 cups all-purpose flour, divided
1 teaspoon each ground cloves, cinnamon, nutmeg, and allspice
3 teaspoons baking soda
2 pounds candied cherries (red and green)
2 pounds candied pineapple (red, green, and yellow)
1 pound dark raisins
1 pound white raisins
6 cups chopped pecans

Preheat oven to 300 degrees.

Cream butter and sugar in large bowl of electric mixer. Add eggs 1 at a time, blending well after each addition. Add bourbon and milk; blend well.

Sift 4½ cups of the flour together with the spices and baking soda. Gradually add to creamed butter mixture, blending well.

Cut up cherries and pineapple; dredge in remaining ½ cup of flour. Stir cherries, pineapple, raisins, and pecans into creamed butter mixture. Mix well with spoon. Drop by teaspoonfuls onto greased baking sheets. Bake for 10 minutes. (Note: Lizzies will keep for months if stored in tins or plastic storage containers.)

Yield: 20 dozen

AUNT LIL'S BROWNIE-FUDGE SQUARES

¾ cup margarine
4 (1-ounce) squares unsweetened chocolate
4 eggs
2 cups sugar
1 teaspoon vanilla extract
1 cup all-purpose flour
½ teaspoon baking powder
1 cup chopped pecans

Preheat oven to 325 degrees.

Melt margarine and chocolate in top of double boiler, stirring to mix; cool. In large bowl of electric mixer, beat eggs until light. Gradually add sugar to eggs, beating thoroughly. Add cooled chocolate mixture to egg mixture. Add vanilla extract and beat.

Sift together flour and baking powder; gradually add to chocolate mixture, blending well after each addition. Stir in chopped pecans.

Grease sides of 9 x 13 x 2-inch pan with vegetable shortening. Line bottom of pan with wax paper. Pour batter into prepared pan, spreading evenly. Bake for 30 minutes. Cool completely. Cut into squares.

Yield: 2 dozen

NICK'S PEANUT BRITTLE

1 cup sugar
½ cup light corn syrup
2 cups raw peanuts
1 square-inch piece of paraffin
pinch of salt
1 heaping teaspoon baking soda

Grease a baking sheet with vegetable shortening. Combine all ingredients except baking soda in medium saucepan. Cook over medium heat, stirring almost constantly, until peanuts are done and candy thermometer reaches 290 degrees (about 12 minutes from time sugar melts). Toward end of cooking time, it is necessary to stir constantly to avoid scorching.

When peanuts are done, remove mixture from heat and quickly stir in baking soda. Pour hot mixture onto prepared pan; quickly spread thin with back of wooden spoon. Allow peanut brittle to cool completely. Twist pan to release candy. Break peanut brittle into pieces.

(Note: It is important to use peanuts that do not have a high moisture content so the syrup will not overcook before the peanuts are done.)

Yield: 1½ pounds

PECAN FUDGE PIE

½ cup butter
3 (1-ounce) squares unsweetened chocolate
4 eggs
3 tablespoons light corn syrup
1½ cups sugar
¼ teaspoon salt
1 teaspoon vanilla extract
1 cup chopped pecans
2 (9-inch) Pie Crusts (recipe on page 194)

Preheat oven to 350 degrees.

Melt butter and chocolate in top of double boiler. Meanwhile, in large mixing bowl, beat eggs with electric hand mixer until light. Beat syrup, sugar, salt, and vanilla extract into eggs. Stir in pecans and slightly cooled chocolate mixture; mix thoroughly with spoon. Pour filling into crusts.

Place pie plates directly on oven rack. Bake for 30-35 minutes, or until filling is set, but still soft inside. Do not overcook.

Yield: 12 servings

BEST EVER ICE CREAM PIE

1½ cups chocolate wafer crumbs
⅓ cup butter, melted
2 (1-ounce) squares unsweetened chocolate
1 tablespoon butter
½ cup sugar
1 (5-ounce) can evaporated milk
1 quart coffee ice cream
½ pint whipping cream, whipped
¼ cup chopped pecans
crème de cacao

Combine chocolate wafer crumbs and ⅓ cup butter in bowl; mix well. Press evenly into 9-inch pie plate; place in freezer.

Melt chocolate and 1 tablespoon butter in top of double boiler. Stir in sugar and evaporated milk. Cook and stir until mixture is smooth and thickened; cool and pour into prepared crust. Return pie crust to freezer for about 30 minutes. In meantime, soften ice cream to spreading consistency. Spread ice cream over chocolate-covered pie crust. Cover and freeze for several hours.

Remove pie from freezer 15 minutes before serving. Spread whipped cream evenly over ice cream. Slice pie. Sprinkle each serving with chopped pecans and crème de cacao.

Yield: 6-8 servings

BISHOP WHIPPLE

2 eggs
½ cup sugar
⅔ cup sifted all-purpose flour
1 teaspoon baking powder
1 cup chopped dates
1 cup chopped pecans
granulated or confectioners' sugar
½ pint whipping cream, whipped with 2 tablespoons XXXX confectioners' sugar

Preheat oven to 350 degrees.

In large bowl of electric mixer, thoroughly beat eggs and sugar. Sift flour and baking powder together; gradually add to egg mixture, beating after each addition. Stir in dates and pecans. Pour mixture into greased 15½ x 10½ x 1-inch pan. Spread mixture to almost cover bottom of pan. Bake for 25 minutes.

Immediately after removing from oven, sprinkle generously with sugar. Loosen warm cake from bottom of pan with spatula; break into pieces. Serve with sweetened whipped cream.

Yield: 6-8 servings

BROWNSTONE FRONT CAKE

2 (1-ounce) squares unsweetened chocolate
½ cup butter or margarine, at room temperature
2 cups dark brown sugar
2 eggs
1 teaspoon vanilla extract
2 cups all-purpose flour
1 teaspoon baking soda
1 teaspoon salt
½ cup water
½ cup buttermilk
Laplanders Icing

Preheat oven to 350 degrees.

Melt chocolate in top of double boiler. In large bowl of electric mixer, cream butter and brown sugar thoroughly. Add melted chocolate and mix well. Add eggs 1 at a time, beating well after each addition. Add vanilla extract; mix well.

Sift flour with baking soda and salt 4 or 5 times. Combine water and buttermilk. Alternately add dry ingredients and liquids to creamed butter mixture, mixing well after each addition.

Cut 2 circles of wax paper to fit the bottoms of 2 (9-inch) round cake pans. Grease sides of pans with vegetable shortening. Place wax paper in bottom of pans. Pour batter into prepared pans. Bake for 30-35 minutes. Immediately turn cake out onto wire racks to cool. After cake has cooled, ice with Laplanders Icing.

Yield: 12-16 servings

LAPLANDERS ICING:

½ cup butter or margarine
1½ cups sugar
8 teaspoons cocoa
¼ teaspoon salt
1 teaspoon vanilla extract
½ cup water
1 egg, well beaten

Mix all ingredients together in heavy saucepan. Cook over medium heat, stirring occasionally. When icing reaches soft ball stage (234 degrees on a candy thermometer), remove from heat. Cool and beat until icing is creamy and of spreading consistency.

SOUR CREAM POUND CAKE

3 cups sugar
1 cup margarine, at room temperature
6 eggs
3 cups all-purpose flour
¼ teaspoon baking soda
¼ teaspoon salt
1 (8-ounce) carton sour cream
1 teaspoon vanilla extract
1½ teaspoons almond extract

Preheat oven to 350 degrees.

Sift sugar 3 times. In large bowl of electric mixer, cream margarine and sugar. Add eggs 1 at a time, beating thoroughly after each addition.

Sift flour with baking soda and salt 3 times. Gradually add flour mixture to creamed margarine and sugar, beating well. Add sour cream and beat thoroughly. Add vanilla extract and almond extract. Mix well.

Pour batter into lightly greased tube pan. Bake for 1 hour and 20 minutes, or until cake tests done. Immediately turn cake out onto wire rack to cool.

Yield: 16 servings

SIN CITY SHEET CAKE

2 cups all-purpose flour
2 cups sugar
¼ teaspoon salt
½ cup butter
½ cup vegetable oil
1 cup water
¼ cup cocoa
2 eggs, slightly beaten
½ cup buttermilk
1 teaspoon baking soda
1 teaspoon vanilla extract
Sin City Icing

Preheat oven to 350 degrees.

Sift flour, sugar, and salt into large mixing bowl; set aside. In medium saucepan, bring butter, vegetable oil, water, and cocoa to boil, stirring to mix. Remove from heat. Cool slightly.

Pour warm mixture over flour mixture. Stir to mix well. Add eggs, buttermilk, baking soda, and vanilla extract. Mix well. Pour batter into greased and floured 17 x 11-inch jellyroll pan. Bake for 20-25 minutes, until cake tests done. Cool slightly. Pour Sin City Icing over warm cake, spreading evenly to cover.

Yield: 24 servings

SIN CITY ICING:

½ cup butter
6 tablespoons cocoa
6 tablespoons whole milk
1 (16-ounce) box XXXX confectioners' sugar, sifted
1 teaspoon vanilla extract
1 cup chopped pecans

Bring butter, cocoa, and milk to boil in medium saucepan, stirring to mix. Remove from heat. Stir in confectioners' sugar and vanilla extract. Beat with spoon to mix well. Stir in pecans.

CARAMEL NUT CAKE

2¾ cups all-purpose flour
2½ teaspoons baking powder
1 teaspoon salt
½ cup butter or margarine, at room temperature
1¾ cups sugar
1½ teaspoons vanilla extract
2 eggs
1¼ cups whole milk
Caramel Nut Icing

Preheat oven to 375 degrees.

Grease and flour 2 (9-inch) round cake pans. Combine flour, baking powder, and salt. In large bowl of electric mixer, cream butter for 30 seconds. Add sugar and vanilla extract; beat until well blended. Add eggs, 1 at a time, beating for 1 minute after each is added. Alternately add dry ingredients and milk to beaten mixture, beating after each addition. Pour batter into prepared pans.

Bake for 30-35 minutes, or until cake tests done. Cool pans for 10 minutes on wire racks. Remove cake from pans; cool on wire racks. Ice cake with Caramel Nut Icing.

Yield: 16 servings

CARAMEL NUT ICING:

2½ cups sugar, divided
1 cup whole milk
½ cup butter
½ teaspoon vanilla extract
1 cup chopped pecans

Place 2 cups sugar, milk, and butter in large saucepan. Cook over medium heat, stirring occasionally, until milk is just under boiling and butter is melted. Reduce heat to low, so that mixture remains very hot (but does not boil) while sugar is being caramelized.

Meanwhile, place remaining ½ cup of sugar in 9-inch iron skillet. Cook over medium heat, stirring constantly, until sugar melts to a rich amber color. Take care not to scorch sugar. Slowly pour caramelized sugar into *hot* milk mixture; stir to mix. Continue to cook over medium heat, stirring occasionally, until mixture reaches soft ball stage (234 degrees on candy thermometer). Cool slightly. As mixture begins to cool, beat with spoon until mixture is creamy and of spreading consistency. Stir in vanilla extract and pecans.

(Note: If caramelized sugar hardens when poured into milk mixture, continue cooking and stirring until it melts and mixture reaches soft ball stage.)

CHEESECAKE

1½ cups graham cracker crumbs
⅓ cup butter or margarine, melted
4 eggs, separated
3 (8-ounce) packages cream cheese, at room temperature
1 cup sugar, divided
1 teaspoon vanilla extract
1 (16-ounce) carton sour cream

Preheat oven to 350 degrees.

Combine graham cracker crumbs and butter in bowl; mix well. Grease bottom and sides of 10-inch springform pan with vegetable shortening. Press cracker crumb mixture into bottom of pan.

In small bowl of electric mixer, beat egg whites until stiff; set aside. In large bowl of electric mixer, combine egg yolks, cream cheese, ¾ cup sugar, and vanilla extract. Beat until smooth. Fold in egg whites. Pour mixture into prepared pan.

Bake for 40-45 minutes, or until slightly browned. In meantime, combine sour cream and remaining ¼ cup sugar; mix well. Increase oven temperature to 450 degrees. Pour sour cream mixture over cake; return to oven for an additional 5 minutes.

After cake cools, refrigerate for at least 12 hours before serving. (Cheesecake is best if taken out of refrigerator 1 hour before serving.) Top with fresh fruit, if desired.

Yield: 12 servings

MAE'S BOILED CUSTARD

1 envelope unflavored gelatin
⅓ cup cold water
4 eggs, beaten
1 cup sugar
⅛ teaspoon salt
4 cups whole milk
1 teaspoon vanilla extract

Dissolve gelatin in water. Place eggs, sugar, salt, and milk in large heavy saucepan; mix well. Cook over medium heat, stirring constantly, until mixture coats a metal spoon (about 20 minutes). Remove from heat.

Stir in gelatin mixture and vanilla extract. Pour into custard cups. Cover with plastic wrap and refrigerate until set.

Yield: 12 servings

HOMEMADE PEACH ICE CREAM

4 eggs
1 cup sugar
½ pint whipping cream
¼ teaspoon salt
2 tablespoons vanilla extract
2 (14-ounce) cans sweetened condensed milk
2½ cups puréed fresh peaches
1 to 1½ quarts whole milk

In large bowl of electric mixer, combine eggs, sugar, cream, salt, and vanilla extract. Mix thoroughly. Pour into ice cream freezer can. Stir in condensed milk; mix well.

Stir in peaches. Add milk to fill line (3-4 inches from top). Do *not* fill to top. Stir to mix. Churn ice cream according to directions accompanying churn.

Yield: 4 quarts

POTPOURRI

BENNY SAUCE

An *excellent* marinade and basting sauce for grilled chicken and pork, Benny Sauce has been a Busbee family favorite for years. The recipe was developed by our "back-door neighbor" in Albany, Benny Lanier. Now a part of our traditional family Thanksgiving dinner, Benny Sauce is a delicious way to turn ordinary roast turkey into something extraordinary.

1 cup vegetable oil
1 cup lemon juice
1 cup red wine vinegar
1½ tablespoons salt
1½ tablespoons fresh black pepper
1½ tablespoons onion salt
1 heaping tablespoon celery salt
1 heaping tablespoon garlic salt
1 tablespoon ground marjoram
1 tablespoon dried thyme
1 tablespoon dried basil
1 tablespoon dried oregano
3 tablespoons soy sauce
3 tablespoons worcestershire sauce
dash Tabasco sauce
5 large cloves garlic, minced
½ teaspoon white pepper

Combine all ingredients in saucepan. Heat to boiling, stirring constantly. Reduce heat and simmer for 1-2 minutes, stirring frequently. Remove from heat; cool.

Sauce can be stored in refrigerator for several weeks, or used immediately. (For optimum flavor, marinate chicken and pork for at least 8 hours before grilling.)

Yield: 4 cups

BROCCOLI SAUCE

In the early, lean days of our marriage, I attended a free cooking school which was sponsored by the local gas company. My motivation was not a desire to improve my cooking skills, but the gas range that was being given away. I didn't win the range, but I did discover a simple sauce recipe that got George and the children to eat broccoli.

½ cup mayonnaise
1 teaspoon sugar
1 teaspoon full-strength prepared horseradish
2 teaspoons prepared mustard
½ teaspoon lemon juice

Combine all ingredients in small bowl; mix well. Serve over cooked broccoli spears.

Yield: about ½ cup

JAN'S SPINACH QUICHE

1 (9-inch) Pie Crust (see recipe below) or frozen deep-dish pie crust
1 (10-ounce) package frozen chopped spinach
1 tablespoon butter
1 medium onion, diced
4 eggs
1 (12-ounce) can evaporated milk
8 ounces Swiss cheese, grated
½ cup grated parmesan cheese, divided
salt and pepper to taste

Preheat oven to 350 degrees. Prebake Pie Crust for 5 minutes.

Cook spinach according to package directions. Drain in colander or strainer, squeezing out all excess moisture with back of spoon. Melt butter in medium skillet; add spinach and onion. Sauté over medium-high heat until onion is transparent. Set aside to cool.

In large bowl, beat eggs. Stir in evaporated milk, Swiss cheese, ¼ cup parmesan cheese, salt, and pepper. Add lukewarm spinach mixture and mix well.

Pour filling into prebaked pie crust. Sprinkle with remaining ¼ cup parmesan cheese. Bake for 45 minutes, or until center is set. Let quiche stand for 10 minutes before cutting.

Yield: 6 servings

PIE CRUST:

1 cup sifted all-purpose flour
½ teaspoon salt
6 tablespoons vegetable shortening
¼ cup ice cold water

Mix flour and salt in small bowl. Cut shortening into flour with pastry blender or 2 knives until particles are size of rice grains. Add cold water, a tablespoon at a time, as you mix with fork. As particles stick together, push to 1 side of bowl. When all water has been added and mixed into flour, gently press dough together into a ball. Avoid over-handling. Wrap dough in plastic wrap; refrigerate for 10 minutes.

On lightly floured board, roll out dough, working from center to edge, forming a 12-inch diameter circle. Carefully wrap pastry around rolling pin; unroll onto 9-inch pie plate. Ease pastry into pie plate; do not stretch. Trim pastry to ½ inch beyond edge of pie plate. Fold under the extra ½ inch of pastry, so that edge of pastry extends slightly beyond rim of plate. Flute edge with fingers. Press fluted edge against rim of pie plate.

Yield: 1 (9-inch) pie crust

BLUE CRAB OMELETTE FOR TWO

5-6 ounces blue crab meat
⅔ cup half-and-half
1 tablespoon sliced green onion
¼ teaspoon dried thyme
⅛ teaspoon salt
3 drops Tabasco sauce
1 tablespoon all-purpose flour
1 tablespoon water
5 eggs
¼ teaspoon salt
dash pepper
1 tablespoon butter or margarine
½ cup grated cheddar cheese

Combine crab meat, half-and-half, onion, thyme, ⅛ teaspoon salt, and Tabasco sauce in medium saucepan. Cook over medium heat until hot, stirring occasionally. Combine flour and water; gradually stir into crab meat mixture. Continue to cook over medium heat, stirring constantly, until mixture thickens. Keep warm while omelette cooks.

Beat eggs with ¼ teaspoon salt and dash pepper. Melt butter in omelette pan over medium-high heat. Pour beaten eggs into pan. When eggs are partially cooked, run a spatula around edge, lifting slightly to allow uncooked egg to flow underneath.

When eggs are almost done, sprinkle cheese on top and cook until cheese melts. Place half of crab meat mixture on 1 side of omelette. Fold other side of omelette over crab meat mixture. Pour remainder of crab meat mixture on top and serve immediately.

Yield: 2 servings

DIRTY RICE

Served with a green salad and crusty bread, Dirty Rice is a delicious and different main dish. It can also be served as a side dish.

2 pounds chicken giblets
salt
black pepper
cayenne pepper
4 cups water
⅓ cup vegetable oil
3 tablespoons all-purpose flour
2 cups chopped onion
1 cup chopped celery
3 cups cooked long-grain white rice
½ cup chopped green onion tops
¼ cup chopped fresh parsley

Season giblets generously with salt, black pepper, and cayenne pepper. Bring water to boil in saucepan; add giblets. Cover and reduce heat; simmer until tender, about 30 minutes. Drain giblets, reserving broth. Mince giblets and set aside.

Heat oil in Dutch oven over medium heat. Add flour. Cook, stirring constantly, until flour is medium brown. Stir in onion and celery. Cook until tender, stirring occasionally. Slowly stir in reserved broth. Add minced giblets. Cook until liquid is reduced and slightly thickened. Stir in cooked rice.

Before serving, toss rice mixture with green onion tops and parsley.

Yield: 6-8 servings

CRACKLIN' BREAD

2 cups plain cornmeal
1 teaspoon salt
½ teaspoon baking powder
¼ cup vegetable oil, divided
⅓ cup whole milk
⅓ cup water
1 cup cracklings

Preheat oven to 400 degrees.

Combine cornmeal, salt, baking powder, and half of the vegetable oil in mixing bowl; mix well. Pour remaining oil into jellyroll pan. Heat oiled pan in oven for 2-3 minutes. Add milk, water, and cracklings to cornmeal mixture; mix well. Drop by rounded tablespoonfuls onto hot pan. Return to oven and bake for 30-35 minutes, or until golden brown.

Yield: 2 dozen

SOUR CREAM BISCUITS

1 cup margarine, melted
1 (8-ounce) carton sour cream
2 cups self-rising flour

Preheat oven to 450 degrees.

Combine margarine and sour cream in large bowl; mix well. Add flour; mix well.

Drop dough by teaspoonfuls into ungreased miniature muffin tins. Bake for 15 minutes.

Yield: 2½ dozen

INDEX

Almond Lace Cookies 127
Ambrosia 99
Angel Biscuits (see Southern Angel Biscuits)
Angel Food Rum Strips 70
Anne's Rice 181

APPETIZERS
  CHEESE
    Boursin Cheese 138
    Cheese Dreams 69
    Cheese Wafers 88
    Garlic Cheese Roll 147
    London Cheese Roll 138
    Melanie's Cheese Ring 147
    Olive Bites 89
    Pecan Cheese Ball 138
    Sherry Cheese Pâté 148
  FISH AND SEAFOOD
    Coulibiac 125
    Crab-Stuffed Mushrooms 148
    Destin Dip 148
    Lobster, Phyllo-Wrapped 125
    Oysters Burton 124
    Oysters Thomas 59
    Shrimp, Marinated Baby 123
    Shrimp Mold 89
    Shrimp Spread, Rena's 149
    Trout, Stuffed 124
  FRUITS
    Kiwi and Prosciutto 122
    Pineapple Chunks, Spiced 67
  MEATS
    Mini Beef Wellington 126
    Prosciutto, Kiwi and 122
    Roast Contrefilet of Beef
      with Dipping Sauce 122
    Sausage Balls 138
  MISCELLANEOUS APPETIZERS
    Peanut Fingers 90
    Sweet'N Sour Rumaki 147
    Toasted Pecans 67
  POULTRY AND GAME
    Chicken Champagnoise 126
    Chicken Drummettes, Marinated .. 149
    Chicken Salad in Toast Cups 137
    Chicken Turnovers 149
    Chicken Williamsburg,
      Puff Shells with 90
    Duck Gallantine
      with Cumberland Sauce 122
  VEGETABLES
    Mushrooms, Crab-Stuffed 148
    Spinach Balls 89
Apple Nut Cake 37
Apples (see Fruits and Desserts)
Apricot Moscovite 104
Artichokes (see Salads and Vegetables)
Asparagus (see Salads and Vegetables)
Asparagus and Artichoke Salad 79
Aspic (see Salads)
Assorted Sandwiches 68
Aunt Lil's Brownie-Fudge Squares 187
Avocado Mousse 36
Baked Beans 110
Baked Eggs 63
Baked Grits 107
Baked Ham 32
Baked Quail 55
Barbecue (see Beef, Pork, and Poultry)
Barbecued Chicken 110
Barbecued Pot Roast and Dumplings 167
Bass (see Fish and Seafood)
Beans (see Vegetables)
Béarnaise Sauce 60

BEEF
- Barbecued Pot Roast and Dumplings .. 167
- Beef Bonaparte 168
- Beef Burgundy 165
- Beef Bourguignonne over Noodles 21
- Beefy Chicken 174
- Charcoal Sirloin Cubes 12
- Filet of Beef Stephanie 60
- Filet Mignon Alfonse 166
- Filet Mignon Sauté 46
- Lasagna 40
- Marinated Flank Steak 166
- Mini Beef Wellington 126
- Old-Fashioned Beef Stew 157
- Pepper Steak 165
- Quick Beef Stroganoff 168
- Roast Contrefilet of Beef
  with Dipping Sauce 122
- Southern Sirloin Tip Roast 167
- Tournedos Monegasques 80

Beef Bonaparte 168
Beef Bourguignonne over Noodles 21
Beef Burgundy 165
Beefy Chicken 174
Benny Sauce 193
Best Ever Ice Cream Pie 188
Beth's Blueberry Muffins 134
Betty Sanders's Peach Punch 71

BEVERAGES
- Eggnog 137
- Golden Summer Punch 71
- Peach Punch, Betty Sanders's 71
- Wassail 88

Bishop Whipple 189
Biscuits (see Breads)
Blue Crab Omelette for Two 195
Blueberry Muffins
  (see Beth's Blueberry Muffins)
Boiled Custard (see Mae's Boiled Custard)
Bourbon Balls 140
Boursin Cheese 138

BREADS
  BISCUITS
  - Buttermilk Biscuits 48
  - Buttermilk Biscuits, Processor 93
  - Cheese Biscuits 13
  - Herb Biscuits 52
  - Sour Cream Biscuits 196
  - Southern Angel Biscuits 99

  CORNBREADS
  - Corn Muffins, Small 33
  - Corn Sticks 30
  - Cornbread 97
  - Cracklin' Bread 196
  - Dressing with Giblet Gravy 97

  MISCELLANEOUS BREADS
  - Garlic Bread, Brennan's 41
  - Herb Bread 21
  - Hushpuppies 74
  - Toast Cups 137
  - Waffles, Workhorse 63

  MUFFINS
  - Blueberry Muffins, Beth's 134
  - Herb Muffins 103
  - Corn Muffins, Small 33

  YEAST BREADS
  - Biscuits, Southern Angel 99
  - Dinner Rolls, Effie's 131
  - Homemade Bread 23

Brennan's Garlic Bread 41
Broccoli (see Vegetables)
Broccoli Casserole 179
Broccoli Sauce 193
Broccoli-Stuffed Tomatoes 17
Brooke's Sweet Potatoes 180
Brownie-Fudge Squares
  (see Aunt Lil's Brownie-Fudge Squares)
Brownies (see Desserts: Cookies)
Brown Sugar Cookies 139
Brownstone Front Cake 189
Butter Cookies 52
Butter Frosting 70
Buttered Noodles with Poppy Seeds 144

Butternut Bake	178
Cabbage (see Vegetables)	
Caesar Sour Cream Dressing	50
Cakes (see Desserts)	
Candied Yams	32
Candies (see Desserts)	
Caramel Nut Cake	191
Caramel Nut Icing	191
Carlton's Fried Rice	181
Carrots (see Vegetables)	
Carrots with Walnuts	178
Chantilly Cream	128
Charcoal Sirloin Cubes	12
Charles Durant's Channel Bass	162
Cheddar Chowder	156
CHEESE	
Boursin Cheese	138
Cheddar Chowder	156
Cheese Biscuits	13
Cheese Dreams	69
Cheese Omelette	22
Cheese Soufflé	134
Cheese Wafers	88
Cheesecake	192
Cream Cheese Open-Faced Sandwiches	68
Garlic Cheese Grits	184
Garlic Cheese Roll	147
London Cheese Roll	138
Macaroni and Cheese, The Best	183
Melanie's Cheese Ring	147
Olive Bites	89
Pecan Cheese Ball	138
Pimiento Cheese Sandwiches, Ribbon	68
Sherry Cheese Pâté	148
Cheese Biscuits	13
Cheese Dreams	69
Cheese Omelette	22
Cheese Soufflé	134
Cheese Wafers	88
Cheesecake	192
Chicken (see Poultry and Game)	
Chicken-Artichoke Bake	174
Chicken Champagnoise	126
Chicken Duxelles	143
Chicken Livers Stroganoff	175
Chicken Parisienne	130
Chicken Salad (see Salads: Poultry and Seafood)	
Chicken Salad in Toast Cups	137
Chicken Soufflé with Sherry Mushroom Sauce	102
Chicken Spaghetti	176
Chicken Tetrazzini	116
Chicken Turnovers	149
Chicken Virginia	93
Chicken Williamsburg	90
Chicken with Tarragon	173
Chilled Cucumber Soup	143
Chocolate Chip Cookies (see Great Chocolate Chip Cookies)	
Chocolate-Dipped Strawberries	127
Chocolate Frosting	111
Chocolate Glaze	128
Chocolate Pound Cake	100
Chocolate Pound Cake Icing	100
Chocolate Truffles	127
Chowders (see Soups and Stews)	
Cold Artichoke Rice Salad	154
Coleslaw	75
Cookies (see Desserts)	
Corn (see Vegetables)	
Corn on the Cob	111
Corn Sticks	30
Cornbread	97
Cornbreads (see Breads)	
Cornish hen (see Poultry and Game)	
Coulibiac	125
Coupe Champagne	13
Crab-Stuffed Mushrooms	148
Cracklin' Bread	196
Cranberries (see Fruits and Salads)	
Cranberry Mold	99
Cranberry Soufflé Salad	82
Cream Cheese Open-Faced Sandwiches	68
Cream of Broccoli Soup	20

Creamed Corn 29
Creamed Shrimp in Puff Pastry Shells 36
Creole Squash 178
Crêpes 144
Crisp Green Beans 37
Crunchy Baked Potatoes 12
Crusty Baked Potatoes 61
Cucumber Soup (see Chilled Cucumber Soup)
Cumberland Sauce 123
Curried Chicken 176
Curried Fruit 18
Custards
  (see Desserts: Puddings and Custards)
DESSERTS
  CAKES
    Apple Nut Cake 37
    Bishop Whipple 189
    Brownstone Front Cake 189
    Caramel Nut Cake 191
    Cheesecake 192
    Frosted Cake Squares 70
    Karidopita 81
    Lemon Cheese Cake 75
    Pound Cake, Chocolate 100
    Pound Cake, Sour Cream 190
    Prune Cake 62
    Sheet Cake, Sin City 190
  CANDIES
    Chocolate Truffles 127
    Fudge, Mrs. Baker's 140
    Haystacks 139
    Mints, Wedding 71
    Peanut Brittle, Nick's 187
    Pralines 127
  COOKIES
    Almond Lace Cookies 127
    Bourbon Balls 140
    Brown Sugar Cookies 139
    Brownie-Fudge Squares, Aunt Lil's .. 187
    Brownies, Heavenly Hash 111
    Butter Cookies 52
    Chocolate Chip Cookies, Great 185
    Fruitcake Cookies 139
    Hello Dollies 186
    Lizzies 186
    Oatmeal Cookies, Jackie Wiggins's .. 185
    Orange Balls 70
    Pecan Crescents 140
    Shortbread Cookies 33
    Sugar Cookies 41
  FRUIT DESSERTS
    Ambrosia 99
    Apricot Moscovite 104
    Chocolate-Dipped Strawberries 127
    Coupe Champagne 13
    Crêpes, Peach Melba 144
    Fruit Parfait 21
    Macedoine of Fruit 52
    Peach Ice Cream, Homemade ... 192
    Strawberry Dessert, Luscious 94
  MISCELLANEOUS DESSERTS
    Angel Food Rum Strips 70
    Ice Cream with Crème de Cassis 33
    Savannah Trifle 47
  PIES AND PASTRIES
    Éclairs, Mini Chocolate 128
    Grasshopper Pie 86
    Ice Cream Pie, Best Ever 188
    Key Lime Pie 131
    Pecan Fudge Pie 188
    Pecan Pie, Southern 30
    Pecan Tassies 90
    Puff Shells filled with Vanilla Ice Cream
      and Fudge Sauce 56
    Rum Cream Pie 84
  PUDDINGS AND CUSTARDS
    Apricot Moscovite 104
    Boiled Custard, Mae's 192
    Irish Mist 117
Destin Dip 148
Dill Sauce 124
Dinner Rolls (see Effie's Dinner Rolls)
Dipping Sauce 122
Dips (see Appetizers)

Dirty Rice 195
Dot's Potatoes Deluxe 180
Dressings (see Salad Dressings)
Dressing with Giblet Gravy 97
Duchess Potatoes on Artichoke Bottoms . . 51
Duck (see Poultry and Game)
Duck Gallantine with Cumberland Sauce . . 122
Duck Terrine 50
Dumplings 167
Durkee's Chicken 173
Earline's Ham Balls 171
Effie's Dinner Rolls 131
Éclairs (see Mini Chocolate Éclairs)
Eggnog 137
EGGS
    Baked Eggs 63
    Eggnog 137
    Eggs Benedict 118
    Omelette, Cheese 22
    Omelette for Two, Blue Crab 195
    Poached Eggs 118
    Scrambled Eggs 48
Eggplant (see Vegetables)
Eggs Benedict 118
Eva Jo's Fruited Pork Loin 169
Family Favorites 145
Filet Mignon Alfonse 166
Filet Mignon Sauté 46
Filet of Beef Stephanie 60
FISH AND SEAFOOD
    MISCELLANEOUS FISH
    AND SEAFOOD
        Blue Crab Omelette for Two 195
        Channel Bass, Charles Durant's 162
        Coulibiac 125
        Crab-Stuffed Mushrooms 148
        Dip, Destin 148
        Fish Chowder, Sapelo Island 156
        Flounder Veronique 45
        Gumbo, Joan's Seafood 163
        Gumbo, Southern 163
        Lobster, Phyllo-Wrapped 125

        Red Snapper Louisiana 162
        Salmon Salad Mold 153
        Seafood Casserole 16
        Seafood Fancy 11
        Swordfish, Grilled 159
        Trout, Fried Rainbow 74
        Trout, Stuffed 124
        Tuna Casserole 159
OYSTERS
    Oyster Stew 54
    Oysters Burton 124
    Oysters Mary 79
    Oysters Thomas 59
    Scalloped Oysters, Mae's 98
SHRIMP
    Creamed Shrimp in Puff Pastry Shells 36
    Marinated Baby Shrimp 123
    Mushroom and Shrimp Bisque 82
    New Orleans Casserole 161
    Shrimp Creole 160
    Shrimp Mold 89
    Shrimp Salad 20
    Shrimp Salad Piquant 153
    Shrimp Spread, Rena's 149
    Shrimp with Green Noodles 161
    Sunbelt Shrimp and Rice 160
Flank Steak (see Marinated Flank Steak)
Flounder Veronique 45
French-Style Green Beans 83
Fresh Green Beans 46
Fresh Mushroom and Romaine Salad 54
Fresh Pole Beans 98
Fried Chicken 28
Fried Grits 48
Fried Okra 29
Fried Rainbow Trout 74
Fried Rice (see Carlton's Fried Rice)
Frosted Cake Squares 70
Frostings (see Icings and Frostings)
Fruit Cup with Ginger Cream Dressing . . . 84
Fruit Parfait 21
Fruitcake Cookies 139

FRUITS
  APPLES
    Apple Nut Cake 37
    Waldorf Salad 32
  CRANBERRIES
    Cranberry Mold 99
    Cranberry Soufflé Salad 82
  MISCELLANEOUS FRUITS
    Ambrosia 99
    Apricot Moscovite 104
    Blueberry Muffins, Beth's 134
    Curried Fruit 18
    Fruit Cup with
      Ginger Cream Dressing 84
    Fruit Parfait 21
    Fruitcake Cookies 139
    Fruited Pork Loin, Eva Jo's 169
    Grape Sauce 93
    Kiwi and Prosciutto 122
    Macedoine of Fruit 52
    Raspberry Cream Mold 151
  PEACHES
    Betty Sanders's Peach Punch 71
    Homemade Peach Ice Cream 192
    Peach Melba Crêpes 144
    Sliced Georgia Peaches and Cream .. 107
  PINEAPPLE
    Pineapple Delight 184
    Spiced Pineapple Chunks 67
  STRAWBERRIES
    Chocolate-Dipped Strawberries 127
    Luscious Strawberry Dessert 94
    Strawberries and Cream 48
Fudge (see Desserts: Candies)
Fudge Sauce 56
Game (see Poultry and Game)
Garden Aspic 18
Garlic Cheese Grits 184
Garlic Cheese Roll 147
Gazpacho Salad in Brandy Snifters 102
German Sausage Chowder 157
Giblet Gravy 97

Ginger Cream Dressing 85
Glaze for Apple Nut Cake 37
Glaze for Baked Ham 32
Glaze for Prune Cake 62
Golden Pheasant Salad 59
Golden Summer Punch 71
Grape Sauce 93
Grasshopper Pie 86
Gravies (see Sauces)
Great Chocolate Chip Cookies 185
Green Beans (see Vegetables)
Green Beans Amandine 32
Green Beans Horseradish 177
Green Pea Timbales 117
Green Peas (see Vegetables)
Green Rice 80
Grilled Pork Loin 169
Grilled Swordfish 159
Grits (see Side Dishes)
Gumbo (see Fish and Seafood)
Ham (see Pork)
Ham Jambalaya 171
Ham Pinwheels 69
Ham Steak with Orange-Currant Sauce ... 83
Haystacks 139
Heavenly Hash Brownies 111
Hello Dollies 186
Herb Biscuits 52
Herb Bread 21
Herb Dressing 54
Herb Muffins 103
Hollandaise Sauce 118
Homemade Bread 23
Homemade Peach Ice Cream 192
Hors d'oeuvres (see Appetizers)
Hot Chicken Salad 153
Hushpuppies 74
Ice Cream (see Desserts)
Ice Cream Pie (see Best Ever Ice Cream Pie)
Ice Cream with Crème de Cassis 33
ICINGS AND FROSTINGS
  Butter Frosting 70

Caramel Nut Icing 191
Chocolate Frosting 111
Chocolate Glaze 128
Chocolate Pound Cake Icing 100
Glaze for Apple Nut Cake 37
Glaze for Prune Cake 62
Karidopita Syrup 81
Laplanders Icing 189
Lemon Cheese Filling 75
7-Minute Icing 76
Sin City Icing 190
Irish Mist 117
Jackie Wiggins's Oatmeal Cookies 185
Jambalaya (see Ham Jambalaya)
Jan's Spinach Quiche 194
Joan's Seafood Gumbo 163
Karidopita 81
Karidopita Syrup 81
Key Lime Pie 131
Kiwi and Prosciutto 122
Lamb (see Roast Leg of Lamb with Mint Sauce)
Laplanders Icing 189
Lasagna 40
Lemon Cheese Cake 75
Lemon Cheese Filling 75
Liver Gratin Forcemeat 123
Lizzies 186
Lobster (see Fish and Seafood)
London Cheese Roll 138
Luscious Strawberry Dessert 94
Macaroni (see Pasta)
Macaroni and Cheese
 (see The Best Macaroni and Cheese)
Macedoine of Fruit 52
Mae's Boiled Custard 192
Mae's Scalloped Oysters 98
Marinated Baby Shrimp 123
Marinated Chicken Drummettes 149
Marinated Flank Steak 166
Meats (see Beef, Lamb, Pork, and Veal)
Medium White Sauce 102
Melanie's Cheese Ring 147

Million-Dollar Marinated Salad 152
Mini Beef Wellington 126
Mini Chocolate Éclairs 128
Mint Sauce 172
Minted Carrots and Peas 130
Mints (see Wedding Mints)
Misty Salad 29
Molded Broccoli Salad 85
Mrs. Baker's Fudge 140
Mrs. Patrick's Eggplant 179
Muffins (see Breads)
Mushroom and Shrimp Bisque 82
Mushroom Duxelles 143
Mushrooms (see Salads, Soups, and Vegetables)
Mustard Dressing 79
New Orleans Casserole 161
Nick's Peanut Brittle 187
Noodles (see Pasta)
NUTS
 ALMONDS
  Almond Lace Cookies 127
  Green Beans Amandine 32
 PEANUTS
  Haystacks 139
  Peanut Brittle, Nick's 187
  Peanut Fingers 90
 PECANS
  Apple Nut Cake 37
  Caramel Nut Cake 191
  Pecan Cheese Ball 138
  Pecan Crescents 140
  Pecan Fudge Pie 188
  Pecan Pie, Southern 30
  Pecan Tassies 90
  Pralines 127
  Toasted Pecans 67
 WALNUTS
  Carrots with Walnuts 178
Oatmeal Cookies
 (see Jackie Wiggins's Oatmeal Cookies)
Oil and Garlic Dressing 102
Okra (see Vegetables)

Old-Fashioned Beef Stew 157
Olive Bites 89
Omelettes (see Eggs)
Onions (see Vegetables)
Onion Soup 45
Orange Balls 70
Orange-Currant Sauce 83
Orange-Glazed Carrots 117
Orange-Glazed Cornish Hen Halves 17
Oriental Chicken Salad 154
Oriental Vegetable Sauté 93
Oven-Barbecued Pork Chops 170
Oyster Stew 54
Oysters (see Fish and Seafood)
Oysters Burton 124
Oysters Mary 79
Oysters Thomas 59
Parsleyed New Potatoes 46
PASTA
   Beef Bourguignonne over Noodles 21
   Buttered Noodles with Poppy Seeds ... 144
   Shrimp with Green Noodles 161
   The Best Macaroni and Cheese 183
Peach Ice Cream
   (see Homemade Peach Ice Cream)
Peach Melba Crêpes 144
Peaches (see Fruits and Desserts)
Peanut Brittle (see Nick's Peanut Brittle)
Peanut Fingers 90
Peanuts (see Nuts)
Peas (see Vegetables)
Pecan Cheese Ball 138
Pecan Crescents 140
Pecan Fudge Pie 188
Pecan Pie (see Southern Pecan Pie)
Pecan Tassies 90
Pecans (see Nuts)
Pepper Steak 165
Phyllo-Wrapped Lobster 125
Pie Crust 194
Pies and Pastries (see Desserts)
Pimiento Cheese
   (see Ribbon Pimiento Cheese Sandwiches)
Pineapple Delight 184
Poached Eggs 118
Poaching Liquid 124
Pole Beans (see Vegetables: Beans)
PORK
   Ham, Baked 32
   Ham Balls, Earline's 171
   Ham Jambalaya 171
   Ham Pinwheels 69
   Ham Steak with Orange-Currant Sauce . 83
   New Orleans Casserole 161
   Pork Chops, Oven-Barbecued 170
   Pork Chops, Swedish 170
   Pork Loin, Eva Jo's Fruited 169
   Pork Loin, Grilled 169
   Prosciutto, Kiwi and 122
   Sausage Balls 138
   Sausage Chowder, German 157
Potatoes au Gratin 83
Potatoes (see Vegetables)
POULTRY AND GAME
   CHICKEN
      Barbecued Chicken 110
      Beefy Chicken 174
      Chicken-Artichoke Bake 174
      Chicken Champagnoise 126
      Chicken Drummettes, Marinated ... 149
      Chicken Duxelles 143
      Chicken Livers Stroganoff 175
      Chicken Parisienne 130
      Chicken Salad, Hot 153
      Chicken Salad in Toast Cups 137
      Chicken Salad, Oriental 154
      Chicken Soufflé with Sherry
         Mushroom Sauce 102
      Chicken Spaghetti 176
      Chicken Tetrazzini 116
      Chicken Turnovers 149
      Chicken Virginia 93
      Chicken Williamsburg,
         Puff Shells with 90

Chicken with Tarragon 173
Curried Chicken 176
Dirty Rice 195
Durkee's Chicken 173
Fried Chicken 28
Sour Cream Marinated Chicken 175
South Georgia Chicken Casserole . . . 175
CORNISH HEN
   Orange-Glazed Cornish Hen Halves . . 17
   Rock Cornish Hen Alexandra 85
DUCK
   Duck Gallantine
      with Cumberland Sauce 122
   Duck Terrine 50
MISCELLANEOUS POULTRY
  AND GAME
   Quail, Baked 55
   Turkey with Benny Sauce, Roast 96
Pound Cake (see Desserts: Cakes)
Pralines 127
Processor Buttermilk Biscuits 93
Prune Cake 62
Puddings (see Desserts: Puddings
  and Custards)
Puff Shells filled with Vanilla Ice Cream
  and Fudge Sauce 56
Puff Shells with Chicken Williamsburg 90
Punch (see Beverages)
Quail (see Poultry and Game)
Quiche (see Jan's Spinach Quiche)
Quick Beef Stroganoff 168
Raspberry Cream Molds 151
Red Bean Soup 155
Red Hot Rice 182
Red Snapper Louisiana 162
Rena's Shrimp Spread 149
Ribbon Pimiento Cheese Sandwiches 68
RICE
   Anne's Rice 181
   Carlton's Fried Rice 181
   Cold Artichoke Rice Salad 154
   Dirty Rice 195

Green Rice 80
Red Hot Rice 182
Rice Chantilly 181
Rice Mingle 18
Sharon's Broccoli-Rice Casserole 183
Shrimp and Rice, Sunbelt 160
Wild Rice Deluxe 85
Yummy Rice Casserole 182
Rice Chantilly 181
Rice Mingle 18
Roast Contrefilet of Beef
  with Dipping Sauce 122
Roast Leg of Lamb with Mint Sauce 172
Roast Turkey with Benny Sauce 96
Rock Cornish Hen Alexandra 85
Rolls (see Breads)
Romaine and Spinach Salad with Caesar
  Sour Cream Dressing 50
Roux 143
Rum Cream Pie 84
Rumaki (see Sweet'N Sour Rumaki)
SALAD DRESSINGS
   Caesar Sour Cream Dressing 50
   Ginger Cream Dressing 85
   Herb Dressing 54
   Mustard Dressing 79
   Oil and Garlic Dressing 102
   Shanghai Dressing 11
   Vinaigrette 46
SALADS
  FRUIT SALADS
   Cranberry Mold 99
   Cranberry Soufflé Salad 82
   Fruit Cup with
      Ginger Cream Dressing 84
   Misty Salad 29
   Raspberry Cream Molds 151
   Sunderland Salad 152
   Waldorf Salad 32
   Yum-Yum Salad 151
  POULTRY AND SEAFOOD SALADS
   Chicken Salad, Hot 153

Chicken Salad, Oriental 154
Chicken Salad in Toast Cups 137
Million-Dollar Marinated Salad 152
Salmon Salad Mold 153
Shrimp Salad 20
Shrimp Salad Piquant 153
VEGETABLE SALADS
   Artichoke Rice Salad, Cold 154
   Asparagus and Artichoke Salad 79
   Avocado Mousse 36
   Broccoli Salad, Molded 85
   Coleslaw 75
   Garden Aspic 18
   Gazpacho Salad in Brandy Snifters .. 102
   Golden Pheasant Salad 59
   Mushroom and Romaine Salad, Fresh 54
   Romaine and Spinach Salad with
      Caesar Sour Cream Dressing 50
   Shanghai Salad 11
   Spinach Mushroom Salad 46
Salmon Salad Mold 153
SANDWICHES
   Cream Cheese Open-Faced Sandwiches 68
   Ham Pinwheels 69
   Ribbon Pimiento Cheese Sandwiches ... 68
Sapelo Island Fish Chowder 156
Sauce for Ham Balls 171
SAUCES
   Béarnaise Sauce 60
   Benny Sauce 193
   Broccoli Sauce 193
   Cumberland Sauce 123
   Dill Sauce 124
   Dipping Sauce 122
   Fudge Sauce 56
   Giblet Gravy 97
   Grape Sauce 93
   Ham Balls, Sauce for 171
   Hollandaise Sauce 118
   Mint Sauce 172
   Orange-Currant Sauce 83
   Sherry Mushroom Sauce 103

   White Sauce, Medium 102
   Wine Sauce 55
Sausage (see Pork)
Sausage Balls 138
Sautéed Mushrooms 12
Sautéed Snow Peas 103
Sautéed Zucchini and Yellow Squash 144
Savannah Trifle 47
Scalloped Oysters
   (see Mae's Scalloped Oysters)
Scrambled Eggs 48
Seafood (see Fish and Seafood)
Seafood Casserole 16
Seafood Fancy 11
7-Minute Icing 76
Shanghai Dressing 11
Shanghai Salad 11
Sharon's Broccoli-Rice Casserole 183
Sheet Cake (see Sin City Sheet Cake)
Sherry Cheese Pâté 148
Sherry Mushroom Sauce 103
Shortbread Cookies 33
Shrimp (see Appetizers, Fish and
   Seafood, Salads, and Soups)
Shrimp Creole 160
Shrimp Mold 89
Shrimp Salad 20
Shrimp Salad Piquant 153
Shrimp Spread (see Rena's Shrimp Spread)
Shrimp with Green Noodles 161
SIDE DISHES
   Baked Grits 107
   Fried Grits 48
   Garlic Cheese Grits 184
   Pasta (see main heading Pasta)
   Pineapple Delight 184
   Rice (see main heading Rice)
Sin City Icing 190
Sin City Sheet Cake 190
Sirloin Tip Roast
   (see Southern Sirloin Tip Roast)
Slaw (see Coleslaw)

Sliced Georgia Peaches and Cream 107
Small Corn Muffins 33
Small Whole Carrots 80
Snow Peas (see Vegetables: Peas)
Soup Supreme 92
SOUPS AND STEWS
  COLD SOUPS
    Cucumber Soup, Chilled 143
    Mushroom and Shrimp Bisque 82
    Vichyssoise 130
    Watercress Soup 116
  HOT SOUPS
    Bean Soup, Red 155
    Bean Soup, Spanish 155
    Broccoli Soup, Cream of 20
    Cheddar Chowder 156
    Fish Chowder, Sapelo Island 156
    Mushroom and Shrimp Bisque 82
    Onion Soup 45
    Sausage Chowder, German 157
    Soup Supreme 92
    Watercress Soup 116
  STEWS
    Oyster Stew 54
    Beef Stew, Old-Fashioned 157
Sour Cream Biscuits 196
Sour Cream Marinated Chicken 175
Sour Cream Pound Cake 190
South Georgia Chicken Casserole 175
Southern Angel Biscuits 99
Southern Gumbo 163
Southern Pecan Pie 30
Southern Sirloin Tip Roast 167
Spaghetti (see Chicken Spaghetti)
Spanish Bean Soup 155
Spiced Pineapple Chunks 67
Spinach (see Salads and Vegetables)
Spinach Balls 89
Spinach Mushroom Salad 46
Spinach Quiche (see Jan's Spinach Quiche)
Spinach-Stuffed Tomatoes 61
Spinach with Sour Cream 179

Squash (see Vegetables)
Squash Casserole 28
Steamed Broccoli with Wine Sauce 55
Stews (see Soups and Stews)
Strawberries (see Fruits)
Strawberries and Cream 48
Stroganoff (see Beef and Poultry)
Stuffed Trout 124
Sue's Marinated Vegetables 177
Sugar Cookies 41
Sunbelt Shrimp and Rice 160
Sunday Vegetable Casserole 178
Sunderland Salad 152
Swedish Pork Chops 170
Sweet'N Sour Rumaki 147
Sweet Potato Soufflé 98
Sweet Potatoes (see Vegetables)
Sweets (see Desserts)
Swordfish (see Fish and Seafood)
Tetrazzini (see Chicken Tetrazzini)
The Best Macaroni and Cheese 183
Timbales (see Green Pea Timbales)
Toast Cups 137
Toasted Pecans 67
Tomatoes (see Vegetables)
Tournedos Monegasques 80
Trifle (see Savannah Trifle)
Trout (see Fish and Seafood)
Truffles (see Chocolate Truffles)
Tuna (see Fish and Seafood)
Tuna Casserole 159
Turkey (see Poultry and Game)
Veal Farce 60
Veal with Mustard Sauce 51
Veal with Peppers 172
Vegetable Medley 21
VEGETABLES
  ARTICHOKES
    Asparagus and Artichoke Salad ... 79
    Chicken-Artichoke Bake 174
    Cold Artichoke Rice Salad 154
    Duchess Potatoes on Artichoke

    Bottoms 51
BEANS
    Baked Beans 110
    Crisp Green Beans 37
    French-Style Green Beans 83
    Fresh Green Beans 46
    Fresh Pole Beans 98
    Green Beans Amandine 32
    Green Beans Horseradish 177
    Red Bean Soup 155
    Spanish Bean Soup 155
BROCCOLI
    Broccoli Casserole 179
    Broccoli-Stuffed Tomatoes 17
    Cream of Broccoli Soup 20
    Molded Broccoli Salad 85
    Sharon's Broccoli-Rice Casserole 183
    Steamed Broccoli with Wine Sauce ... 55
CARROTS
    Carrots with Walnuts 178
    Minted Carrots and Peas 130
    Orange-Glazed Carrots 117
    Small Whole Carrots 80
CORN
    Corn on the Cob 111
    Creamed Corn 29
MISCELLANEOUS VEGETABLES
    Asparagus and Artichoke Salad 79
    Coleslaw 75
    Cucumber Soup, Chilled 143
    Eggplant, Mrs. Patrick's 179
    Marinated Vegetables, Sue's 177
    Okra, Fried 29
    Oriental Vegetable Sauté 93
    Pepper Steak 165
    Peppers, Veal with 172
    Sunday Vegetable Casserole 178
    Vegetable Medley 21
    Watercress Soup 116
MUSHROOMS
    Crab-Stuffed Mushrooms 148
    Fresh Mushroom and Romaine Salad . 54
    Mushroom and Shrimp Bisque 82
    Mushroom Duxelles 143
    Sautéed Mushrooms 12
    Spinach Mushroom Salad 46
    Sherry Mushroom Sauce 103
ONIONS
    Onion Soup 45
    Zapped Vidalia Onions 180
PEAS
    Green Pea Timbales 117
    Minted Carrots and Peas 130
    Sautéed Snow Peas 103
POTATOES (see also Sweet Potatoes)
    Crunchy Baked Potatoes 12
    Crusty Baked Potatoes 61
    Dot's Potatoes Deluxe 180
    Duchess Potatoes on Artichoke
      Bottoms 51
    Parsleyed New Potatoes 46
    Potatoes au Gratin 83
SPINACH
    Jan's Spinach Quiche 194
    Romaine and Spinach Salad with Caesar
      Sour Cream Dressing 50
    Spinach Balls 89
    Spinach Mushroom Salad 46
    Spinach-Stuffed Tomatoes 61
    Spinach with Sour Cream 179
SQUASH
    Butternut Bake 178
    Creole Squash 178
    Sautéed Zucchini and Yellow Squash . 144
    Squash Casserole 28
SWEET POTATOES
    Brooke's Sweet Potatoes 180
    Candied Yams 32
    Sweet Potato Soufflé 98
    Yam Balls 56
TOMATOES
    Broccoli-Stuffed Tomatoes 17
    Spinach-Stuffed Tomatoes 61
Vichyssoise 130

Vidalia Onions (see Vegetables: Onions)
Vinaigrette 46
Waffles (see Workhorse Waffles)
Waldorf Salad 32
Wassail 88
Watercress Soup 116
Wedding Mints 71
White Sauce (see Medium White Sauce)
Wild Rice Deluxe 85
Wine Sauce 55
Workhorse Waffles 63
Yam Balls 56
Yams (see Vegetables: Sweet Potatoes)
Yeast Breads (see Breads)
Yummy Rice Casserole 182
Yum-Yum Salad 151
Zapped Vidalia Onions 180
Zucchini (see Vegetables: Squash)

MARY BETH TALBOT BUSBEE was born in Ruston, Louisiana, and for eight years served as First Lady for the state of Georgia.

JAN BUSBEE CURTIS graduated *magna cum laude* from the University of Georgia and is a free-lance writer.